RECOLLECTIONS OF A RACKETEER

Patrick Lane was born in England in 1946. He was found guilty of racketeering in 1988 and served two years in prison in the US. Now a full-time writer, he lives in France with his wife and two small dogs.

RECOLLECTIONS OF A RACKETEER

SMUGGLING HASH AND CASH AROUND THE WORLD

PATRICK LANE

MAINSTREAM
PUBLISHING

EDINBURGH AND LONDON

Copyright © Patrick Lane, 2009
All rights reserved
The moral right of the author has been asserted

First published in Great Britain in 2009 by
MAINSTREAM PUBLISHING COMPANY
(EDINBURGH) LTD
7 Albany Street
Edinburgh EH1 3UG

ISBN 9781845964337

This book is a work of non-fiction based on the life,
experiences and recollections of the author. In some instances,
names of people, places, dates, sequences or the detail of events
have been changed for artistic purposes and to protect the privacy of
others. The author has stated to the publishers that, except in such
respects, not affecting the substantial accuracy of the work,
the contents of this book are true

A catalogue record for this book is available
from the British Library

Typeset in Badhouse, Caslon and Ticket

Printed in Great Britain by
CPI Mackays, Chatham ME5 8TD

To Jude.
For all the love.

CONTENTS

islands and across the shores of remote Irish lochs and sometimes even Scottish 'fjords'. Eventually, some of us, including Howard, were arrested and stood trial in the Central Criminal Court, the Old Bailey, for what was, certainly in 1980, the biggest pot-smuggling case in history. I was lucky and escaped first to the Continent and then to America, living as a fugitive for several years.

But nothing changed and the Great Game continued until 1988, when the law-enforcement authorities from some 13 countries dragged us from all over the world into a South Florida courtroom, where we were finally charged with, and convicted of, federal conspiracy and racketeering.

When I came out of prison in 1990, I decided to put the past behind me and create a new and different life as a corporate executive. Many of my friends, however, decided to write about our mutual experiences. These various books describe our numerous adventures in exhaustive detail and there is certainly no need for yet another book covering the same ground. But while these books describe the How and the Who, the Where and the When, not to mention the How Much and the Howard, I feel that they missed the Why and the What: What did it feel like to be a smuggler? Why on earth did we do such silly things? And that is the real reason I decided to write this book.

My book does not offer a chronological description of those years, nor does it give a grand view. I never had a grand view; I just stumbled from one rather ludicrous situation into another, often amused and usually confused. It is that bewildering sense of the ridiculousness of those years that I hope to convey.

I am in my 60s now and have decided that I am old enough to put it all into perspective. I've had a very good life, blessed with good friends and good family. I've had a lot of adventures, a lot of fun and a lot of luck. Ever since my birth, I've also received a lot of love – more than I deserve and much more than I've been able to return. My experience has always been that most people are kind and decent, and this book is my way of saying thank you while I'm still young enough to remember.

Patrick Lane

[1]

THE SUITCASES

Though I hate to generalise, it's safe to say that the professional luggage of choice among international money launderers is Hartmann. The company was established in the Midwest more than 100 years ago and Hartmann luggage epitomises the traditional American virtues of simplicity and unassuming strength that the international courier has learned to appreciate.

France's Louis Vuitton also offers fine luggage but it tends to be a little showy and attracts attention, which really is something to avoid if possible. Hartmann cases have clean lines and are understated and easily overlooked. My own preference was always the Hartmann Woodbox Pullman; its spacious interior would hold 16 stacks of £20 notes (2 rows of 8). With a depth of 9 in., each stack could contain about 800 notes, which meant each case could comfortably accommodate £250,000.

The two cases on the floor beside me held £500,000 between them, half a million pounds sterling, which, back in the 1970s, was quite a hefty sum. It was heavy, too. The popular image of money launderers as corpulent parasites lounging in the shadows or holding sinister meetings in expensive Washington DC restaurants belies the challenge of the profession. This is no job for the laggard. Rather than have the taxi drop me off outside the door of the bank, I asked to be set down a few hundred yards away, around the corner. It was only after the taxi had left and I was certain that nobody had followed me that I picked up the suitcases and walked to the bank. The true professional carries two heavy suitcases full of cash with a nonchalant gait, as though he had just picked up some silk lingerie for his girlfriend. Staggering along the street huffing and puffing and setting the cases down every few yards is the sign of an amateur who would not survive five minutes in an international airport.

The bank was more like a gentlemen's club than a financial institution. From time to time, a young man would glide past carrying anonymous folders beneath his dark-suited arm and, in the distance, I could hear the soft chatter of telex machines; but there were no bank tellers and there was certainly no cash. The room in which I sat was panelled in oak, which decades of polish had given a subtle inner glow. The chairs were upholstered in a dark leather that might once have been green but, rubbed by generations of worsted pinstriped bottoms, had acquired an indeterminate patina. The carpet was a fine Bokhara, probably brought back from the Anglo-Afghan Wars by one of the bank's original founders who had been a nineteenth-century explorer in Central Asia.

In fact, it was the great-great-grandson of that very founding director, Charles Latimer, whom everyone in the room was waiting to meet. He was the chairman and his assistant had assured us that he would be joining us presently. In the meantime, we were to make ourselves comfortable. The only person in the room whom I knew was Alec Singh. The other four men had been introduced to me as directors of the bank but I had immediately forgotten their names as I struggled to present a relaxed and respectable demeanour. There was some desultory small talk as we waited for the chairman to join us and everyone studiously ignored the two large suitcases, which I'd placed beside the door. Compared with their Louis Vuitton equivalents, the Hartmann cases were unassuming but, nevertheless, in the respectable, club-like surroundings of this merchant bank, they seemed as blatantly indiscreet as a couple of hookers in a monastery. I was horribly aware that the cases contained half a million pounds – in wrinkled, grubby cash.

The problem was that we had too much money to deal with. Back in the 1970s, depositing large sums of money in a bank was not usually a major problem. There were few anti-money-laundering laws and as long as the cash did not actually have blood on it, very few questions were asked. One or two hundred thousand pounds could easily be fed through a few central London banks in a week without attracting attention. But since we had 20 tons of Colombian marijuana deposited in various warehouses and rented castles around the British Isles, the amount of cash we were generating each week was approaching embarrassing levels. There was no way of feeding it into the regular system without attracting comment. I needed to establish a system whereby I could deposit more than half a million pounds each week and have it transferred out of the country quickly. Our Colombian suppliers and the New York financiers were anxious to recoup their investment and I was equally anxious not to disappoint them. Although they were nice people to be nice to, I suspected that they were not very nice people not to be nice to. The sooner they were paid off, the sooner I could relax.

If I had not become an accountant, I would never have met Alec Singh and if I had not met Singh, I would not have been standing in Latimer's Merchant Bank with two discreet but nevertheless incriminating suitcases that morning. That I had chosen to become an accountant was purely an alphabetical accident in the first place. Back in 1968, despite being one of the first medically documented examples of an MSA (a multiple substance abuser), I had somehow managed to graduate from Sussex University with an honours degree in English literature with a minor in philosophy. Not knowing what to do with the rest of my life but realising I would need to do something if I was not to die very soon of a drug overdose like so many of my friends, I consulted the government publication *Opportunities for Graduates*. This was a thick book that listed every possible profession from A to Z and explained not only what qualifications were needed and what salary might be expected but also what each profession involved and what a typical day's work might entail.

I read the book slowly over the space of several weeks in the summer of 1968, during which Robert Kennedy lay wounded in a Los Angeles hotel kitchen and Russian tanks rolled into Czechoslovakia. The Prague Spring and the dreams of Camelot died while I sat at the kitchen table in Brighton and contemplated my future. At the time, I was living on a diet of hashish, cocaine, heroin and Methedrine, most of which I received legally as a registered addict. Diligently, I worked through *Opportunities for Graduates* page by page, rejecting each alphabetically ordered profession. The trouble was that whatever job I considered, and however enticing it might appear, I could simply not imagine myself being a Film Producer or Petroleum Engineer, for example, for the rest of my life. At that age, of course, you cannot imagine being anything for the rest of your life. Eventually, I reached the final entry, Zoologist, and swiftly eliminated that one. Bad enough to be cleaning out elephant shit for a living but working with venomous snakes and large beasts with sharp teeth certainly held no appeal for me. Rock Idol was not listed as an option and there was no explanation of how Mick Jagger had got his job. I closed the book in disgust. Nothing suited me. I was doomed to remain a hopeless drug addict for the rest of my pathetically short life.

'To heck with it!' I said, or words to that effect. 'They're all the same so I'll just pick the first one on the list.' I opened the book to the first page and that is how I became an Accountant rather than a Banker, a Chiropodist or a Deep-Sea Diver. My timing was fortuitous, because Price, Waterhouse & Co. had recently made the decision to begin hiring university graduates without any accounting background. They were looking for young gentlemen with an arts degree who would be at home in the boardroom and better able to mix with captains of industry. I quit heroin cold turkey and, after six rather unpleasant months, I presented myself, with a haircut and a borrowed suit, at the head office of Price, Waterhouse & Co., or 'PW', for the interview.

My parents were obviously pleased that I was finally getting a proper job but they were surprised at my choice of profession.

'But you'll have to cut your hair and wear one of those silly bowler hats,' my mother said.

'And you can't add,' my father protested. 'You've always been innumerate.'

My father, who had studied nuclear physics at Cambridge, was very good at maths and was always disappointed by my inability to perform rapid mental calculations. 'Come on,' he'd say. 'It's not difficult. Just think.' The trouble was I could not think; my brain would grind to a halt under the pressure and my mind became more and more blank as he protested.

Although I can perform basic maths, I have absolutely no sense of numbers and what they mean, and I was in fact rather concerned that being innumerate might prove a hindrance to a career as an accountant. However, Edward Welsh, the Price Waterhouse partner who interviewed me, dismissed my worries and asked me if I liked canoeing. He seemed pleased when I nodded enthusiastically and assured him I loved canoeing, even though I'd not been in a canoe since I was a small boy. The conversation then moved on to Greek tragedy, which we both loved, and finally Edward asked me if I could start work at PW the following week. The interview was over and I'd got the job. I was probably 22 years old at the time of that interview and I'm 62 years old now but I still sometimes lie awake at night wondering what relevance canoeing can possibly have had to a career in high finance. I later discovered that Edward was discreetly gay and I wondered whether 'canoeing' was some sort of secret code word, like 'cottaging'. But if it was, he never followed up and offered to paddle me or share my canoe. Some things in life we are just not supposed to understand.

I reported for duty at PW's head office at Old Jewry, in the very heart of the medieval City of London. It was a Dickensian setting, near Lombard Street, just around the corner from the Stock Exchange and the Bank of England. In those days, Bank of England employees still wore silk top hats and tails to work. Stockbrokers wore black jackets, striped trousers and bowler hats. As chartered accountants, we also wore bowler hats but with either a black or a pinstripe suit. All three groups also carried a copy of *The Times* and a tightly furled umbrella, which a gentleman never opened, even in the rain, except to escort and protect a lady. In 1968, there were very few ladies in the City of London and umbrellas were seldom unfurled. Bankers, brokers and accountants would all crowd together in the pubs at lunchtime for shepherd's pie or sausage and mash. The three-martini lunch was never a British tradition but five or six pints of beer at lunchtime was standard fare. Is it just that we were younger and stronger then or was the beer weaker?

I met Alec Singh soon after I started working at PW. We both worked for the same senior partner. However, I was still a mere articled clerk while Singh, just a couple of years older than me, was already a manager. He had a terrible reputation in the office for doing everything by the book, for being a stickler for dress codes and a workaholic. Despite his English-sounding first name, he was a dark-skinned Indian and we all secretly made fun of his accent, doing Peter Sellers-style impressions. My fellow clerks were sympathetic when it was announced that Singh and I were to spend two weeks together doing an out-of-town audit in Bedford. 'No civvies for you,' I was told. 'Singh will make you wear your suit and tie till you go to bed.'

At head office, the only acceptable attire was a three-piece black or pinstripe suit worn with highly polished black shoes and a bowler hat. However, one of the perks of doing an audit away from London was that most managers and partners relaxed the dress code for the duration of the visit. Clerks were permitted to wear tweed jackets with brown shoes, and a more colourful selection of ties was considered acceptable. Not for Alec Singh, however. 'We are representing the company,' he told me. 'We must show these fellows that we have standards and that we plan to maintain them.' He spoke as though the citizens of Bedfordshire were some unruly mob of ignorant yokels who needed to be shown the flag. 'You may remove your bowler hat when you return to the hotel after work,' he finally conceded.

The job itself was fine. We audited the books of the Swiss company Suchard, which produced Toblerone chocolate in a factory just outside Bedford. They had a generous policy of allowing staff and visitors (including auditors) to eat as much chocolate as they liked. The idea was that the sooner people became sick of chocolate the sooner they would stop trying to steal it. New staff and visitors fell upon the triangular bars and gorged themselves as though they were in paradise. The day we arrived to begin our audit, a group of local schoolboys was being given the run of the factory and, as sugar mixed with teenage hormones in their bloodstream, they ran shrieking in all directions, inflamed with God knows what beastly desires.

'We will not participate,' Singh informed me. 'Not only would it be most improper for auditors to benefit from a client's assets and place us in a most difficult ethical situation – but,' and here he indicated the rampaging schoolboys, 'it would be most undignified and reflect badly on PW.'

Bedford is a provincial market town on the River Great Ouse, which, as its name suggests, oozes slowly through East Anglia till it reaches the Wash and meanders into the North Sea. This is the flattest part of the British Isles and sleepy villages lie beneath a vast and peaceful sky, immortalised for ever in the paintings of John Constable. Our hotel was situated a mile or so outside of Bedford, with views across the flat meadows to where the river wound its languid course three miles further to the east.

Bedford no doubt has a lively social scene these days but it didn't in 1968. Sex, drugs and rock 'n' roll were strictly limited to London and Brighton in those days, with faint stirrings in Oxford and Cambridge – but not in Bedford. I'd be surprised if they even had a Chinese takeaway or a pub with a jukebox. Alec Singh and I went to the cinema a couple of times in our suits and ties but otherwise there was little to do after work. Evenings were spent enjoying classic English hotel cuisine (stewed cabbage and overcooked beef) while discussing Singh's various theories concerning double-entry bookkeeping. His white collar was always highly starched and the knot in his tie small and tight. Even after dinner, he would forbid me to loosen my tie in the bar. 'We represent standards out here,' he reminded me. I hated the man and did everything I could to irritate him and defy his rules. Alone in my room, I gorged on dark Toblerone chocolate.

One evening, I can't remember why, we left work early and had time for a drink before dinner. We both ordered a pint of best bitter and walked out onto the hotel terrace to enjoy the tranquillity of an English twilight.

It was a scene straight out of a Constable painting. From the terrace, we could see the spires of at least three village churches emerging from the distant woodlands. Their bells tolled the hour, almost but not quite in unison. Immediately in front of us, on a village green, two cricket teams made the most of the fading light to finish their game. The sound of leather on willow and the unhurried enthusiasm of an English cricket team provide memories as timeless as they are clichéd. In the further distance, we could see the sails of large barges taking their cargoes of beetroot and Brussels sprouts down to the sea at King's Lynn. The rising mists and the fading light gave everything a hazy, dreamlike quality. As we leaned on the balustrade, holding our beer glasses and silently savouring this classic English twilight, I noticed that Singh was quietly murmuring to himself. I leaned closer and realised he was reciting from Gray's *Elegy Written in a Country Churchyard*:

> The curfew tolls the knell of parting day,
> The lowing herd winds slowly o'er the lea,
> The ploughman homeward plods his weary way,
> And leaves the world to darkness and to me.

Englishmen do not normally recite poetry to each other (it's considered bad form), so I was not sure of the proper response.

'Ah, England!' I said, and swept my arm vaguely towards the rustic scene. 'Jolly nice view,' I added. 'But always wet and muddy.'

Singh turned to face me and his eyes were wild. 'You can never understand,' he said, grasping my arm. 'You can never imagine the dryness and the heat of the land I come from.' He let go of my arm and stared again towards the distant river. 'I come from Rajasthan, on the plains of northern India. Nothing grows there. No rains come. I watched my parents and their parents claw at the stony ground with their bare hands, but nothing grows.'

Not quite sure how to handle this dramatic outburst, I watched as the cricketers pulled up their stumps and put their bats in their bags. I noticed the lushness of the green and the sponginess of the turf beneath their feet. Mists were rising over the river and the low-lying land beside the banks was rich and dark and fertile.

'It was the missionaries who saved me,' Singh continued. 'They took me away from there and gave me an education. I worked hard and I won prizes and they sent me to England and a job with Price, Waterhouse & Co.'

I still did not know what to say or how to react. The cricketers had moved away now and I could hear the sound of car doors slamming and a few 'cheerio's. Singh was transfixed by the scene, almost as though he had forgotten my presence.

'If only they could see me now,' he said. 'The people in my village would not believe it.' He turned to me sadly and said, 'My parents are dead now. They will never know. But, one day, I would like the people in my village to know.' He leaned on the balustrade again and sipped his beer, looking towards the river. 'They would say, "Oh, Alec, look at you. Staying in a fine English hotel, sharing a beer with an English gentleman. Look at you, watching the cricket and the green, growing things in the fields. Look at you, one of the bosses, dressed in a suit and tie."' He paused a little and his eyes were wet when he quietly added, 'They would say, "We are so proud of you."'

Looking at those sad dark eyes, so suddenly vulnerable, I wanted to put my arms around him and tell him that his parents were looking down on him and proud of what he had achieved. But Englishmen are not trained for handling such confidences and so I looked at my watch and said, 'Getting bloody late. Time for a spot of dinner, I think. Don't know about you but I'm starving.' After a final turn of the head to look at the river, Singh said, 'Good idea! I could eat a horse.'

We never discussed that evening again. He seldom mentioned his background after that and certainly never again recited poetry. Nonetheless, my feelings about him were never the same after I'd watched him reveal his vulnerability. After that evening, I stopped fighting him and later, back at head office, made a point of treating him with more formality and deference. After seeing him so emotionally naked, I always wanted to protect him or at least demonstrate the respect that his poor parents would never be able to display. Consequently, we remained friends long after I left accountancy and became an international smuggler. Singh left Price Waterhouse himself a few years later and took a senior position with Latimer's Merchant Bank. Latimer's had been established in the second half of the nineteenth century, partly to finance Britain's colonial wars against the Russians on the north-west Indian frontier – a dusty land where nothing grows.

So in 1979, when I found myself with this river of cash that I needed to transfer out of the country, I could think of no better person to ask for advice than my old friend Alec Singh. 'Nothing to be worrying yourself for,' he assured me. 'This is the sort of matter on which the British Empire was truly built. My bank is extremely well connected throughout the Empire.' He added, 'We also have contacts in New York and Switzerland.' Over the course of a couple of lunches, Singh advised me to fly to Guernsey in the Channel Islands, establish a company there and open a local bank account. He provided the names of a friendly local lawyer and a bank that had a close relationship with Latimer's Merchant Bank.

Singh had developed professionally far beyond the awkward manager of our Price Waterhouse days. The tie was still knotted tightly but these days it was made of silk and the suit was a hand-tailored lambswool job from Savile Row. I doubted whether the people of his village would recognise him now and I wondered if he would even care. He spoke of credit lines and offshore funds, of currency markets and fiscal havens. He told me about Liechtenstein and the Cayman Islands. He never once mentioned the plains of Rajasthan or his village where nothing grows.

The scheme that I devised, based on Singh's advice, was elegant but simple. The Guernsey-based Overseas United Investors Inc. (me) would send their representative (me) to open an account with Latimer's in the City. Latimer's would then alert various banks in the West End that they were to expect cash deposits of fifty or a hundred thousand pounds per week on behalf of the bank. The cash would be deposited in the various banks in the heart of the West End (close to the Mayfair casinos, the Saudi Embassy and Harrods), where cash was a common commodity. The funds would stay overnight in the bank of deposit (thus earning interest for the banks) and would then be transferred to Latimer's. Latimer's would immediately transfer the funds to Guernsey, retaining 2 per cent as its normal banking fee. Within 36 hours of receiving cash in London, I would be able to disperse it anywhere in the world that my investors requested. That would make them very happy.

The only problem was that so far the matter had gone no further than discussions between Alec Singh and me. I had certainly told him that cash was involved but he had never asked me whether this would be crisp new bills issued by the Bank of England in official wrappers from the Royal Mint or whether it would be wads of street cash, redolent of sweat and paranoia. I had not raised this issue either. I had developed the plan with Singh while speaking in the abstract. We used the word 'funds' a lot. We spoke of 'transfers' and 'deposits'. But we seldom mentioned the word 'cash'.

I'd never before met anybody else from his bank and had not really thought about the visceral reality of street cash until that morning at 11 a.m., sitting in the conference room with Alec Singh. I had put my fate in the hands of an Indian immigrant with nineteenth-century Kiplingesque visions of a long-departed Empire while we sat in a room full of crisp, white, old-school English bankers. Singh had told me that he had discussed my proposal with his directors and that they had agreed that the first transaction should be run through their own branch. As I sat there waiting, I reflected that the terms used had all been 'transfers' and 'transactions'. Nobody had said anything about 'suitcases full of dirty money'.

Singh went strangely silent during the wait. Having been encouraging for so many weeks, he retreated into a corner while we waited for the chairman to join us. Perhaps it was because he was only a manager while all the rest were directors. Perhaps it was because he was a dark-skinned Indian while all the rest were white English aristocrats. Perhaps it was because he'd suddenly realised that he had no idea where my money had come from and that for all he knew he was responsible for bringing into the hallowed halls of this imperial institution a criminal canker that could eventually cause its demise (although by this point I had at least prepared a cover story, involving rock groups, gigs and T-shirts). Whatever the reason, Singh went silent and I was forced to smile awkwardly and try not to look at the suitcases.

Eventually, the chairman arrived. 'Charles Latimer,' he introduced himself, offering a soft, white and perfectly manicured hand. 'How d'you do? Call me Charles.' His handshake was limp and un-enthusiastic.

From what I understood, his great-great-grandfather spent three nights during the siege of Chitral alone and armed only with a revolver, holding off several thousand local insurgents inflamed by agents of the Russian Tsar. Apparently, he was saved by the copy of Aeschylus's *Oresteia* that he always carried in his breast pocket and which absorbed two of the bullets aimed at his remote ledge in the High Pamirs.

Though it was hard to imagine the great-great-grandson bestriding any Central Asian battlefields, Charles had all the warrior attributes required for the twentieth-century boardroom. His collar was stiffly starched, his cheeks and pink jowls were closely shaved and his eyes were small and cold.

'I've heard a lot about you from Singh,' he said.

There was an awkward silence while I desperately tried to summon an appropriate reply. 'Me too,' I said.

'Shall we?' he asked.

'Why not?' I responded.

He stalked out of the room and all the other directors went with him. Singh paused momentarily and then followed the others, as though dissociating himself from me. The message on his face was more eloquent than all the words he had used years before while the two of us stood watching England's glory in the fading light by the Great Ouse: 'Please, Patrick. Please don't fuck up!'

My main challenge was to carry the two suitcases without stumbling. Nobody had volunteered to assist me, so I lifted them both and followed the rest of them along the corridor and up the stairs, attempting to look relaxed while the tendons on my arms strained and I tried to think of soft, silk feminine underthings. From the moment I had arrived in the bank, nobody had acknowledged the two suitcases. A doorman had taken my coat and my scarf but had ignored my heavy load. All the directors and Singh had taken my hand but ignored the suitcases.

We proceeded up the stairs and through the private banking section to the boardroom. I am sure that in the original Charles Latimer's bullet-scarred copy of Aeschylus there is a scene in which a still-bleeding corpse is dragged through the public areas of the city, leaving a dark-red smudge to mark its bloody progress. That's how I felt about my Hartmann cases – they were conspicuous, incriminating and heavy. These did not contain any silk lingerie, nor even cotton pyjamas – nothing but cash. I felt as though I were dragging a butchered carcass as I passed through the various departments of the prestigious merchant bank, expecting at any moment to be denounced.

When I entered the boardroom, all the others were waiting for me. The room was dominated by the largest and most deeply polished table I have ever seen. It could easily have seated two dozen portly directors and accommodated all their files and folders of important documents. But there were no important documents and the table was revealed in all its gleaming emptiness. There were no directors sitting around it, either; they were all standing, looking at me and my two suitcases.

That was the moment when I finally understood what a colossal mistake I had made and how Singh and I must have misunderstood each other. I should have confessed to him: 'This is dope dealer's cash, collected off the streets and exchanged in back-street pubs. It even smells of pot. This can have no place in a respectable institution such as Latimer's.'

I lowered the two suitcases to the floor and shot Singh an anguished glance. If we had not been on the third floor of the bank, I think I would have jumped out the window. Singh smiled at me and gave a discreet but encouraging nod. I lifted one of the Hartmann cases and placed it on the polished surface of the table. The brass locks gave a resounding click when I opened them. I had come too far to stop now, so I raised the lid and spilled the contents of the case onto the table. Bundles of £20 notes, wrapped in rubber bands, bounced in all directions. Swiftly, I emptied the contents of the second case on top of the first.

There was a long silence while the directors of the bank surveyed the pile of cash on the polished table. Nobody moved. There was a silence in the heavens while we all digested the sight of the bundles of filthy lucre. Finally, the chairman moved forward and gingerly lifted a wad of notes as though to confirm by touch what his disbelieving eyes had witnessed. The pink folds of his neck seemed to glow above the tight starch of his collar and his eyes, smaller than before, had acquired a fierce glow.

'Gentlemen,' he said, in a voice of hushed reverence edged with lust, 'this is what banking is all about. We need to count it.'

He ran his hands lovingly through the collection of banknotes and his fellow directors fell gleefully upon the cash like small boys in a chocolate factory. Singh smiled.

2

BEST SERVED COLD

The first time I really got to know Michael Durani was back in the early '70s, on a Boeing 747 flying first class to New York from Switzerland. Michael always flew first class.

He had purchased two large boxes of Cuban cigars at the airport in Geneva and after we had finished our first glass of Scotch and the pilot released the seat-belt sign, he gave me one of the boxes and told me to follow his example. Carefully, using his small gold Dunhill pocketknife, we removed the Havana labels from the outside of each box. We then took off the seals that showed that tax had been paid to Cuba's Communist government. Finally, we carefully emptied a box each of twenty-four cigars into our laps and replaced them one by one, after removing the individual labels.

'There!' Michael said, closing the boxes and slipping them into his Hartmann carry-on case. 'I do this each time I come to New York. Americans are crazy for Cuban cigars but they're not allowed to import them.'

I was impressed by the experienced way he handled the cigars and added that to the growing list of 'Durani-isms' that I was compiling for my own later use. Though probably only four or five years older than me, Michael Durani seemed to be of another, more worldly and sophisticated generation. Since I had first made his acquaintance, he had been my hero, and I found myself adopting many of his mannerisms.

Whenever he visited London, Michael always stayed at Brown's

Hotel on Albemarle Street in Mayfair and I would often drive my partner Graham Plinston there to discuss business, or else I'd collect Michael and bring him to our offices in Little Venice. He was always extremely polite and courteous to me but I was aware that I was the junior partner and he saved his conversation for my seniors. A trusted friend of government officials, customs inspectors and shipping agents throughout the Middle East, he was Graham's most important partner.

He was a tall man and his slim figure was accentuated by the elegant suits he always wore. One reason he liked staying at Brown's, he once told me, was because it was only a short walk to his tailor on Savile Row. It was Michael who first introduced me to the style of blue striped shirts with stiff white collars and who explained the finer details of tailor-made worsted suits.

'Make sure the buttonholes on the sleeves are real, not decorative,' he confided. 'That way you can undo them and roll your sleeves up if you're involved in a knife fight.' I tucked that away as useful information, though remaining rather vague on its practical application. It would certainly be an advantage if I was ever in a knife fight with somebody wearing a cheap suit. In the late '60s, when 'cool' was everything, Michael Durani was the epitome of classic cool – rather like James Bond. Graham, Howard and I had grown beyond our hippy phase but nevertheless we still favoured long hair and liked leather jackets. Michael, however, maintained a conservative hairstyle and always wore a suit and tie.

And he was always cool in his manner; whatever the pressure, he always looked relaxed and calm. One of the first times I worked with him was in the Swiss capital, Berne. In late 1972, Graham was detained by the German authorities and our Swiss bank account was frozen. Michael Durani called me from his home in Geneva with the bad news and told me to get on the next plane. He met me at Geneva airport and accompanied me by train to Berne.

'Don't worry about it,' he told me. 'They're as embarrassed by this as you are. They don't want to lose your business. Some busybody bureaucrat in Interpol must be jealous of Graham and he's slandered him to the Swiss. What do you think of this wine?'

We were eating an excellent lunch on the train to Berne. The food was good, the service was excellent and the forests of the Jura glided past the dining-car window. 'I'm normally not too fond of Swiss wine,' Michael continued, 'But this Aigle les Murailles is excellent.' It is impossible to think of Michael without thinking of good food, excellent wine and civilised company. Michael truly dedicated his life to savouring its most refined pleasures.

My previous experience of the legal system had been limited to British justice, and to very minor cases indeed. At the age of 18, I was busted for importing pornography into England. Prior to going to university, I'd spent a year hitch-hiking around the USA where I'd bought books and shipped them back to England after I had finished reading them and had no more room in my backpack. Many of the books I shipped back were simply not known in England at that time, like John Updike, and others were forbidden, like Henry Miller. In 1965, Her Majesty's Customs intercepted a parcel I had sent myself that contained a copy of Henry Miller's *Sexus* and eventually I received a summons to appear at their office, in the shadow of the Tower of London.

'Do you know,' a red-faced officer yelled at me, 'that this chapter alone contains the word "cunt" more than 30 times?' He paused and waved the book at me. 'We have counted them,' he added, rather unnecessarily, I thought. The book was certainly well thumbed and all the other officers looked equally outraged and offended by the filth they had been forced to examine in the execution of their official duties.

At the time, I was a newly enrolled student in the literature department at Sussex University. Following the recent *Lady Chatterley* trial at the Old Bailey, there was no shortage of young professors eager to defend my entitlement to enjoy the word and abstract concept, if not the physical reality, of 'cunt' as an Englishman's God-given right. Her Majesty's Customs quickly dropped the case. Lord Byron's complaint that 'cant is so much stronger than cunt nowadays' could never have been applied to England in the '60s.

My next brush with the law occurred in 1968, when the Brighton police raided my flat and found a joint of hashish. They were quite nice about it and confided that the only reason they had raided the house was because of the psychedelic artwork we had painted on the door and exterior walls; the lead detective's wife was a professional decorator and loved what we had done. Following my arrest, she visited the house and became quite friendly with my landlady. They discussed colours and techniques till the small hours.

I appeared at Brighton Magistrates' Court the next week, pleaded guilty to possession and was fined £50. With hindsight, I can see that I was a lost soul at the time and the arrest was a blessing. I'd managed to graduate but had no idea what I wanted to do with my life, other than have sex as often as possible. So I spent most of my time – well, actually all of my time – taking drugs and thinking about sex. Getting busted for a joint of hash finally persuaded me to give up all the heroin, cocaine and Methedrine with which I was slowly destroying myself.

Within months, I had (with my plan to become a chartered accountant in mind) moved back to my parents' house in Staffordshire, successfully quit drugs, got a temporary job teaching English and philosophy at a local college, acquired a lovely girlfriend with horses and finally, week by week, paid off the £50 fine for my drug bust. I was finally growing up.

The day I sent off the final payment in the mail, I decided to celebrate. A fellow college lecturer, Tony Ledbetter, and I set out to enjoy the alcoholic delights of Birmingham. I had not been to Birmingham since I was a small boy, when my father had wanted to prove it was possible to drive there and back from London in a day. Tony would drive us there and I had arranged to spend the night at his flat. Having no driving responsibilities and knowing I would not be seeing my parents, I proceeded to get disgustingly drunk. At some point during the night, after returning to Tony's flat, I decided I needed more cigarettes. The cigarette machine at the local gas station swallowed my money but gave me no cigarettes in return. Furious, I punched the machine, broke the glass and removed a packet.

'Oi!' yelled a passing carload of good citizens who had witnessed my assault on the machine. 'Fucking wanker's nicking bloody fags!' They leaped out of their car and rushed towards me. My only escape, or so it appeared to me at the time, was through the plate-glass window of the car showroom. The first time I threw myself against it, I bounced back and landed on the concrete floor, somewhat bruised. The second, more determined leap resulted in a satisfying explosion of glass in all directions as I landed in a bleeding heap inside the showroom. Weaving my way through a proud display of Hillman Imp motor cars, I crossed the room and hurled myself through a second plate-glass window on the other side. Pouring blood, I lurched into the darkness and somehow found my way back to Tony's flat. It was on the seventh floor of a council block; I forced my way up the outside stairs, pumping blood with each step. Tony opened the door and I collapsed inside.

The headlines in the *Staffordshire Times* the following day proclaimed: 'Police Follow Trail of Blood to College Lecturer's Hideout'. Apparently, using the latest in crime-detection techniques, they had followed the bloody trail to Tony's flat, collected my unconscious body and taken me to the Stafford police cells without me being aware of anything.

The first thing I knew about the whole business was waking up with the mother of all hangovers and hearing the sound of my own mother's voice. I gradually realised that I was lying in a bloody mess on the floor of a police cell and that my mother was on the other side of the bars talking with the chief constable of Staffordshire – the head of the police force for the whole county. My parents were major social figures in Staffordshire and knew everybody. My father, as managing director of English Electric, was the biggest employer in the region. My parents had significant influence.

Nevertheless, despite all of my mother's heartfelt pleading, the chief constable remained inflexible. 'I'm sorry, ma'am, I really am. But we are just not allowed to flog prisoners any more. I quite agree that nine lashes with a whip, or whatever comes to hand, would do your son the world of good, but it is simply no longer permitted.'

My mother was a big advocate of flogging and was convinced that it would solve most of the world's ills. 'Don't lock them up,' she would argue. 'It's the taxpayers who have to pay for their food and their lodging while they sit there watching TV. They should be flogged and then they will think twice before they do it again.' She was also a big believer in hanging, though not necessarily for being drunk and disorderly.

I am eternally grateful to that policeman for standing up to my mother and refusing to have me flogged.

'They don't allow it any more,' he said wistfully.

'It's the socialists, isn't it?' my mother said bitterly.

'And the Europeans,' the chief said, hinting darkly at high politics.

He sighed and my mother sighed at the foolishness of the modern world and the slow erosion of British traditions.

I sighed, too.

So, although I had had some experience with The Law, none of my three adventures was sufficient to prepare me for what Michael Durani was now suggesting. Apparently, Graham had been apprehended by the German authorities in Rheinfelden as he was crossing over the border into Switzerland. They had found $100,000 in dollar bills in the car and also details of a bank account in Geneva. While holding Graham on suspicion of being suspicious, the Germans had asked the Swiss federal authorities to investigate the bank account and see if it was legitimate. The account was in the name of Zeitgeist Ltd, a company owned by Graham and me. All the money we made from smuggling hashish around the world was kept in the account and Zeitgeist would then 'loan' money to our various other companies for whatever venture needed financing. Obviously, the truth would not please the German authorities or help alleviate Graham's current predicament.

'All you have to do is appear before the tribunal,' Michael explained. 'Give them whatever cock-and-bull story you like, as long as you keep saying the cash is legitimate. The Swiss want to believe you. They like your business.'

Without Michael Durani's calming and urbane presence, I would never have had the courage or the skill to carry off so blatant a deception. The tribunal met in the federal justice building in the centre of Berne and consisted of four interrogating magistrates. They sat on the far side of a long table, wearing black robes and grey horsehair wigs. Durani and I sat at a lower level, facing them. Durani introduced himself as the local representative of Zeitgeist Ltd and me as the London-based managing director. Graham was described as 'an extremely well-regarded senior executive'.

Michael then proceeded to spin the most extraordinary story – a reverse version of today's Nigerian letter scam. He explained to the tribunal that our respectable English company had been approached by a Nigerian prince whose family had been massacred during the recent fighting in Biafra. Apparently, the prince still had access to about 50 million dollars in various family holdings and needed our assistance in transferring the money surreptitiously out of Nigeria. For a fee of 10 per cent, we were collecting his money in various European countries and moving it to our Swiss account for eventual dispersal to its rightful owner.

From time to time, Michael would turn and ask me to confirm some detail, a name, place or date that he was unsure of. None of this had been rehearsed, so my responses were all spontaneous. I just invented things. It was great fun and I was starting to enjoy myself. Michael sensed my change of mood and his story started getting more and more outrageous. He invented a sister for the prince, called Sonja. 'Remind me, Patrick,' he asked, 'was that by the father's first or second wife?'

'Neither. Sonja's mother was the third wife,' I answered, and then explained to the tribunal, 'It was a Muslim family.'

'Before they were butchered by the anti-Muslim government,' Michael added gravely.

He explained that Sonja had been kidnapped after escaping from Nigeria and was now being held for ransom. Graham had driven to Germany with some cash in an effort to contact the kidnappers. 'That he was returning alone and still in possession of the cash concerns me greatly,' Michael concluded. 'I fear for the girl's safety.'

Our bank account was unfrozen within the hour and the Germans were advised to release Graham immediately.

He joined Michael and me later that evening in Geneva and the three of us had dinner on the Quai des Bergues, near the bank. I was extremely excited and proud of what we had achieved, and I wanted to talk about it and boast all evening. But Michael dismissed the whole thing as a minor incident not worth discussing, so instead we spent the evening listening to Graham's grumbles about the appalling conditions in German police cells. From that day on, I was never to lose my admiration for Michael's cool *savoir faire* and grace under pressure.

Many people claimed that Michael was of royal blood, related to the Afghan royal family, but I never heard Michael himself make such claims. In fact, he rarely spoke about his past life. Certainly, he dressed like a prince and his English was impeccable and cultured. Whatever his lineage, it was commonly agreed that he had been educated at Harrow and Sandhurst. He spoke French fluently and also German – not to mention Dari, Pashto and Farsi.

By the time I joined Michael on that plane to New York, he was my biggest hero and I was delighted with this opportunity to learn from the master. We landed at Kennedy airport and proceeded to customs. 'Anything to declare?' the officer asked.

Michael opened his Hartmann carry-on for the man to examine. 'Just a bottle of Black Label and two boxes of cigars,' he said.

The customs agent removed the two cigar boxes and examined them casually. Removing the cigars, he reached to the bottom of each box and pulled out a small label in Spanish, which he translated for us: 'Genuine Cuban cigars. Fabricated and packaged in Havana.' With a deadpan face, he handed it to Michael to read.

With a bow of the head and a faint smile, Michael acknowledged that we'd been busted. He grinned at the agent. 'I always forget that final label,' he confessed.

'Most people do,' the agent replied.

The two men looked at each other. The agent put the cigars back in the box and handed it to Michael. 'Welcome to America,' he said. 'Have a nice day.'

The reason we were in New York was to watch and purchase movies. This was in the days when Bollywood films from India were banned in Pakistan and most movies shown there had to be imported from America. The trouble was that the money earned by the US film companies was paid locally in rupees and could not be exported back to America. Michael Durani and his friend Shemsi had therefore established a company in Karachi that purchased the US film companies' rupees for a nominal fee. The rupees were used to purchase hashish, which we then exported to Europe and the US. The US film companies were eventually paid dollars in America after the hashish had been sold. It was a win–win situation.

It was important that the movies shown in Pakistan appealed to local taste and were successful, otherwise they wouldn't generate enough rupees to pay for all the hashish. Michael therefore made it his job to visit New York every few months and spend his afternoons in Times Square movie houses with a stopwatch.

'Why the stopwatch?' I asked him.

'For the kissing,' he explained. 'Pakistan is a Muslim country and we cannot show people kissing in the movies. We have to remove those scenes. If there is too much kissing, then the film will be too short and the people will be angry.' He clicked the stopwatch to emphasise his point. 'So you and me, we watch the movies and we use the stopwatch to time the kissing.'

So my first visit to New York as a professional racketeer was spent in a seedy movie theatre watching endless Hollywood films selected by an Afghan prince and writing down the amount of time spent kissing. Many of the movies he selected starred Elvis Presley and I can confidently assure you that when he was not actually singing, the King spent a lot of time kissing.

Like the King, Durani also apparently spent a lot of time kissing. I'd visited his home in Geneva, where he lived with his wife and a bevy of permanent and very beautiful girlfriends. Whenever I visited, there was always an air of amusement and of barely suppressed sexuality in the house. I sensed that I was the only person not in on the joke – or not invited to the orgy – and I always felt like some awkward provincial cousin. Michael had a similar set-up in New York and, as far as I could tell, everywhere else that he travelled. Each time we went to New York on our movie-watching trips we were immediately joined for the duration by several attractive young women and, as I recall, a lot of time was spent kissing. We would take the girls for expensive meals in fashionable restaurants and entertain them in our suite at the Waldorf Towers or the Plaza and they in turn would introduce us to Maxwell's Plum on the Upper East Side, Studio 54 or CBGB's when such places were still new and hot.

Michael seemed to spend most of his time in Geneva and New York. I think he had a place in Paris and another in Rome but I was never invited to visit. He travelled to Karachi regularly but did not like it. 'Very smelly,' he explained. He did not have a permanent base in England, unless you counted Brown's Hotel, and visited seldom. 'I always feel I am still considered a wog when I'm in England,' he said rather sadly.

Of course, there was other work to be done while we were in New York. We had to collect suitcases of cash from our US distributors (which was when Michael introduced me to the benefits of Hartmann luggage). We would visit the Midtown offices of the various Hollywood film companies and pay them in dollars for the rupees they had originally given us in Karachi. At the same time, we would order new movies with the kissing scenes removed. The balance of the money I would then take down to Wall Street and give to a new contact that I had made through an associate in Zurich. Juan Dejesus had an office high above Manhattan in the World Trade Center, from where he would transfer all my New York cash to Switzerland and the account of Zeitgeist Ltd. But that's another story.

In fact, on that first New York trip with Michael, the hashish had already been sold in Europe and so there was no cash to collect from our US distributors. Michael had therefore secreted the money for the film companies in the lining of his suitcase before leaving Geneva and then distracted the US customs officer with his Cuban cigars.

'Busting us with Cuban cigars made him happy,' Michael explained to me. 'He could have been officious and confiscated them or even fined us. Or he could be the nice guy and let us through. Makes no difference. Either way he was happy. He had won and we were busted. He had done his job and was ready for the next people in line.'

That was one of the most important smuggling lessons that I learned from Michael: always cause a distraction. 'It is impossible to stand still, to do nothing and look innocent,' Michael told me. 'The professionals will spot you immediately. You must be pre-emptive and distract them. If the legal limit is two bottles of wine, carry three and argue about it. They will either let you through or charge you extra duty. Either way, they feel in control. Even while standing passively in line waiting for passport control, you must take the initiative. You know they are observing you behind their one-way mirrors; don't just stand their feeling guilty. Look for a pretty girl also standing in line, undress her with your eyes, imagine sharing a cab with her outside the airport . . .' Michael was serious when he explained all this. 'Focus. Don't embarrass the girl or make any sort of scene but let the intensity of your stare burn away her clothes and fill your mind with images of wild and wanton pleasure. Empty your mind of everything but pure lust. Anyone watching you will recognise the signs and you'll be stuck in the "dirty young man" category.' He grinned as he confided, 'I always like to approach the customs officer in a distracted condition of mild tumescence.'

During these New York trips, when we were not watching boring movies with stopwatches and when we were not wandering around Wall Street with heavy suitcases, we were usually sitting in elegant restaurants with beautiful girls who listened with adoring eyes to everything that Michael Durani said. It was at one of these dinners that I learned that Michael was not of the Afghani royal blood and had not been educated at Harrow or Sandhurst. Apparently, he came from a humble background in Pakistan, had been orphaned at a young age and found himself as a teenager owning a small trading stall in Dubai with a partner named Muhammad. The two of them were ambitious and resourceful, which is how they had acquired the stall in the first place. They realised that although they could make a decent living where they were in Dubai, selling the same cheap Indian jewellery and Egyptian cottons as everyone else, they would never be able to grow. They would never save enough money to purchase brides worthy of their ambitions. They needed fresh ideas; they needed new and unique goods to trade.

Michael was telling this story at dinner one night at Elaine's when a girl we'd not met before joined our group at the table. Apart from Michael and myself, there were Jenny and Heather, who always joined us when we were in town, Cindy, a friend of Heather's, and this new girl, Clair.

Clair had recently been dumped by her boyfriend Chuck and wanted revenge, so Jenny had invited her to dinner to calm her down and 'take her mind off of things'. Michael, sensing a fresh challenge, focused his energies on consoling Clair, while I, more than happy to console anybody, focused on Jenny, Heather and Cindy. As a young male, I would never have described myself as selective. I worshipped and desired all women.

Clair was describing to Michael her desire for revenge on this man who had hurt and humiliated her and Michael was explaining that revenge is a destructive emotion that does more harm to the person seeking it than to the object of the hatred. 'You need to move on,' he explained. 'You need to focus on growing and enriching your own life, not on harming the life of another. You need to seek your own peace and let God deal with the other person.'

As I think I've already suggested, Michael had a seductive charm that attracted all women – particularly when the subject of his conversation was love and revenge. I quickly became invisible as Michael pursued his story. The four girls leaned towards him with increasing intensity as Michael revealed hitherto hidden aspects of his previous life. Already, I could tell that the story of the trading stall in Dubai was working its oriental magic, like a tale of Sinbad the Sailor. The mystic allure of the East was mesmerising these women with the hint of exotic romance. Michael's good looks merely speeded up the inevitable.

'My partner Muhammad betrayed me,' Michael told Clair. 'Just like this young man Chuck betrayed you.'

Michael explained how the two of them had tossed a coin to decide which one would explore Europe for contacts and trading partners. 'It was a gold dirham,' he said, 'and I kept it close to my heart for all the two years that I was away.'

Michael had 'won' the toss and it was he who went to Europe on behalf of the partnership. While he was away, he signed over power of attorney to Muhammad so that he had full control of the business during Michael's absence.

The trip to Europe was unsuccessful. Michael learned how to behave like a French or English businessman but he was still treated like a 'Westernised oriental gentleman', 'a wog' – or 'a nigger', as he finally explained. The large and luminous eyes of the young ladies were wide with Western grief and guilt at this point and they were full of sympathy as Michael described his humiliating return to Dubai. He had no new contacts, no new goods and no money.

'I even had to sell my lucky gold dirham to pay for the final boat trip from Basra. "What did you say your name is?" asked Muhammad. "I have no partner called Michael Durani. What are you saying? Be careful or I shall call the police."'

By this time, we were all leaning into the table and listening to Michael's story. The girls' eyes were ablaze with the drama of the tale while Michael's were distant and lost in the sadness of memory. I was invisible to all of them.

'He denied you?' Cindy was aghast.

'As Peter denied Christ in the garden,' Michael responded.

We both knew of Cindy's fundamentalist Christian upbringing and worked hard to indulge it without spoiling her proclivity for imaginative sexual positions.

'So what did you do,' Clair asked, 'after he betrayed you like that?'

'What could I do?' Michael responded. 'He had the paperwork, he had the local contacts. He had the upper hand. There are times when you need to move forward with your life.'

In those days, smoking was acceptable at the dinner table. Michael spent some time heating, igniting and finally drawing upon his Cuban cigar. 'Genuine Cuban cigars have no wrappers,' he explained solemnly, although it was unlikely that the girls had even noticed this detail.

'You let him screw you and get away with it?' Clair asked.

'I assure you, my dear, that there was no sex involved.'

Visibly flustered, Clair said, 'Of course not. That's not what I meant at all. But you must have had strong feelings about it. Surely you wanted to punish him?'

'Punishment is for God to give,' Michael said, turning again to Cindy, 'not man.'

'In any event,' Michael hastened on, as though knowing he was pushing the holy martyr image too far, 'I had my life to live. I had to rebuild everything from scratch. I had nothing.' He looked each girl frankly in the eye. 'I could not start a family. I could not ask any decent girl to join me. I had no time for revenge. I had to start over with my life. From scratch.'

There was no need to ask if Michael had succeeded. The choice of this restaurant alone, to say nothing of his selection from the menu or the way he was dressed, more than demonstrated his material success.

'So what happened to Muhammad?' Jenny finally asked. 'Is he still in Dubai? Is he happy? Is he married? Is he rich?'

'So many questions,' Michael laughed. 'He is no longer in Dubai but if he is happy or if he is married, I have no idea.'

'But you are still in touch?' Heather asked.

'From time to time.'

We all looked surprised. 'I assume you spit in his face when you see him,' Clair said, obviously still angry with Chuck despite all Michael's advice.

'Absolutely not,' Michael said, horrified at the very suggestion. 'I am always very polite and friendly.'

'What do you say to him?' I asked.

Michael shrugged. 'I don't know. Whatever seems appropriate at the time. But I always insist on saying how pleased I am to see him. I always make a point of shaking his hand enthusiastically and asking "How's business?"'

Even I was impressed by this demonstration of wisdom and forgiveness. I could see that the girls were starry eyed as they listened to Michael's story. They all wanted to rub their naked bodies over his face and comfort him for his hurt and suffering while they licked away his pain.

'How often do you see him?' Heather asked, her voice already thick with desire.

'Maybe five, six times each year,' Michael said, 'whenever I'm in Paris.'

'He lives in Paris?'

'Yes,' Michael said. 'He has a shoeshine stand outside my hotel on the Avenue George V. I always let him know how delighted I am to see him whenever I stay there. Poor fellow, it's the least I can do.'

3

DRIVING TO WALES

Part of my childhood was spent living in South Wales while my father had a job in Bridgend, near Cardiff. My brother George was born there when I was six, and my sister Natasha and I would torment him unmercifully for years by jeering that he was Welsh and not English. Life was much slower in those days, especially in Wales, and the milkman delivered from a horse-drawn cart. My mother would hear the sound of the milk bottles as they rattled along the street towards us. 'Take the spade and run,' she would tell me. 'Quickly, before the other boys get there!'

I would dash towards the milkman's cart, looking for the fresh and steaming horse droppings that were left in its wake. I would use the spade to shovel as much as I could into a big aluminium bucket before the other boys could get them. On a good day, I could proudly give my mother a heavy bucket of horseshit that she could use to fertilise her rose bushes. It's the first gift I can remember giving her. Years later, when I travelled on school trips to France, I would proudly bring back bottles of Nuits de Paris perfume. What as a young boy I thought exotic and romantic, was, I now realise, as powerfully cloying as it was cheap. Each time I saw my mother in an evening dress preparing to go out with my father, I would make sure she was wearing a generous helping of Nuits de Paris. 'Dear me, I quite forgot my perfume,' she would smile gracefully as she turned to my father. 'How lucky that Patrick remembered.'

With guilty hindsight, I see now that, as gifts, my buckets of horseshit were far more welcome and fragrant than the cheap French perfume I was so proud of. My mother is dead now and has no grave, else I would gather horseshit and plant roses till the end of days.

The British Isles used to be much bigger in the 1950s. There was no motorway system and towns were linked by two-lane roads, so traffic moved at the pace of the slowest lorry or horse-drawn milk cart. From London, it would take three days or more to drive to Cornwall and a day or two to drive to Wales. Moving from Wales to Stevenage, near London, as we did when I was about seven, felt like going to New York or the moon – both equally inconceivable in those days. As for Scotland, that would require a two-week holiday.

I remember when the M1 motorway was first opened in 1959. The Saturday after it opened, my father piled us all into the family's Hillman Minx and we drove north from Stevenage to Birmingham. We all admired the wide and neatly mown grass verges and the graceful poured-concrete flyovers as we drove at a steady 75 mph. 'This is the twenty-first century,' my father announced, and we all agreed.

The biggest excitement, of course, was a visit to the Blue Boar service station at Watford Gap. For English kids in the '50s, a motorway service station was the equivalent of a visit to Disney's Magic Kingdom today, and Watford Gap was the first service station to be built in the UK. 'It's like being in America,' my father told us, and we all believed him. We gorged ourselves on Wimpy hamburgers with lashings of Heinz tomato ketchup poured over our skinny chips and washed it down with cups of Tizer. It was so exotic that for years afterwards we would beg my father to take us back to Watford Gap.

In the early '60s, the service station became the centre of the nascent English rock scene. The Beatles, the Rolling Stones, the Who, the Birds, the Faces and all the other young hopefuls with their roadies and their Bedford vans crammed full of guitars and drum kits, rushing through the night to gigs, from one end of the country to the other, would stagger bleary-eyed into the Blue Boar to play the jukebox or grab a cup of tea and a bacon sandwich. It was eventually immortalised by Roy Harper on his album *Bullinamingvase*:

DRIVING TO WALES

Watford Gap, Watford Gap,
A plate of grease and a load of crap.

As soon as we reached Birmingham, my father turned the car around and we drove back home again. However, before we left, he allowed us to stop at a petrol station and buy one of those souvenir plastic flags, which said 'Birmingham'. The back window of the family car was gradually getting covered with little flags of all the places we had visited: Bedford, London, Baldock, Hitchin, Swansea, Cambridge and now Birmingham. My father was simply excited by the concept of driving all the way to Birmingham and back in a single day. 'This is the way of the future,' he told us, and we knew he was right. We had been mesmerised for the whole journey, so excited by the speed and the distance we were covering that my sister Natasha and I did not even fight with each other and completely forgot to tease George and Judy and make them cry, which was our usual form of entertainment in the back seat.

The following Monday, my teacher asked the class how we had spent the weekend. I could barely restrain myself and had my hand in the air immediately. 'Please, Miss,' I said, 'we went to Birmingham on Saturday.'

'That's a long way to go,' she replied. 'Where did you stay? Did you stay in a hotel or do you have family in Birmingham?'

'We didn't, Miss,' I said proudly. 'We drove back the same day.' I looked around the class and said, 'We drove at more than 75 miles an hour!'

'Don't be ridiculous, boy!' she snapped. 'You cannot drive to Birmingham and back in one day. Put out your hand.'

I held my hand out and she lashed it twice with her ruler. 'That's for telling lies,' she said. It was around this period that I started to entertain doubts about authority figures.

Twelve years later, the state of England's roads had improved enormously but there was still nothing like today's motorway system. Even setting out from Oxford, driving to Wales and back remained a major undertaking. The M4 motorway was not an option in 1971, so we had to follow the two-lane A4 and take advantage of the occasional bypass. Most of the time, even though we were in Graham's large and powerful Jaguar, the journey was frustratingly slow. When we weren't stuck behind some diesel-belching lorry, we had to stop at traffic lights and slow down to pass through villages where kids were returning from school and women were pushing prams home from the local shop.

It was especially frustrating because we were in a hurry and desperately needed to be in Wales as soon as possible. Graham was driving and Howard Marks sat next to him, shifting in his seat with impatience and lighting up endless joints. Dutch Nik and I sprawled in the back seat and watched the English countryside crawl past the window. We were all uptight and on edge, and the slowness of the drive just increased the tension. Graham was tense because it was his money at stake; Howard was tense because it was his hash; Nik was tense because it was one of his crew who had stolen the hash. I was tense because everyone else was tense and it seemed the polite thing to be.

'All we need is a flock of fucking sheep in the road,' Graham grumbled. Graham hated the countryside and was always uncomfortable when he had to leave London. Howard told me that Graham had even hated his years at Oxford and had left for London the day his final exam was finished.

'Don't even mention it,' Howard replied, filling his lungs with smoke from the joint. 'Wales is full of sheep and half of them are on the roads.' Oddly enough, Howard also came from South Wales, near Bridgend, where I had lived. We might even have played rugby against each other when we were schoolboys. But we never met each other until we'd both graduated from university and were living in London, members of Graham's gang of dope smugglers.

For more than a year, we had been transporting large wooden crates full of hashish from Michael Durani's contacts in Pakistan. They were flown direct to Shannon airport in Ireland, where we persuaded the IRA to unload them, giving them the impression that the containers were filled with guns and explosives for 'the boys in the north'. We rented a small, remote farm overlooking the Shannon estuary in a place called Paradise. There we would pack the hashish inside the door panels of Ford Capri cars that we'd rented and driven over from London. To begin with, Howard and I took turns driving the dope-packed cars south to Cork, where we would board the ferry to Swansea in Wales and then drive (slowly and carefully) across England to London. After a while, we started using old college friends to drive the cars and would pay them £2,000 per trip. This had been going on for about a year and was providing a nice steady income and employment, as well as satisfying the British appetite for quality hashish, which had been growing since the Beatles and the Rolling Stones made the drug fashionable in the late '60s.

The four men in the Jaguar inching its way across the country that afternoon in 1971 were probably responsible for most of the hashish in England. Graham had been a major importer and distributor since his days at Oxford. He had contacts all over the Middle East as well as in California and he financed most of the smuggling operations in and out of Europe. Howard had been Graham's friend at Oxford. He'd spent most of his student days getting stoned and getting laid, or shagging, as he preferred to describe it. He had only joined the business side of things in the past few years. He was Graham's right-hand man on the dope side of the business, as I was Graham's right-hand man on the business side of the business. But already Howard was a major figure in his own right, well on his way to becoming the most famous British smuggler in history and a legend in his own lifetime; indeed, he was already a legend in his own mind.

I was the junior member of the team. Officially, I was Graham's partner in his various business ventures, like the property company and the carpet shop owned by Zeitgeist Ltd, our holding company. In reality, I was the money launderer, thanks to my time as an auditor with Price, Waterhouse & Co. I was also Graham's troubleshooter: the person sent to clear the air, test the waters or muddy them as the situation demanded.

Dutch Nik was a gentle giant of a man who lived on a converted barge in Amsterdam. His brother Diederik worked as a chef on the oil tankers that sailed between the Iranian Gulf and Rotterdam and he would occasionally deliver a few loads of hash from the Middle East. Nik ran an army of couriers all over Europe. He delivered carloads of Dutch and German underground newspapers to England and he delivered English underground magazines to Berlin and Paris. He had trucks that delivered Marvel Comics, which he imported from the US, and pirated Pirelli calendars, which he brought up from Milan. Nik's people were crossing European frontiers day in and day out, and after initial suspicion of these bearded hippies, most customs officers and border guards accepted them as part of the routine.

And, of course, Nik delivered our dope for us. The biggest European market for hash at that time was still England but for logistical reasons we often found ourselves bringing it in from Europe, especially Germany. Many of our flights from Pakistan and Lebanon would land in Frankfurt, so we would still have the problem of bringing the dope from Germany to the UK. That was Nik's speciality and he was excellent at it.

When our old college friends had all become too rich driving cars for us and no longer wanted to do the Irish deliveries, we turned to Nik to provide drivers. For the past few months, his people had been taking the ferry from Ireland and delivering the cars to an underground car park near Leicester Square. There was a drop-off box for the car keys and the car-park stub. This system allowed us to collect the car and unload it within a few hours of delivery. We would pay Nik for each car delivered and he would pay his drivers.

We were expecting a Saturday delivery from one of Nik's guys, Pieter, and became concerned when the box remained empty. We called Nik in Amsterdam. 'Don't worry,' said Nik. 'Pieter already called me when he was leaving Swansea. Everything is fine. Maybe he met some girl. Don't worry.' When there was still no news late on Sunday night, even Nik started to sound concerned. 'Don't worry. I'll come over,' he said. 'See you tomorrow.'

The news Nik brought on Monday morning was confusing. Apparently, Pieter had phoned Nik's wife and told her he'd dropped off the car. He'd said that we must have lost the keys or we were trying to cheat Nik out of his payment. Graham, Nik and I were sitting in the Warwick Castle pub, next door to our office in Little Venice, when Howard phoned. We were having a quick pint of beer before lunch. People usually phoned the pub before calling the office because that was where we spent most of our time. Howard was calling from Oxford, where he'd been making enquiries about Pieter.

'He's on a farm in Wales,' he told us. 'He drove the car there to meet some of his mates. They must have planned this some weeks ago. They'll hide out for a while and then drive the dope to Holland. He's ripped us off.'

As far as I can recall, this was the first 'dishonest' act I had ever witnessed during my career as a professional racketeer. Obviously, since we were smugglers and money launderers, our operation's very existence was criminal but we never stole anything or told lies, and the idea that one of us would deliberately steal came as a shock to all of us. We had no idea what to do.

'Do you have the address of the farm?' Graham asked.

'I can get it,' Howard replied.

'We'll be at your place in a couple of hours.'

We climbed into the car and drove to Oxford. These days, drug dealing is a byword for brutality but in those days we knew nothing of violence. Using his Welsh contacts, Howard had found the address of the farm, which was in a remote part of the Brecon Beacons.

'North of Merthyr Tydfil and west of Abergavenny,' Howard said, his unmistakable Welsh brogue savouring the sounds of the local names. 'There will be a lot of fucking sheep out there and not much else,' he grinned.

'Except for sheep-fucking,' Graham added with the city boy's eternal suspicion of country living.

We set off in high spirits. It was a sunny day, the car was spacious and we had an errand to perform – a mission, an adventure. I don't want to give the impression that we were arrogant and swollen-headed, at least no more so than any other group of young men in their early 20s. Nevertheless, we knew the significance of who we were and what we symbolised. Between us, we represented the aristocracy of European drug smuggling. For some ignorant, out-of-work Dutch sailor to think that he could insolently steal the fruits of our labour was more than insulting: as far as we were concerned, it threatened the very fabric of society. It represented total disrespect for who we were and the position we held in the hierarchy of dope smugglers. If we permitted this miserable Pieter to get away unpunished, then the very structure we had worked so hard to build might simply collapse. Drug smuggling as we knew it would never again be the same. For the sake of the smuggling community, we needed to act decisively.

The Jag moved west along the A4, leaving the Vale of Oxford behind us and climbing into the Cotswolds. The villages were smaller now and the buildings acquired a uniformity of colour and style, built in mellow Cotswold stone, reminding us that we were crossing through England's heartland. Like King Arthur's knights, we felt we were on a noble quest. As we passed road signs pointing to the ancient hamlets of Chipping Norton and Stow-on-the-Wold, I thought of Rupert Brooke's England:

> Stands the Church clock at ten to three?
> And is there honey still for tea?

'If we let Pieter get away with this,' Graham warned darkly, 'then all the others will think it's OK to steal from us.'

'We can't let it happen,' Howard added. 'Otherwise we lose all control.'

'Trust me,' Nik said, feeling guilty and responsible for the theft, 'Pieter will have to know who he is dealing with. It's not some petty gang of dopers in Amsterdam.' Nik leaned towards the front of the car and addressed Graham and Howard directly. 'I never told him who was involved. I never told him your names. Why should I?' Graham nodded at the wisdom of Nik's decision. Howard took a long slow drag on his joint. 'He thought he was just ripping off from me,' Nik continued. 'He had no idea he was stealing from you.'

'Ignorance is no excuse under the law,' Graham intoned rather pompously. 'Your friend Pieter is about to learn a very serious lesson.'

Comfortably replete with self-righteous indignation, we moved steadily west towards the mountains of Wales. Dusk was already falling when we reached the River Severn and it was dark by the time we left

England and crossed the border into the ancient province of Gwent. As we climbed into the uplands of Brecon, the roads became narrower and ever more twisting. Often, a white, ghostlike shape would force us to a halt and Howard would have to get out and push a sheep to the side of the road. 'Come on, Howard!' Graham would yell out the window. 'You can shag it later. We've got work to do.'

Eventually, after several false alarms and dramatic U-turns, we arrived at the farm.

'Look!' Nik said, pointing excitedly. 'There's the Capri we rented for Pieter in London. He's still here!'

'And the dope, too,' Howard added, equally excited.

We were all in such high spirits after the long ride and so filled with our sense of purpose that we had never actually formulated a plan. We got out of the Jag and moved together through a cluster of Land Rovers and large motorbikes parked around the main farmhouse door.

Beside me, Nik chuckled. 'I can't wait to see the expression on Pieter's face when he sees us here. I wonder what excuse he'll offer.'

The man who eventually opened the door in response to our loud knocking was not Pieter. He was a large bearded guy with a bare chest and a long ponytail, and in his hand he carried an axe. He wore leather trousers and a leather waistcoat that displayed the thickness of his chest hair. The axe was the same shape, although larger, as the one my father let me use when we went camping in these same Welsh hills as a child. My father's axe was used for splitting small branches for kindling when we lit campfires. He always watched protectively to make sure I did not chop myself; he knew my mother would never have approved if she'd learned he let me use it. There are some things fathers and sons need to do together that women will never understand.

Behind the man at the door, we could see a large room at the end of a dark hallway, filled with people. A wood fire burned in the stone fireplace and the flickering light reminded me of tales from Norse mythology. From what I could see, all the others were also bearded giants and this increased my sense of having stumbled into the Hall of the Mountain King. The Rolling Stones' *Sticky Fingers*, released a few months earlier, was playing in the background. As we stood in the doorway, 'Brown Sugar' started to blare out. Jagger's swaggering lyrics filled the hallway and someone turned the volume up. The energy level and the noise in the room down the hall increased and the smell of hashish was overwhelming.

The giant gripped the axe with one hand just under the head. I doubt whether his axe would have been much help with kindling. It was the sort of tool that you would use to split large logs, take down trees or confront a mountain lion with a certain degree of confidence. Certainly, the man holding it exuded an air of absolute confidence.

'Can I help you?' he asked politely.

'Sorry to bother you so late,' Graham said, 'but we believe a friend of ours might be staying here.'

'His car is parked over there,' Howard pointed helpfully.

'We're looking for Pieter,' said Nik.

'Ah,' the man said, and looked at us slowly, one by one. His voice was soft but his eyes were piercing. He moved the axe into his other hand. 'Let me see if Pieter is available.'

He turned and closed the door softly behind him. There was a long pause while we all looked at each other by the light of the coach lamp above the door.

'Seemed like a nice chap,' I said brightly.

Graham turned on me furiously. 'Patrick! We don't need any more of your horseshit. Just shut the fuck up.'

Understandably, he was still feeling tense. We continued to wait in silence.

Eventually, the door opened again and the large man smiled at us. He stood in the doorway, holding his axe. Behind him I could hear laughter and the crackle of the wood fire. It looked warm and inviting down the hall and I suddenly realised how tired and hungry I was. We'd been travelling all day and had eaten nothing.

'Pieter's sort of busy at the moment,' the guy said, giving an apologetic shrug. 'He's not really receiving visitors. Maybe some other time.'

Behind him, the music had switched to the Grateful Dead's 'Truckin''.

The four of us stood facing the axeman. 'Busy?' Graham repeated.

The man nodded and smiled sympathetically. His head moved in time to the music.

> Sometimes the light's all shinin' on me;
> Other times I can barely see.
> Lately it occurs to me
> What a long, strange trip it's been.

He waited patiently, holding his axe and nodding his head to the rhythm, but he was obviously anxious to rejoin his friends beside the warm fire, with the food and drink and the 200 kg of hashish that had recently been delivered from Ireland.

'Let's go,' Graham said tightly, and we all turned and walked back to the car, careful not to knock over any of the Harley-Davidsons. The axeman waved farewell from the doorway as he watched to see that we left the property.

It was a long drive back to Oxford, conducted mostly in silence while we all sat with our own thoughts, and it was almost dawn by the time we arrived. Howard's stunningly and unforgettably beautiful girlfriend Rosie got out of bed and cooked us a large English breakfast but we still didn't speak much. It had been a quiet drive back and, as I'd sat thinking, I'd remembered my father driving us up the M1 to Birmingham and then turning around and driving home again, without ever accomplishing anything. At least on that trip we'd got to visit the Watford Gap service station and come home with a souvenir flag of Birmingham to justify the trip.

The mood in the car had not improved when Howard announced that he was out of hash. 'I rolled the last joint just before we got there,' he grumbled.

'Oh,' I joked, 'we should have asked the man with the axe if he could spare some for the ride back.'

They all rounded on me at once. 'Patrick! Just shut the fuck up!'

At least my mother always appreciated my horseshit.

4

SMUGGLING

Unlike most other English boys, I never wanted to be an engine driver or a fireman or even a policeman like my uncles. I always wanted to be a smuggler. I never planned on being a racketeer, either – that was an unexpected honour bestowed upon me by the US government.

From an early age, I loved reading books about smugglers on the south coast of England bringing in contraband barrels of brandy from Napoleonic France. I could picture the secret caves in the cliff face, the tunnels that led to some innocent-looking Kentish cottage, where the smugglers would gather at midnight and divide up their latest haul. I could hear the sound of the tide hissing over the pebbles as we waited in the dark shadow of the cliff, watching with bated breath for the sight of a hooded lantern to tell us our boat was coming in. Even a poem as innocent as Matthew Arnold's 'Dover Beach' would fire my imagination with thoughts of illicit acts:

> The sea is calm to-night.
> The tide is full, the moon lies fair
> Upon the straits; on the French coast the light
> Gleams and is gone; the cliffs of England stand,
> Glimmering and vast, out in the tranquil bay.

I loved tales of derring-do in which the wily villagers outwitted the stupid revenue men. My favourite author was John Buchan. Although none of his very proper English heroes were actual smugglers, they were always slipping across international borders and working with local smugglers who would guide them over mountain passes when the moon was low or row them across rivers with blanket-muffled oars. His characters were all smugglers at heart. My dream was to be a Buchan hero like Sandy Arbuthnot. The following passage from Buchan's *Greenmantle* describes my youthful ambitions better than I could ever express:

> Lean brown men from the ends of the earth may be seen on the London pavements now and then in creased clothes, walking with the light outland step, slinking into clubs as if they could not remember whether or not they belonged to them.
>
> From them you may get news of Sandy. Better still, you will hear of him at little forgotten fishing ports where the Albanian mountains dip to the Adriatic. If you struck a Mecca pilgrimage the odds are you would meet a dozen of Sandy's friends in it. In shepherds' huts in the Caucasus you will find bits of his cast-off clothing, for he has a knack of shedding garments as he goes. In the caravanserais of Bokhara and Samarkand he is known, and there are shikaris in the Pamirs who still speak of him round their fires. If you were going to visit Petrograd or Rome or Cairo it would be no use asking him for introductions; if he gave them, they would lead you into strange haunts. But if Fate compelled you to go to Llasa or Yarkand or Seistan he could map out your road for you and pass the word to potent friends.
>
> . . . In old days he would have led a crusade or discovered a new road to the Indies. Today he merely roamed as the spirit moved him, till the war swept him up and dumped him down in my battalion.

Eventually, I outgrew John Buchan and discovered sex (which Buchan's heroes apparently never did, other than once observing that some young lady looked 'rather jolly'). But my fascination with smuggling continued as I learned that smugglers cavorted around exotic Caribbean beaches with bikini-clad beauties, sipping rum drinks and smoking pot. So when Howard Marks, a friend whom

I'd met when he was doing his MA at Sussex University, invited me to join him in a bit of smuggling, I was already prepared and ready to jump on board.

My first smuggling experience had occurred many years before Howard and I even met. When I was about seven, my parents decided to go on a driving tour of southern Ireland. My four-year-old sister Natasha was too young to come with us, so we left her at my grandmother's house in Belfast. 'You can't come with us because you're a baby,' I told her. 'We're going to stay in hotels and you'd only pee the bed. Anyway, you're just a girl, and Mummy and Daddy don't like you.'

Natasha did not say anything because her mouth was full of food. It was one of her tricks. If she did not like her food, she would shove it in her mouth till her plate was empty and then leave the table and spit it out somewhere, sometimes in my bed but usually in my school satchel. Instead of saying anything in reply to my taunts, she suddenly stabbed her fork into the back of my hand, drawing blood, and when we set off for the South the next morning my hand was still wrapped in a bandage.

Fifty-three years later, I can still remember the holiday incredibly clearly. It was wonderful – just me and my parents. At the time, the only other member of our little family was Natasha and we'd got rid of her in Belfast. Eventually, by the time I was nineteen, I had three sisters and two brothers, all younger than me: Natasha, George, Judy, Masha and Marcus. After that short trip to Killarney, the Gap of Dunloe and the Isle of Valencia, I never again had time alone with my parents. I was always surrounded by babies and nappies, and I always got blamed for setting the younger ones a bad example. I suffered a surfeit of siblings. No wonder I now live on the other side of the world and have nothing to do with any of them.

At the end of the trip, crossing back into Northern Ireland, we needed to show our passports. My parents had got me a passport for the trip but Natasha, of course, had not needed one because she was staying in Belfast. 'Mummy and Daddy got me a passport because I'm grown up,' I told her before we left on the trip. 'They didn't get you one because you're adopted and we're going to give you back to the Gypsies because you made my hand bleed.' Unfortunately,

Natasha's mouth was empty of food at that time, so when she bit my arm her sharp teeth were able to break the skin.

We approached the customs post late in the afternoon. After examining our passports, the officer put a large, official inked stamp in each one to show that we were re-entering the United Kingdom. I already had a stamp in my passport from when we had entered the Republic of Ireland seven days earlier. Now I had two stamps. I could not wait to show Natasha. I was sure she would be impressed but I hoped she wouldn't bite me again.

As I grew older and went on school trips, I loved collecting international entry and exit stamps. I was delighted when immigration officials had trouble finding enough blank space to place their stamp in my crowded passport. Later, of course, when I became a smuggler, the opposite was true: the stamps and dates became a professional nightmare. I was constantly juggling new and false passports to confuse my travel history.

After checking our passports, the officer asked us if we had anything to declare. My father, who was always very prepared and organised in everything he did, had made a list of all our purchases in the Republic of Ireland.

'Only some butter,' he smiled. We loved the creamy Irish butter and had bought several pounds to take home with us. Ice chests and coolers did not exist in the 1950s but my father had wrapped the packs of butter in wet newspaper and then in some towels and put them on the back seat.

'Butter? Would you be showing me what you've got?' the officer asked. My father retrieved the butter, after which he and the officer vanished into the customs shed to discuss it.

My mother turned to me and hissed, 'Don't sit up. Don't move. Stay asleep!'

When my father returned, he was empty-handed and furious. 'They charged me two shillings duty on each pack and then they confiscated them.' He pulled the throttle to start the car but was so angry that he flooded the engine and it was a while before we were able to move again. 'Apparently, you're not allowed to bring more than one packet of Irish butter into the United Kingdom,' he said. 'I told them to keep it.' He turned to my mother, his voice rising: 'I was tempted to tell them where they could stick it.'

'They should stick it up their bottom,' I said from the back seat, sitting up at last.

'That's enough, Patrick,' my father said. 'I was talking to your mother and I do not like you talking like that. Go back to sleep.'

My father remained in a bad mood until we reached my grandmother's house. I was disappointed that we had returned to Belfast, as I'd hoped my parents would forget Natasha and we would go straight back home to England.

While we unpacked the car, I helped my mother to raise the back seat, where I had been sleeping. She had hidden several bottles of Powers and Bushmills Irish whiskey as well as a couple of cartons of Capstan Full Strength and Player's Navy Cut cigarettes under my sleeping body.

My father was livid.

'But they're so much cheaper down there,' she protested.

'We could have been arrested and thrown into prison,' my father said.

'Don't be silly,' she replied.

'What sort of example are you setting for Patrick? How is this going to affect him when he grows older?'

I barely noted my father's remark at the time, I was so proud of my performance, pretending to be asleep, without moving and barely opening my eyes to peep at the customs officer. However, many years later, alone with my thoughts, unable to sleep in my cell in Atlanta Federal Penitentiary, I suddenly remembered what my father had said. It all came back to me.

'It's all my mother's fault,' I said to the large black man in the bunk above mine. 'She made me a smuggler.'

'Least y'all had a mother,' Leroy replied.

Leroy tended to be morose, especially on the subject of family. He'd been abandoned by his mother when he was about four years old, the same age as Natasha when we left her in Belfast. His mother, though, had never come back to collect him and he'd been raised by a succession of aunts and probation officers. Leroy was more of a dealer than a smuggler. He never blamed his upbringing for his fate and, except for that one short outburst, neither did I. The truth was that I always wanted to be a smuggler and my mother could never have stopped me. It was my vocation.

My first attempt at smuggling pot was an inauspicious prelude to my subsequent career. With my girlfriend Sue, I hitch-hiked to Morocco during the school holidays. We took a room overlooking Djemaa el Fna, the main market square in Marrakesh, where we would watch the snake charmers. On a clear day, we could see the distant peaks of the High Atlas Mountains from our window. We smoked a lot of kief, Moroccan hash, and spent our evenings sitting in cafés having pretentious conversations about existentialism and reading French poetry to each other. Ah, youth!

In Tangier, as we walked towards the ferry terminal, on our way back to Spain, Sue had one of those horrible moments of feminine intuition. 'Patrick, are you carrying dope?' She stopped in the street and put her bags down. 'Because if you are, I'm not coming with you.'

Whatever it was that I mumbled had no effect on her. 'How could you be so stupid?' she asked. 'Hitch-hike across Spain with a load of dope? Cross the border into France with a load of dope? Go through British customs with a load of dope? Are you insane? Do you know what Spanish jails are like?'

Franco was still running the show in Spain and his prisons certainly had a sinister reputation. That's the awful thing about women. We hate what they say and try not to listen to it but they do have an unfortunate and irritating habit of being right. In truth, I'd become increasingly nervous as we approached the port and knew I'd made a foolish decision.

I saw a young tourist who had obviously just arrived and was walking into town. I pulled three large slabs of Moroccan hash out of my bag and gave them to him. 'Welcome to Tangier,' I said.

'And the pipes,' Sue said. 'I know you've hidden those, too.'

I reached back into my bag, pulled out two elaborate water pipes and gave them to the surprised young man.

'Wow! Cool, man! Far out!'

We passed though customs in Gibraltar, in Spain, in France and finally at Dover. Our bags were not examined once. 'See what you made me do?' I shouted. 'We could have made a fortune. I was going to buy you that Biba dress you wanted. And now I've thrown away all my savings.' I got a lot of mileage out of that and continued to sulk for months.

The following Easter, I drove across Europe to Turkey with my friend John. I had just completed my A levels and was preparing for university. During my last year at school, I had studied the balance of power in nineteenth-century Europe, so I considered myself an authority on the Balkans. After the colour and gaiety of Italy and Austria, the monochrome grimness of Communist Yugoslavia under Tito was striking. As we drove through the monotonous, dreary villages and observed the surly or blank expressions on the faces of the population, I became increasingly depressed.

'It's all gone,' I told John. 'All their glorious history has been lost.' With the arrogance and pomposity of an educated schoolboy, I told him about the Bosnians and the Serbo-Croats. I described the ancient enmities of the Montenegrins and the Herzegovinians and the tensions between the Catholics, the Orthodox Christians and the Muslims.

'Look at them,' I said, pointing out the window at a resigned and silent crowd of men and women standing in line for a bus. 'They have no concept of their rich and glorious heritage. The Communists have drained all their passion and their memories. They have forgotten everything.'

I am still embarrassed when I remember that little speech and the certitude with which I gave it. Thankfully, John was bored and didn't listen to any of my ramblings, but, nonetheless, I would have felt even sillier about my confidently expressed opinions if we hadn't lost contact long before the recent wars in Bosnia.

In Istanbul, we purchased a load of what was claimed to be Lebanese hash from the Bekaa Valley, although I had my doubts. We had spent days in the shady quarters of Istanbul looking for somebody who could supply us with hash and who was not an obvious police informer. With his ever-shifting eyes, Mohamed certainly looked the part, and at least the hash was good enough to get us stoned. I was not going to waste time arguing with him over provenance – even though we had to pay more for 'Lebanese' than for local Turkish hash. Besides, Mohamed carried a large and wicked-looking knife.

For the return journey, we hid the hash under the back seat, just like my mother had done with the whiskey in Ireland. Hashish had not become popular on the European mainland in the 1960s, so we were not too concerned about the European border crossings. However, England was a different matter and customs at Newhaven were increasingly on the alert for young men with long hair and strange cigarettes.

The car ferry from Dieppe on the Normandy coast took some four hours to cross the Channel and the sea was rough. The deliberately lethal mixture of brandy, wine, beer, cigarettes, chocolate and whisky I consumed soon had the desired effect, and I started vomiting into a series of plastic bags. When the ferry reached Newhaven, we went below deck to the car and I lay on the back seat, still retching. John emptied the contents of the bags onto the front of my body, trying not to spill too much onto the seat of his car.

Even with all the windows open, the stench was overwhelming and John himself started to look green. The customs officer looked disgusted and barely examined our passports before waving us through. That was my first successful smuggling operation and with the profits I was able to buy a stereophonic LP player and a round-trip ticket to America via Iceland. John bought himself a replacement second-hand car that did not smell of old vomit.

I had won a place at Sussex University but postponed it for a year, until 1965, in order to spend 18 months hitch-hiking around the USA with my school friend Charles. It was in America that I had my second successful smuggling experience.

At one stage during our travels, we found ourselves completely destitute in El Paso, Texas. El Paso is across the river from its twin city, Ciudad Juárez, on the Mexican side of the Rio Grande. Three bridges joined the two cities over the tepid brown water of the river. In 1964, they were both squalid border towns and not good places to be down on your luck. The following year, on *Highway 61 Revisited*, Bob Dylan used Juárez as the setting for 'Just Like Tom

Thumb's Blues', a terrifying vision of urban desolation and the perils of hungry women.

A helpful man whom we met in a rather seedy bar offered to pay us for every bottle of Bacardi rum that we could bring him from Mexico. The price differential on Bacardi was enough for him to pay us a satisfying amount for each bottle we brought across the border. Each person was allowed to bring through one bottle per day and, since there were three border crossings in those days and three guard shifts per day, this meant that between us we were able to transport and sell eighteen bottles daily. Within a couple of months, we had saved enough money to be able to move on. It wasn't smuggling on a grand scale, I admit, but smuggling nevertheless, even if we did declare each bottle.

It was with Howard Marks that I started smuggling on a professional scale. Our first jobs were simple airport affairs. Graham Plinston, Howard's college friend from Oxford, would ship suitcases filled with hash from Pakistan to Frankfurt in Germany. Graham's research showed him that even though the flight from Karachi terminated in Frankfurt, the plane itself might continue on to another city in Germany such as Hanover under a different flight number. Graham's contacts in Karachi airport would therefore label the suitcase, with the appropriate flight number, for delivery in Hanover. I would board the plane in Frankfurt for the short domestic flight to Hanover and then exit the airport with my suitcase and no need to clear customs. Suitcases with little roller wheels had not been invented in the early 1970s and carrying a 200-lb case through an airport without looking obvious required considerable stamina. But there was very little official scrutiny in small provincial airports and we were never stopped. In today's post-9/11 world, with its sophisticated surveillance techniques, such a scheme would never work; it was all so much more innocent back then.

I'd rent a car at the airport, drive to a prearranged spot such as an old gravel quarry in the woods outside of town and rendezvous with Dutch Nik and a team of cars. The load would be divided among the drivers, Nik and I would stand in the gravel pit and swap gossip, and a few days later I'd pay him for his services in a London pub.

Not glamorous work, but it was steady, it paid the rent and it helped satisfy the insatiable English demand for 'Black Pak'.

The Irish operation was far more sophisticated and much more profitable. Once the hash had been unloaded by our IRA contacts at Shannon airport, the next task was to get it into Britain. I had tested various rental cars in London and decided that Ford Capris had the greatest amount of space behind the door panels and under the back seat. I would rent a Capri, drive across England to Wales and take the overnight ferry from Swansea to Cork. From Cork, there was a delightful three-hour drive across the green hills of southern Ireland to Limerick. After the car was loaded up, I'd spend the evening drinking far too much Guinness with Jim McCann, 'our man in the IRA', at Durty Nelly's pub on the River Shannon. The next day, nursing a giant hangover, I'd drive carefully back to Cork. Having checked out all the ladies' corsetry shops in Limerick, I would stop off in Killarney or Tipperary on my way to the ferry and collect the names and, if possible, business cards of shops that sold ladies' undergarments.

I'd drive carefully because the Irish, like the French, are among the world's worst drivers. The French are inept and reckless drivers at high speeds and the road accidents in France during those years were as spectacular as they were inevitable. The Irish, on the other hand, are inept drivers at low speeds. There were very few cars on the roads of Ireland in the early '70s and you could drive for hours without seeing another vehicle. Unfortunately, when you did see another car it was quite likely to crash into you. Even at low speed, a car crashing through the door panel of my Ford Capri could have caused considerable embarrassment.

I would take the night ferry from Cork and have a few more pints of Guinness in the bar before retiring to my bunk. We'd arrive at Swansea at dawn and catch the early-morning shift at the customs house. The examination was usually brief. An English passport and a London-registered car aroused little interest, especially in those days, when the IRA had not yet turned its attention to the British mainland. In any event, I was well prepared. My cover story was that I was a ladies' underwear representative. I was equipped with a set of business cards, a collection of marketing materials from various corsetry manufacturers and a suitcase filled with ladies' undergarments. I had, I told the customs officers, spent the past few days in Ireland visiting my various accounts.

The modern reader no doubt assumes I had selected this cover in order to carry a selection of racy marketing materials and a suitcase filled with brightly coloured G-strings and fluorescent thongs. Unfortunately, this was in the days before Victoria's Secret and heart-themed, brightly coloured pieces of flimsy lace were invented. My product line consisted of three colours: beige, taupe or flesh. As far as I could ascertain, the only size was gargantuan.

In fact, I had selected this particular profession because I counted on the natural reticence of the British male whenever the subject of ladies' underthings happens to be mentioned.

'Been in Ireland long, then?'

'No, just a couple of days.'

'On holiday, like?'

'No, business trip.'

'What's your line of business, then?'

'Sales rep.'

'Oh, aye. What do you sell?'

'Ladies' undergarments.'

'Here's your passport back.'

I always affected a slightly effeminate voice during these exchanges and it had the same effect as the vomit on the back seat had had when I'd come through Newhaven customs with John. They'd seen enough and they knew my type. They wanted me out of there.

Ladies' undergarments in those days were the real thing. They were thick, ugly and uncomfortable, and real men were even more uncomfortable thinking about them. Those were the days when even slim, 16-year-old virgins wore rubberised, roll-on elasticated girdles. In many instances, that was why they remained virgins for so long. Those things were very difficult to remove in the back seat of your mother's car, especially when you were both awkwardly smoking and pretending to each other that nothing was happening.

The ladies' underthings persona remained my major cover for many years and even today I think I would still use it if I were in the smuggling business. It is so obviously out of date. It's like telling people that you have the exclusive North American distribution for Betamax. The listener can only feel embarrassed and sorry for you, which is exactly how you want them to feel if you are a professional smuggler.

The overnight ferry from Cork would arrive at dawn and I had usually cleared customs at Swansea by nine in the morning. It would take a full 12 hours to drive across Wales and England, and I'd reach London just before the pubs closed at 11.00 p.m. Howard or Graham would be waiting in the Warwick Castle and we'd see how much Guinness we could drink before closing time. Somebody else would drive my car away for unloading.

Even today, more than 30 years later, I still remember those drives across England with a sense of joy. The previous night on the Cork–Swansea ferry was always a time of tension as I practised my ladies' underwear routine and prayed that the Welsh police had not yet introduced sniffer dogs. Two hundred kilos of Pakistani hash stuffed in a hot car has an unmistakable pungency. Luckily, it was a smell not yet widely recognised in south-west Wales.

'Rubber,' I'd say if asked.

'Rubber?'

'Yes. They weave rubber into all the garments. That's what the smell is: rubber. Helps keep everything in its place. Very important, that.' I'd add, 'Our customers are very particular about their support.'

I'd even leave a kilo of hash in my bag of samples overnight on the ferry, so that the smells all matched. Of course, it was very important that I remembered to remove the hash before going through customs.

So the long drive across England was always accompanied by a sense of relief and elation. In 1971, the Monty Python team had released 'The Lumberjack Song', a version of which I would sing loudly to myself alone in the car as the villages and green fields of England floated slowly past:

> I'm a smuggler, and I'm OK,
> I sleep all night and I work all day.
> I smuggle hash, I eat my lunch,

I go to the lava'try.

I sell women's underclothing

And have buttered scones for tea.

In my memory, those rides always took place in sunshine and the English countryside was a vision of verdant meadows and leafy woodland. I had completed another successful smuggling operation and I was returning to collect my reward, the recognition and accolades of my peers. Those are days of my youth that I recall as being among the happiest. I was a young man who had found his calling. Of course, a cynic might argue that, even with all the car windows open, 12 hours breathing the aroma of 200 kg of hash would make anybody feel giddy with happiness.

However, as the 1970s progressed, the nature of smuggling changed and the projects became larger, more complex and less personal. As we worked more closely with the Americans, we spent less time stealthily crossing moonlit beaches and more time calculating return on investment. Smuggling became a matter of counterfeiting bills of lading and exchanging air waybill numbers and international carnets. Obviously, my training as an auditor made me ideal for this sort of work but nevertheless I missed the romance of the early days. I remembered the cure for boredom suggested in Buchan's *John Macnab*: 'I advise you to steal a horse in some part of the world where a horse-thief is usually hanged.' For me, the golden age of smuggling was the early 1970s, when we ran yachts filled with hash from Lebanon and Morocco or crossed the deserts of Central Asia in Land Rovers.

❋ ❋ ❋

When, in 1973, former prime minister Mohammad Daoud staged a coup and seized control of Afghanistan, all Graham's contacts in Kabul airport were suddenly useless. Unfortunately, Big Dave and I already had 600 kg of the best Afghani hash in our Kabul warehouse and now we had nowhere to deliver it. The airport was closed down. I had barely made it into the country.

Big Dave was Graham's man in Afghanistan and he was paid to live there, liaise with the farmers and buy the best quality hash at harvest time. Graham or I would fly into Kabul after the crop had been gathered, transfer the cash through the Kabul money market and arrange delivery to the airport, where Graham's contacts would handle the paperwork and loading while we flew back to Europe. It was just one of those routine, seasonal things that one did in those days.

Big Dave liked the slow pace of life in Afghanistan, he liked the houses we rented for him and he liked the unlimited access to hashish that we made possible. Over the years, he had developed a network of friends and contacts throughout Central Asia. He was truly one of John Buchan's 'lean brown men from the ends of the earth'.

He also purchased carpets for us, which we exported to England and sold in our London carpet shop, Hamdullah. That was one of our none too sophisticated cover stories for travelling in Central Asia. I strongly suspected that ladies' underwear salesman would not work in Afghanistan, so I became an oriental-carpet dealer instead. Dave had been living in Central Asia for many years when I first met him and had developed an affinity for the Eastern way of life. With the money we paid him, he bought a houseboat on a lake in Kashmir and a flat in London.

I don't know where the 'Big' nickname originated but at 6 ft 6 in., it certainly suited him. Although he was the same age as the rest of us, there was a sort of ancient wisdom about him, especially when he spoke. He had a cockney accent but he spoke softly in long mellifluous sentences and when he was on a roll nothing could stop him.

Big Dave, having lived in the area for so long, knew the culture and all the stories. Most of the year, he survived in the silence of high, lonely places, so when he had an audience the words just flowed from him in a poetic torrent. I loved listening to him. It was during that trip in 1973 that Dave told me about the naked virgins of the High Pamirs.

I had just flown in from London on a nerve-racking 14-hour flight with Ariana Airlines. They had made us all get off the plane at Istanbul while they removed the seats and then screwed them back into the floor closer together. This allowed them to fit in an extra dozen passengers for the next leg, to Bombay. Flying on the national airline of Afghanistan in those days made you remember that these were the same people who drove overloaded buses crammed with passengers – hanging off the side and clinging to the roof – as well as goats, and which plunged over the edge of mountain precipices on a regular basis.

When I finally arrived in Kabul in the wake of the *coup d'état*, it was to find the airport crawling with armed troops and about ten military checkpoints to navigate before my taxi reached the city. At the checkpoints I heard Russian being spoken. By the time I reached Big Dave's house, I was in need of a stiff drink and was more than happy to listen as he told me about the latest harvest. Alcohol was freely available in Kabul in those days and we stretched out in Dave's house with a bottle of Scotch while he told me his story.

'Even though I can't remember much else,' he began slowly and ponderously as he rolled us a joint, 'what I remember as clear as yesterday are the naked girls. Well, it's what blokes think about, isn't it? That's the sort of thing we remember: a quick glance up a short skirt climbing on the bus; a sudden glimpse of cleavage when the barmaid leans over; the swelling of a hard nipple through a thin cotton T-shirt. I don't know about you, but I live for those stolen moments.'

He paused while he reflected on this. 'Not that I've been on a bus for a while and the last time I looked down a barmaid's cleavage was in Fulham. Still, you never forget, do you? This was more like a vision of paradise. The naked girls were all around me, their golden skin shimmering in the bright sunlight. They knew I was looking. Maybe all girls do.

'It was noon and very hot, especially at that height, where the air is thin and clear. We were in a valley high in the Hindu Kush, on the north-east border of Afghanistan, probably no more than 30 miles as the crow flies from Soviet Tajikistan. Not that any crows could have flown at that altitude – and if they could, the hawks would soon rip them to shreds.

'It's a lovely part of the country, where that finger of Afghanistan pokes across the High Pamirs to touch China. Above the treeline, it's austere and bare, with granite rocks and massive boulders tumbled from unimaginable heights above. But down in the valley, where we'd spent the night, orchards surround the houses and the bright fields are lush with crops. From where we sat, high on the slope of the valley among the apple trees, we could see the snow-covered peaks of the Pamirs, seeming almost close enough to touch. Splendid, they are; they always bring a shiver to my spine each time I see them. They're so remote, even when they seem so close. So high. So mysterious.'

Dave passed me the joint. He knew he had captured his audience. 'It was a beautiful late-summer morning,' he continued, 'near the end of September, when warm sunny days become rare and precious. It was almost noon when we arrived at the field, and we had set out from the valley floor soon after sunrise. For a short while, we had followed the banks of a river, the headwaters of the Oxus, but from the moment we'd left the village, we'd been climbing. The rocky path snaked between fields of grain and trees heavy with fruit. There were apples, pears and plums for the picking as we passed through the orchards. With my knife, I made two holes in the skin of a pomegranate and sucked the juice till it ran down my chin and stained the front of my shirt purple. All the time, the path climbed higher and higher, until, looking over a crag when the trail doubled back on itself, we saw the village small and distant below us. We must have been climbing for more than three hours before we reached our destination. We flung ourselves onto the grass, exhausted.

'Most of the farmers were elsewhere, keeping guard, and occasionally you'd glimpse a bearded man with his rifle silhouetted above a rocky outcrop. Others were working in the fields below, while the rest maintained guard in the village.

'Our farmers are from the Wakhi tribe, Ismailis. Lovely people. From what I could tell, this particular group was a breakaway sect, possibly descended from the Assassins, after the Mongols destroyed their mountain strongholds further to the west, near the Caspian Sea. On my travels, I was always hoping to find the fabled pleasure gardens of the Assassins. That's where young men lounged around in the gardens, smoking hashish with the dancing girls, then slipping away to kill their enemies. They had none of that fundamentalist nonsense. They were all into pleasure domes, singing, dancing, music – gardens of delight and all that stuff. The Ismailis were famous for their poetry and paintings, and our farmers were no different, always singing and making music.'

Of course, Dave was telling me this story in 1973, when legends of the Muslim Assassins had not acquired such a sinister significance in the West.

'Our farmers' women wore brightly coloured shawls of silk and finely woven pashminas. They displayed gold jewellery and happy smiling faces, not like some poor women in the rest of the country, hidden in shame behind their dark robes like lepers. And, of course, as I mentioned earlier, our girls got naked for the harvest.

'The harvest made the area particularly dangerous and meant the men had to be extra vigilant in their guard duty. The valley had the best hashish in Afghanistan. This was a site that required serious protection. The rows of hash plants stretched around the steeply sloping hillside in all directions. The plants were thick and leafy, standing about five feet tall and planted in rows about two feet apart. Even from where we sat, we could see the sticky buds on each plant, swollen with pollen and ready to burst. The thin mountain air had a sweet, thick taste; it was like inhaling honey.

'That's when I realised, halfway up the side of a bloody Himalayan mountain, surrounded by towering snow-covered peaks, while the noonday sun beat down upon us, and the thick pollen filled the air, that I was completely, utterly and hopelessly stoned. Just by sitting in a field and breathing the fresh air, I had become a floating, dreaming speck in the vast panorama of the Hindu Kush.

'By then, the women had moved out into the field. I don't know where they had come from but they had positioned themselves in pairs at the end of each row. Maybe they had climbed the hill behind us or maybe they had been there all the time, though it would have been hard to miss them in their bright silk shawls. Each pair looked like mother and daughter, certainly there was one older and one younger woman. I don't know where the musicians came from, either, but suddenly there was music all around us.

'When the music started, we were really spacing out on the hash-laden air. The view from where we sat was so stunning that my mind was drifting, cloudlike, above the valley towards the high peaks, until the subtle rhythms of tablas and dayerehs pulled me back to earth. And then the tula player got going, with high-sounding notes that swooped and swirled in bright sparks of pure sound all around the immense valley. The music was a joyous affirmation of life, like the call to prayer from the muezzin.

'The sound of the pipes must have been a signal, because at the end of each row a girl stepped out of her brightly coloured wrap, which she handed to the older woman. Their hair, normally worn long and flowing, was tightly bound into white turbans so that not a single strand showed, but beneath their wraps the girls stood proud and completely naked. Young women, I should say; they were poised, with firm breasts and slim, sinuous bodies that swayed to the rhythm of the tablas. Completely unselfconscious, they began to run down the rows between the plants.

'Even though I was stoned, I can still remember every minute detail. To me, it wasn't a sexual thing. It was more than that; it was a vision of unattainable loveliness, a glimpse of paradise, a fleeting dream from which you fear to wake. Above all, it was beautiful and the girls were full of grace. You can have no idea of the beauty or the solemn innocence the ceremony conveyed. I don't know how to describe the effect it had, except it made you feel privileged. You knew you were in a holy place. And all the time, the music of the pipes swooped and flew through the rows of hashish, caressing the young female bodies and celebrating the majesty of the distant peaks.

'As the girls ran down the lines of plants, their movements fanned the air and disturbed the pollen, which gathered in fine clouds above the sticky buds. Their supple bodies were generally hidden by the plants but sometimes they could be glimpsed between the leaves as they disturbed the foliage in passing. When each girl reached the end of her row, she burst into the open and her body was fully revealed before she turned and ran back through the thickening air. The midday sun and their efforts had caused the girls to sweat and there was a glistening sheen to their bare skin, which reflected the sun into our eyes. But, gradually, as the pollen stuck to their flesh, it formed a delicate covering and the bright sheen slowly faded.

'The music of the pipes was swirling all around us now, swooping along the rows and wrapping itself around naked limbs. I turned my head in all directions and everywhere I looked I saw the same green lushness of the plants and the same lithe movement of the nubile bodies.

'After every second turn, the girls would stand on a white muslin cloth while the older women scraped their skin with a bone instrument, a cross between a knife blade and a shoehorn. The girls' skin was uniformly tanned, without the pale bikini marks you see on Western women. When they were standing upon the cloths, their skin was at first dark and dull but as the women's fast-moving fingers removed the pollen, the breasts, the belly, all the skin was quickly revealed in its glory. The thick pollen paste that had accumulated on the girls' bodies was scraped into bowls and then the girls would run down the rows again until the golden dust had covered them once more.

'For some two hours, the girls continued to run the lines, until eventually there was no more powder to dust their perfect skin. All the available pollen had been gathered into bowls or dissipated into the air, an offering to the Gods of High Places.

'And then it was over, as suddenly as it had begun. After scraping the girls' bodies carefully for the final time, the older women wiped them clean and dry with strips of white cloth. The girls were once more dressed in their brightly coloured wraps. Walking in a line like schoolchildren, flashing shy, curious glances in our direction, they were led back down the path to the village far below, and I found myself lying on a bare hillside wondering if it had all been a dream.

'The older women brought their bowls close to where we sat and arranged themselves in a large and cheerful circle. The musicians also moved closer and, while their wild music continued to surround us, the women kneaded the mixture of pollen and perspiration into a thick paste, which they pressed between their palms to mould small discs of pure hashish. As each disc was finished, it was passed to us for inspection. I'm afraid I was not much use: I was still picturing the beautiful bodies, retracing in my mind their gazelle-like steps between the plants.

'It was late afternoon before the final disc was wrapped in one of the white cloths used to wipe off the girls' skin. The air had already turned chilly as we followed the chattering women down the steep mountainside. The farmers walked behind us with the wrapped discs packed into large hemp sacks, which they carried on their backs.

'We left the village at first light the next day with four donkeys. It still took us two days of hard hiking over narrow tracks to reach the main road to Feyzabad, past the ancient mines of lapis lazuli. We had a truck waiting in Feyzabad and drove it down to Kabul last month.'

Big Dave rolled another joint. He'd submitted his report on another successful harvest. Now it was time to relax. He smiled contentedly. 'You can tell Graham that we've now got 600 kg of the finest hash to ever reach Europe sitting in his warehouse. First-blush pollen, brushed from the naked breasts of virgins.'

My voice was thick when I finally spoke. 'Dave, next year I want to come with you. It's not fair to make you do all this alone.'

Dave smiled. 'I rather thought you might.'

Unfortunately, Daoud's *coup d'état* proved to be more serious than we had thought. It wasn't as if we were unaccustomed to coups and revolutions. We were used to political unrest in those parts of the world where hashish is grown. Normally, one would just hunker down in a hotel until the Scotch ran out. The main thing was to steer clear of military checkpoints and avoid looking too conspicuously 'foreign'. We expected no more than a few days of disruption before it was once more business as usual. Daoud, however, had other ideas and, despite his conservative Pashtun background, he was pro-Soviet. His men had been trained and armed by the Russians; it was the first step in a Communist takeover.

All the old guard were out and there would be no more business as usual. Our contacts at the airport had all been arrested or executed or had gone to ground. We had 600 kg of the best virginal hash and nowhere to go. Big Dave and I both knew that Graham would not be satisfied with a harvest-load of primo Afghani hash stuck in a warehouse in Kabul just because the airport had closed down due to a political coup.

'That's no bloody excuse,' he said when I eventually called him on the phone from the money market. 'Tell Big Dave to use Plan B,' he said before the connection cut off.

'What's Plan B?' I asked when I eventually got through all the checkpoints and returned to Dave's house.

'We'll have to drive it overland to the Gulf,' he explained.

'Do what?' I enquired.

'It's our Plan B. We drive through Baluchistan across the desert to Persia and Graham knows this Dutch guy who works on oil tankers in the Gulf. We'll give it to him and we'll be all right.'

Simple as that.

Once we left Kabul, having loaded the harvest into a Land Rover, there were no more checkpoints. Daoud's rule did not yet extend beyond the capital. One of Big Dave's many friends, Mohammad, greeted us when we arrived in Kandahar. Somehow or other, he knew exactly when to expect us and had hot tea ready and waiting. He was a tall man with a full beard and a big, loud, booming laugh. He carried a large curved knife in his belt and a rifle slung over his shoulder. Mohammad was a member of the Baluchi tribe and they had no master but Allah. They did not recognise the Daoud (or any other) government in Kabul, no more than they recognised the Shah in Iran or Zulfikar Ali Bhutto's government in Islamabad. The ancient tribal lands of the Baluchis included areas of Iran, Pakistan and Afghanistan, and as far as the Baluchis were concerned, those national borders were just pencil lines on a foreign map. Mohammad and his people were to be our companions for the rest of the journey, and that made me happy.

The first part of the trip was routine. We followed the valley of the Darya-ye Helmand to Rudbar, where we turned off the road and headed south into the land of the Baluchi. It's a tough country; the reason the Baluchis have remained masters of their domain is that nobody else can survive there. The first day's drive took us across the salt flats of Gowd-e Zereh and the landscape does not get much more bleak and desolate than that. But there is a wild beauty about the land and when you travel with people whose fathers and grandfathers – all the way back to Alexander the Great – have been physically fighting for every rock and wind-blown dune, you can sense their mystic unity with the earth, however harsh and barren it might be.

Late in the afternoon of the second day, we arrived at a tribal campsite near the town of Mashki Chah and Mohammad told me that we were now in Pakistan. His cousin had been expecting us and a feast had been prepared.

As we sat back after the meal, listening to the low murmur of voices, Big Dave explained to me the appeal of his vocation. 'Whenever people back in England ask me why I never settled down and got a normal job in London, when they ask why I lead the kind of life I do, I always want to tell them about evenings like this. But I never know what to say or how to explain the magic. Well, of course, they don't eat goat back home anyway, so they wouldn't understand the special taste it has when it's cooked over open flames and you're eating it with your fingers. It's hard to explain the pleasure of sitting on the ground around a large fire or the special look on people's faces in the flickering light from the flames.'

I too was enchanted as I looked around me at the other faces. Only men were allowed to eat at the fire, all of them bearded, with large turbans and eyes that glinted in the light of the flames. They all carried in their belts curved knives with wicked, sharp blades, which they used to cut the meat. After the meal, when we leaned back and looked up at the sky, there were a million stars hanging there, more than you could ever dream of seeing in the grey skies of England.

Dave's voice was solemn as he pointed to the heavens: 'Some nights in the desert, looking up at the stars, you know you've seen the face of God. Those are the moments that I live for. That's why I love to smuggle hashish.'

After going through the big ritual farewell with Mohammad's cousins, we headed south-west into the desert and within a day Mohammad said that we had crossed the border into Iran. Even though we were skirting south of the terrible Kerman Desert, the southern part of the vast Dasht-e Lut, the crossing wasn't easy and sometimes you'd see the bones of travellers who'd failed to make it. It's an empty, unforgiving part of the world and in the next three days we didn't see another living being, just towering dunes of fine red sand and dry riverbeds. The sand got in our hair and in our mouths. It slipped between our teeth and lodged there and you could feel its gritty irritations on your eyeballs, making you want to rub them all the more. It blocked your nose and dried out the skin inside your throat until you thought you were going mad. But we survived and eventually we rejoined civilisation, and the road, at a small village where another of Mohammad's cousins was waiting to greet us.

That evening, we ate roast mutton as well as goat and we drank fresh yogurt. The stars were graced by a waxing moon and the surrounding desert had a silvery incandescent glow. That night, there was music and singing to follow the food.

In the morning, we bought carpets. Baluchi rugs are not my favourite. I much prefer those of the Afshar and the Qashqai, further to the north and west. I find Baluchis the least interesting of all the tribal rugs but in Baluchistan that's all you can buy. Big Dave sat on a stool, the carpets were thrown on the ground in front of him one after another, and he would quickly nod or shake his head. Eventually, after he had selected about 60 rugs and paid for them with gold sovereigns, we loaded them into Land Rovers and headed towards the sea.

We reached a small village on the Persian Gulf almost two weeks after setting out from Kabul, some two thousand miles away. We were dirty and exhausted. Our eyes were inflamed and we were unshaven.

Mohammad's men loaded the sacks of hashish into a large dhow moored along the water's edge and I stood guard on the boat for the next 24 hours. Meanwhile, Big Dave and Mohammad drove north about ten miles to the oil terminal of Chabahar to make sure our transport was ready. Making the connection with the tanker was, apparently, always the hardest part. There were too many variables when you were driving across deserts to ever be sure of when you would arrive. At the same time, the oil tankers had to be fairly flexible in their schedule, depending on the weather; a big storm rounding the Cape could throw everything out by a week. As Big Dave put it, 'You could find yourself sitting in a small boat in some godforsaken village full of bearded desperados guarding a million dollars worth of pot for a week or more and thinking there had to be an easier way to earn a living.'

But we were in luck. Dave climbed down into the boat and said, 'Diederik will be ready for us at dawn.' While Mohammad and his men stayed behind to guard the cars and the carpets, the dhow's crew raised the sail at around 3.30 a.m. and, without a sound, we glided away from the village and out into the dark waters of the Gulf. The moon was still full and everything was bathed in silver light so that even the vast array of pipes, tanks and cooling towers of the Chabahar oil terminal took on a romantic glow, like some ghostly palace from the *Thousand and One Nights*.

We reached our destination just as the huge crimson disc of the sun appeared above the water behind us. It was a vast, supersized oil tanker, bigger than any of the towns we had visited in the past couple of weeks. It even seemed bigger than Kabul and from where we sat in our dhow, low upon the water, it looked taller than the city of New York.

Diederik was waiting for us at the loading door with a bunch of his crewmen. 'Hey, Big Dave! I hear you've been out in the desert shagging goats again,' he shouted down to us.

'Oh, I'm sorry,' Dave said. 'I thought they were your sisters.'

Diederik, Dutch Nik's brother, lived on a houseboat in Amsterdam when he wasn't working on an oil tanker somewhere in the Indian Ocean. He was the ship's cook. He had a kitchen staff of four men and his rule was law. There was a crew of over 40 men to feed and sometimes the tanker would be at sea for several months. The kitchens were huge and the freezers were vast. Before setting off on a voyage, Diederik supervised the loading of all the provisions. Fruit and vegetables were always picked up at the last moment so that they would be as fresh as possible. Lifting 600 kg of hashish into the hold of the tanker and stashing it deep inside the freezer was the work of just a few moments. If anyone saw the chef loading goods onto the ship, he would assume it was fresh food. Nobody knew what was there, except for Diederik and a couple of his trusted helpers. When the tanker arrived at Rotterdam, the unloading of provisions from the freezers would be equally discreet and efficient.

It was a big relief when the cargo was finally stashed in Diederik's freezer and out of our hands. We sat at the main table in the kitchen and Diederik opened a bottle of schnapps and poured each of us a glass. My job was done and I could finally relax. Mohammad and his boys drove us to the local airstrip, where we loaded all the carpets onto a small plane, in which Dave and I flew to Tehran, the capital. There, it took at least three days and several gold sovereigns for Big Dave's contact in the Shah's bureaucracy to update the entry stamps in our passports and complete the paperwork on all sixty carpets. Everything had to be completed in triplicate and stamped and countersigned, and it took for ever, but when the carpets were finally sold from our shop in London, their provenance and origin would be fully and exhaustively documented, something that Graham always insisted upon.

That was our final Afghanistan deal. Daoud's ineffective government was eventually replaced by the Russians and none of us ever made it back to Kabul. My brother George had moved to the Afghan capital during that period and he stayed on under Daoud's rule until eventually he too was kicked out. He moved to Iran just in time for its own Islamic revolution. But that's another story.

Big Dave told his story about the harvest ceremony to everyone when he next visited England, and Howard, of course, was as anxious as I was to join him for the next harvest. But there were to be no more Afghan harvests for us. Many years later, after the Russians had been expelled, Howard surreptitiously crossed into southern Afghanistan to inspect a hashish harvest but the Taliban were in charge by that time and there were no more naked virgins.

* * *

In the early '80s, after I had quit the smuggling business and moved to Santa Cruz in California, I used to play tennis every morning at dawn with my friend Bob. The tennis courts were located above the cliffs and offered a clear view of Monterey Bay. Usually, at that time of day, we had the area to ourselves, with nobody to disturb us, but one morning we arrived to find a group of scruffy hippies standing near the courts and looking silently out to sea. They were there the following morning and the next, always gazing towards the horizon with the same fixed intensity. Bob didn't like the hippies in Santa Cruz. They would pee in the doorway of his jewellery store at night and he would have to clean away the yellow stains in the morning.

'Go and get a proper job,' he'd mutter when we saw them in the morning, gathered for their silent vigil. 'Probably all smoking dope and sleeping with each other's girlfriends.' Bob had little patience for what he called 'dopers'. Obviously, he knew nothing of my history; he liked me because he usually beat me at tennis.

And then one morning the kids stopped coming and we never saw them again. 'Wonder what that was all about?' Bob said. 'I guess we'll never know.' But I knew what it was about. They'd been waiting all night for their boat to come in.

At the time, I was a fugitive and nobody knew I was living in Santa Cruz. Even my sister Natasha had no idea. (Natasha and I had remained close friends since childhood. She had forgiven my elder-brother bullying and I had forgiven the occasional stabbings and bitings. Indeed, we remain the closest of friends to this day.) Nevertheless, when she set sail from the Pacific coast of Colombia in a yacht, by pure coincidence her rendezvous destination happened to be Santa Cruz. It is a small world after all. Her planned arrival time, I was to learn much later, coincided with the couple of weeks when Bob and I had company for our morning tennis matches. Apparently, it was Natasha's boat that the Santa Cruz hippies were waiting for.

Their wait was in vain, because Natasha had been intercepted by the Mexican navy just off the coast of Tijuana. According to subsequent reports in the Mexican press, the yacht was so heavily loaded with bales of pot that there was nowhere for the crew to sit. Natasha spent the next couple of years in Tijuana's La Mesa State Penitentiary – one of the roughest prisons in South America. Once again, she had no passport. Had my parents only abandoned her in Belfast as I had originally suggested, this could all have been avoided.

|5|

NORWEGIAN SHIT

By the late '70s, all the romance had gone out of drug smuggling. During the middle of the decade, we were moving vast quantities of hashish around the world, hidden inside the sound equipment of international rock groups. We had containers flying into New York and Los Angeles, and, of course, all this activity generated vast quantities of cash. My focus therefore moved from hash to cash and thus I began my new career as an international money launderer. But Howard and I always retained a hankering for the adventure and romance of the old days and that was why the Scottish caper, with boats on the high seas, remote castles and moonlit beaches, was so appealing to us.

Howard and I realised early on that the scheme would require some muscle. Arthur Goldman, a New York contact, offered to introduce us to some soldiers who might be able to help. He thought it was important we meet some of them so that we could form our own opinion of their potential. Which was why, in the summer of 1979, we found ourselves in a New York bar struggling to make ourselves understood by two marines who, Arthur assured us, had never left the Bronx except for basic training. It is true that Howard has a Welsh accent, of which he is immensely proud, but he can speak with no trace of it if the need arises. I like to think that I speak with no accent at all, but I suppose we all think that.

As far as Arthur was concerned, the evening was a disaster. It took him at least half an hour of discreet but agitated persuasion to convince the marines, Vinnie and Billy, that Howard and I were not a couple of 'faggots'. The rest of the evening was spent with Arthur translating Vinnie's and Billy's utterances for us; the two of them just looked blank at everything we said. In some ways, this was lucky because neither Howard nor I knew anything about the current state of New York sports and that was all the two soldiers wanted to discuss. Fortunately, Goldman followed both baseball and football, so he was able to translate my 'I haven't got the faintest idea what you fellows are talking about' into 'Did ya see that fuckin' catch by Sudowski on third?'

'What do you think?' Goldman asked after we'd left the soldiers in a strip bar with $100 each in singles.

'Communication might prove a problem,' Howard said.

St Paul had his moment of insight on the road to Damascus. I had mine in a cheap bar in Glasgow a few weeks after meeting the two soldiers. I asked the barman to recommend the best local beer and I could not comprehend a word he said in reply. I also quickly gathered that he could not understand me or anything I said to him. I turned to another man at the bar for help and still have no idea what he said to me. Forget about being in a foreign country, I was on another planet! The Scots were impossible to understand.

'Brilliant!' Howard said when I told him.

'We'll fly the soldiers to Scotland and tell them they're in Norway.'

'Brilliant!' Howard said.

'They won't have a clue where they are and they won't understand anything anybody says. Then we can fly them to Oslo after the operation, let them hang out in the airport for a few hours and fly them back to New York. If they ever talk, they'll talk about Norway and a bunch of Norwegians they couldn't understand.'

'Brilliant!' Howard said.

* * *

Howard and I could never agree on books. We were both avid readers but I think the only writer we both enjoyed was John Le Carré. We both loved the George Smiley books and when the BBC adapted *Tinker, Tailor, Soldier, Spy* with Alec Guinness in the late '70s, Howard and I would fly to his London apartment from wherever in the world we were at the time to watch the weekly episode. Howard had a Sony Betamax, which was state-of-the-art technology in those days, purchased in the US. Unfortunately, there was no preprogramming and you had to physically press the 'record' button to tape the show. We quickly assimilated all of Le Carré's 'tradecraft' and for the Scottish operation we went strictly by 'Moscow Rules'.

But apart from Le Carré, we seldom liked the same authors. I read Patricia Highsmith and he read Wilbur Smith. This was in the days before I discovered Marcel Proust! In fact it was Wilbur Smith who started the whole Scottish adventure. One day, Howard handed me *Hungry as the Sea* and asked me to read it. I quickly understood why. The novel was about salvage vessels, which patrol the world's oceans waiting for shipwrecks to happen. They are fast and powerful boats, designed to go anywhere in the world faster than their competitors. They are equipped with the latest technology so that they can legitimately evade surveillance while they track and observe the world's shipping. The salvage industry has a love–hate relationship with Lloyd's of London and with the governments of the developed world. But the important fact was that salvage is a legitimate business and the evasive and secretive tactics of the vessels are regarded as normal commercial practice.

'Salvage vessels zigzag across the ocean,' Howard explained. 'They are supposed to be evasive and unpredictable. Government agencies accept that the international salvage fleet performs a vital role. If you are a registered salvage vessel, the US Coast Guard, the British Navy, the DEA [the US Drug Enforcement Administration] will ignore you. You're supposed to scurry around being mysterious.'

'Even if you'd picked up a load of pot from Colombia and dropped it off the coast of Scotland before going to Norway,' I suggested.

'Exactly,' said Howard.

'Brilliant!' I said.

The plan was quite simple. We asked Ernie Combs, our long-time partner in California, to finance several million dollars for one of the Colombian cartels to shift 20 tons of top-quality marijuana out to sea, where arrangements had been made for it to be picked up by an international salvage vessel, the *Karob*, which would immediately shoot down to the Falkland Islands and then vanish into the wastes of Antarctica.

Ernie was a founding member of the Brotherhood of Eternal Love, a group of mystic dope dealers based in Laguna Beach, California, and he handled all of our American business. He gave the project to Santo Trafficante, the head of the Florida Mafia, and to Louis Ippolito, who had strong links with the Colombians. Louis was based in New York and he introduced us to Arthur Goldman, a Jewish vegetarian shopkeeper who claimed to have contacts in the US military that provided him with soldiers for unloading boats off the coast of Long Island, Connecticut and elsewhere in New England. Whether these really were genuine soldiers or just the back-up band for the Village People, we never found out. But they were muscular, they had impressive tattoos and they got the job done. They were also all vegetarian, as Arthur insisted that anyone who worked for him must be a practising veggie.

Meanwhile, on the other side of the world, my sister Natasha contacted her friend Stuart, who had a fleet of yachts anchored on the Isle of Mull in the Inner Hebrides. Ostensibly, Stuart's fleet was used for sailing rich Americans and Germans around the Western Isles but every now and again one of the yachts would go south 'for repairs'. Usually, it would go to Morocco but sometimes it would sail across the Mediterranean to Lebanon or Egypt. After several months, the yacht would return, the crew looking suntanned but otherwise unchanged. Inside, the yacht would be filled either with hashish, kief or pot, or else with bundles of cash wrapped in rubber bands. Sometimes the whole fleet would move south and winter in the Greek Islands. Stuart was a Californian and his band of merry sailors brought along their wives, girlfriends and kids, who all lived together in communal bliss and material plenty.

In Howard's autobiography *Mr Nice* and in my sister's book *Mrs Marks and Mr Nice*, they both claim that only 15 tons was imported but I distinctly remember 20 tons as the amount we brought in. Possibly they kept 5 tons for themselves. But who cares after all these years and what's 5 tons among family? In any event, despite being a chartered accountant, I have always been hopeless with numbers.

As a cover for our operation, Howard and I wrote a film script based on a short story about an unhappy young countess suffering the pangs of unrequited love in her family castle on the shores of an Austrian lake, which we changed to a Scottish loch. (One of the problems with Austria, of which the Habsburgs were painfully aware, is its lack of a seacoast. Lake shores are fine for movies and brooding, beautiful aristocrats but absolutely hopeless for unloading deep-sea salvage vessels.) We used our office on Carlisle Street in Soho to hire a director and four or five actors to make our film for us. Using one of my offshore companies, World-Wide Entertainments (incorporated in Liberia), we rented a castle on the shores of Loch Linnhe for £1,000 per week. The place, Conaglen House, was in reality more of a mansion but we, romantically, always thought of it as a castle.

Loch Linnhe lies at the southern end of the Caledonian Canal – a great, largely natural waterway that splits Scotland from north-east to south-west. Starting at Inverness, it moves down through Loch Ness, past the monster, all the way to the town of Fort William, where it opens into Loch Linnhe. From Fort William the sea loch flows past our 'Austrian' castle and south to Mull, where Stuart's fleet of yachts was anchored and waiting.

Stuart's fleet was waiting for a signal from the mysterious *Karob*, which had last been heard of somewhere in the Antarctic. At some point in time, from some unknown and ever-changing point on the globe, the *Karob* was expected to suddenly race across the Atlantic and transfer the 20 tons of pot into Stuart's fleet of yachts.

Howard and I would be waiting close by in our rented castle, which boasted a five-mile stretch of coast as well as hundreds of acres of prime stag-hunting mountains and glens. To justify our presence – since neither of us looked the type to hunt stags – we explained that we were waiting for the actors and directors to arrive from London and Paris to shoot the film. We spent a lot of time on the shore making measurements and calculating camera angles from which to film the sad and brooding countess awaiting her love.

As soon as Stuart's boats were loaded with the pot, the salvage vessel would leave at full speed for Japan or Panama or God knows where. None of our business. The crew had been paid by our New York investors and we would never see them again.

Stuart's fleet would sail up Loch Linnhe and unload the pot into a couple of 15-ft Zodiac inflatable boats that we had brought up from London and stashed in one of the many barns that surrounded the castle. In order to crew the Zodiacs and load them with pot from Stuart's yachts, transport the pot from the shore to the castle quickly and then load all 20 tons onto trucks for transport south to England – all in one night – we had hired ourselves a platoon of tough US marines from New York.

This was the dangerous part of the plan. Apart from Howard, Stuart, Dutch Nik, Ernie's right-hand man Tom Sunde and me, nobody else knew where and when the pot was being landed or how much had been imported. It was very important that as few people as possible knew that 20 tons were involved. Such an amount would generate intense heat from the authorities if we were ever suspected; what was more, the price of pot on the UK market, following the inexorable laws of supply and demand, was bound to plummet if word got out that we were sitting on 20 tons. Having a platoon of drunken marines knowing exactly where, when and how much pot we had imported therefore made us extremely vulnerable.

'We could always kill them when the operation is over,' Tom had suggested brightly. The trouble with Tom was that you never knew when he was joking. I suspect he didn't know the difference either.

I explained to him our idea about telling the soldiers they were going to Norway. 'They can't understand anyone without a Bronx accent and nobody can understand the Scots anyway, so if we tell them they're in Norway, they'll never know the difference.'

Tom liked it. 'That's so cool, man. And if they start mouthing off and boasting in a bar when they're back in New York, all the heat will be on Norway. Cool. Where the fuck is Norway?'

'It's near Scotland, Tom. Don't worry about it.'

So, altogether, we had quite a few people hanging around waiting for the word from the salvage ship. We had the US marines on standby. We had a bunch of professional but innocent actors and a director waiting in London to come north for the filming. We had Stuart's sailors and crewmen hanging out on the Isle of Mull. And we had the bailie in charge of the castle and all the estate workers wondering what the hell Howard and I were really up to.

Conaglen House was usually rented to groups of wealthy businessmen who went shooting all day, ate and drank uproariously all night, spent tons of money and provided local employment to all. Two shifty-looking southerners with their occasional suspicious and hippy-looking visitors were making the bailie and his staff somewhat uncomfortable. Our image was not helped when we were found hiding up a tree, where we had taken refuge from a herd of longhorn Highland cattle that had emerged suddenly from the mists. 'Just checking camera angles,' I muttered shamefacedly to the bailie as we climbed down, carefully keeping our distance from the primeval-looking beasts, which continued to chew placidly and, like all the other locals, watch us with a bovine but baleful suspicion.

The only things in our favour were having the rent fully paid up in advance and the promise that the film would involve actresses coming up from London and possibly over from Paris. Everyone knew what that meant. Tits! The prospect of naked breasts and disgusting sexual activities, however remote a possibility, was sufficient for the locals' grudging acceptance.

We had been subtle in our approach.

'So why don't you shoot it in Austria, then?' the bailie had asked when we first described the screenplay to him.

Howard and I exchanged awkward glances.

'The Austrians . . .' Howard began.

'Very repressed people, you know,' I explained.

'Hitler was Austrian,' Howard added.

'They don't like nudity,' I confessed.

'Nude scenes, are there?' the bailie asked.

'Only some,' I said.

'Just the women,' Howard emphasised.

'Up in the hills,' I said.

'And in the woods,' Howard added.

'Not by the shore?' the bailie asked.

'No, not by the shore,' Howard and I replied together.

'Water's too cold,' I explained.

Howard pointed to where his nipples were hidden deep under several sweaters, a jacket and a thick overcoat. 'Makes them stand out. Stiff, you know.'

'This is an art film,' I explained. 'We can't have stiff nipples.'

The bailie left soon after that, no doubt stumbling back to his cottage for a quick dram of whisky. My guess was that it was the second reference to stiff nipples that broke him. But that was the end of the questions. After that, all we were asked about was when we might be expecting the young lassies from London.

'And Paris, you said?'

'Maybe Paris. Perhaps Italy, even.'

The idea of stiff Italian nipples was more than the strongest man could bear and that finished the interrogation.

The word finally arrived in late December 1979 that the *Karob* was in the Azores, off the coast of Portugal in the middle of the Atlantic, and expected to meet with Stuart's fleet a few days after Christmas near Mull. It was time to call in the marines.

Ernie's consigliere Tom Sunde had been put in charge of the soldiers and even though he had a Californian accent, they seemed to understand him and respect him. Somehow, he managed to fly them from New York to Oslo, where they spent several hours in the airport bar listening to drunken businessmen talk loudly in Norwegian. Before taking the flight to Glasgow, Tom encouraged the marines to buy souvenir bottles of Linie aquavit for their wives and hairy troll dolls or model Viking boats for their kids. He flew them to Glasgow, told them they were still in Norway and then got them on the train for the Highlands.

I collected the platoon of marines at Fort William railway station on 30 January. Tom immediately corrected me. 'It's not a platoon, man,' he told me, slurring slightly, 'it's just a couple of squads.' In any event, there were ten beefy-looking (though vegetarian) soldiers in civvies and Tom. The combination of a transatlantic flight, jet lag, their first time out of the USA and a considerable amount of alcohol had made the soldiers very mellow and we were able to guide them from the railway station to the bus I had rented without causing any disturbances.

'Do they think they're still in Norway?' I asked Tom as we drove along the side of the loch from Fort William towards our castle.

'The bright ones do,' Tom grinned. 'The rest of them think they're in Canada.'

The first night was easy. The men were tired and drunk and ready for bed. We had prepared a large room for them with a dozen bunk beds.

The bailie had been very concerned about all the bunk beds.

'The lassies will no be sleeping down here?' he'd asked, the metal frames and army blankets dispelling any visions of soft breasts and stiff nipples.

'Absolutely not,' Howard reassured him, 'but there will be cameramen and people like that coming with them.'

'Clapper boys,' I added helpfully.

'Exactly,' said Howard. 'We've got to keep them away from the girls, you see. We don't want anything untoward happening.'

'Good, good,' the bailie said. 'I'll get you some extra blankets. Don't want those clapper boys getting cold and seeking some extra warmth.'

Howard and I had smiled reassuringly.

We were lucky, at first. The marines slept till late morning. Unfortunately, as soon as they woke they became restless and wanted to go outside and exercise. These were guys who, whether they were in prison, in the army or even at home, liked hanging out at the gym and lifting weights. We explained to them that they had to remain hidden till nightfall because Norway was a Communist country and we would all be shot if they were seen.

Tom was very persuasive. 'It's not like America,' he said. 'Little kids at school are taught to spy on their parents. In Norway, people are paid to look out their windows and report what their neighbours are doing.' The marines looked shocked. 'Can you imagine what would happen if one of our Norwegian neighbours looked out her window and saw two squads of US marines in the garden next door?'

'World War Three?'

'Exactly,' said Tom. 'Fucking World War Three, man!'

Fear of the Third World War lasted for about an hour but soon after lunch it became obvious that the only way to keep the marines indoors and reasonably quiet would be to provide serious supplies of alcohol. Our stock of beer had been consumed immediately, within minutes of the soldiers waking. The nearest shops were in Fort William, more than an hour's drive away.

'What about The Highlander?' I asked. The Highlander was a nearby pub, a few miles down the loch. Howard and I had paid several visits while building up our cover of being movie producers setting up a shoot.

'They only sell Scotch,' Howard objected. 'Single malts,' he added for Tom's benefit. It was true; apart from pints of draught beer, the pub sold nothing but whisky. I've liked Scotch since I was a boy, when I used to steal sips at night from my father's extensive collection. When I was finally caught, my father explained that I was being punished not for stealing his single malt but for sneakily replacing it with water.

The Highlander had the most impressive collection of Scotch whisky I had ever seen but no bourbon, no vodka, no Budweiser for our thirsty American soldiers.

'So why not buy them Scotch?' Tom asked.

'They'll read the labels,' I told him. 'You wouldn't be able to get a dozen bottles of single-malt Scotch from a remote local bar in Norway. They'll know they're in Scotland.'

'We'll relabel them,' Howard announced, 'tell them it's local Norwegian hooch, home-made by farmers.'

'Aquavit,' Tom said.

'Exactly. Home-brewed aquavit with handwritten labels. We can write something in Norwegian on the labels.'

I looked sceptical. 'We don't know any Norwegian. How do we write it?'

Tom pulled a packet of Marlboro cigarettes out of his pocket. 'I bought these in the airport at Oslo.' He pointed to what looked like a health warning in some strange Nordic-looking language. 'Look, that's got Norwegian shit on it.'

'Brilliant!' Howard said. 'We can copy that onto the labels.'

'Toothpaste!' Tom suddenly said and raced to his bedroom. 'I bought a tube of Colgate at the airport. That's got tons of Norwegian shit written on the package.'

I left Tom and Howard at the kitchen table excitedly designing phony aquavit labels to put on the bottles, carefully copying the Norwegian words from the cigarette and toothpaste packaging.

The Highlander was getting ready to close for the afternoon when I arrived and it was empty except for the landlord and the bailie.

'Could I have a case of Scotch, Mr Drummond?' I asked.

The bailie looked at me curiously while the landlord went into a back room to get the Scotch. 'Is it a wee party then?' he asked. 'The French lass from Paris, is she here yet?'

'No, no actresses yet,' I said. 'Not till the end of the week, I expect. But since it's New Year's Eve tonight, I thought I'd better have some Scotch in the house. We're expecting to have some more equipment delivered this afternoon – cameras, lights and stuff. The drivers will probably stay the night and enjoy a little drink for the New Year.'

The two men helped carry the case of Scotch to my car and stood in the road watching me as I drove back towards the castle. I felt sure that they hadn't believed a word I'd said.

Back in the kitchen, Tom and Howard were waiting with a pile of labels covered in strange Nordic runes. Apparently, Tom had an artistic bent. The fine penmanship on his labels was very convincing. Nevertheless, it broke my heart to scrape away the original labels from the bottles. There was the legendary name of Ledaig from Tobermory on the Isle of Mull, rare labels of Bruichladdich and Laphroaig from Islay, as well as selections from the more common Glenfiddich and Macallan distilleries. We replaced the magical labels of the Inner Hebrides with runic warnings about the perils of smoking and the importance of flossing.

'What the fuck is this?' demanded Vinnie, the squad leader, when we arrived with the bottles.

'Aquavit,' Tom told him. 'Norwegian firewater. The farmers around here make it themselves.' Tom was always more comfortable telling lies than telling the truth. The truth for Tom was very much an admission of failure, a last resort. 'The Communist government has a monopoly on Russian vodka and charges terrible taxes, so the locals make this stuff themselves.'

Ignoring the labels, the soldiers started pouring drinks into the plastic tumblers and coffee mugs we had provided. 'It's OK, this Norwegian shit,' they finally told us. Encouraged by the thought that they were defying the Communist government and striking a blow for freedom, they threw themselves into their work with gusto and quickly demolished a bottle of Laphroaig labelled 'Sigaretten er dårlig til deres sunnhet'.

In the late afternoon, Dutch Nik arrived from London with two of his friends and three very large furniture removal vans. They were too large to hide inside any of the barns, so we parked them in the inner courtyard of the castle. I just prayed that the bailie would not see them and decide we were going to empty the castle of all its antique furniture and suits of armour.

At 7 p.m., one of Stuart's men arrived on a motorbike with the news that Stuart's two main yachts, *Bagheera* and *Salammbô*, had set sail. They planned to rendezvous with the *Karob* in the open water south of Mull and make the transfer during the final hour of daylight. Stuart expected to be in the loch opposite the castle by 9 p.m. The timing was perfect, as we calculated that all the locals would be either in the pub or in their houses preparing to welcome the New Year in traditional Scottish style with copious amounts of alcohol.

The main road from Fort William ran along the side of the loch, passing between the castle and the shore. Our main point of exposure was crossing the road with the soldiers and the large rubber Zodiacs. My job was to guard the main road and communicate with Howard on the shore using one of the military-issue walkie-talkies that the marines had provided.

When we went to collect the soldiers for the trip across the road in preparation for the arrival of the fleet, we were horrified to discover that they had finished all the whisky and were clamouring for more. 'It's going to get ugly, man, if they don't get some,' Tom said, looking worried. 'It's going to be a long night and these boys are going to be thirsty.'

Nik and I took two separate cars to The Highlander. The plan was to leave one of the cars outside the pub with the keys hidden in the exhaust pipe. If things got ugly at the castle later on, this would provide us with a back-up escape plan.

The Highlander was full, thick with pipe and cigarette smoke and the deafening sound of Scottish males reciting Rabbie Burns and criticising the English or whatever it is they do to prepare for Hogmanay. The room fell silent when Nik and I entered.

'Evening, Mr Drummond,' I said, leaning casually against the bar. 'My friend and I fancied a drop of your fine malt.' Conversation gradually returned to its normal pitch as Nik and I sipped from our glasses and lit our cigarettes. The bailie was in his usual corner beside the bar, watching us intently.

'One of yon drivers?' he finally asked, nodding at Nik.

'Yes,' I said. 'He brought up a load of sound equipment from London.'

'Oh, aye,' said the bailie, 'from London.' He repeated this as though no good could possibly come of it.

'And how was the malt?' asked the landlord. 'Have you no tried a wee taste from your bottles yet?' Conversation had paused, the bar was quiet again and I realised that the whole neighbourhood had learned about our purchase earlier in the afternoon. It was not every day that English visitors bought 12 bottles of single-malt whisky.

'Excellent,' I said, as nonchalantly as I could. 'In fact, I'd like to purchase a little more, if I may.'

'How many would you like?' Mr Drummond asked. The bar was completely silent now.

'Oh, I don't know,' I said offhandedly, my voice squeaking with the strain, 'maybe two or three more cases, if that's OK.' There was a murmur of excitement in the room as they all discussed this latest turn of events.

'So have we got visitors then?' the bailie enquired.

'Just some drivers and technicians.'

'None of the acting folk?'

'Not yet. Maybe two or three days more. I'd like them here by Friday,' I said, hoping I'd be far away by then, far from the randy rustics.

The landlord and a couple of helpers carried the three cases outside to the car. I had paid in cash and twenty pairs of eyes watched as the landlord slowly counted the thick wad of twenties that I handed him. I smiled lamely as I left the silent room. So much for my plan to keep things low key.

'Happy New Year, everyone,' I said with a brave smile as I left the pub, receiving a couple of surly nods in response.

'Not so friendly these Scots,' Nik observed as we drove away.

'They're a dour folk,' I told him.

'In Holland, we're told they all wear skirts,' Nik said.

'Right! And in Holland you all wear wooden clogs and stick your fingers in dykes.'

Despite the fact that a salvage vessel, fresh from Antarctica, had to transfer twenty tons of marijuana to two yachts crewed by a bunch of stoned Californian hippies on the high seas and that the two yachts subsequently had to unload those twenty tons in the middle of a Scottish loch in the dark to a bunch of drunken soldiers in Zodiacs, who then had to carry the heavy bales up a beach and across a main highway to a castle before loading them into three large lorries without anybody noticing, it all went like clockwork. By 11 p.m., it was all over.

I'd spent most of the time guarding the main road, watching for passing motorists and ready to alert the others. I was nearly knocked over by a man riding a bicycle with no lights who approached me from behind. 'Evening,' he muttered as he wobbled back into the darkness. I prayed he was too drunk to wonder why I was standing in the middle of a deserted road in the dark holding a large military walkie-talkie and wearing night-vision goggles.

The radios and goggles had been provided by the marines and were very state-of-the-art in 1979; in other words, they were about ten times the size of today's models and totally useless. In theory, I was maintaining contact with Howard down on the shore and with Nik up at the castle but most of the communication consisted of loud static and people saying 'What?' to each other.

'I didn't say anything.'

'What?'

'Who's that?'

'What?'

The night-vision glasses were very uncomfortable and I had no side vision. I had to keep turning my whole body in order to see properly, which was why I didn't notice the drunken cyclist until he was upon me.

At one point, Tom emerged from the trees leading a couple of soldiers, all three of them carrying large bales of pot. He shone his flashlight at my face as he approached and the night-vision goggles magnified the light to the power of ten suns. It was as though a sword had been plunged into the side of my head, and I fell to the ground, blinded, dropping the walkie-talkie with a loud cackle of static.

'What?' I heard Howard say.

'What?' Nik responded.

'Who said that?'

I ripped the goggles off my head and threw them violently into some bushes.

'Hey!' Vinnie protested. 'Them's government property. Suppose the Commies get their hands on them.'

'Fuck the Commies!' I said.

For the first time in our relationship, Vinnie heard me and understood what I was saying. I was speaking his language.

He nodded approvingly. 'Fuck the Commies.'

Eventually, all the pot was carried across the road and up to the castle, where Dutch Nik and his boys loaded it into the lorries. It was with a sense of restrained elation that we finally watched them drive towards the main road to begin the long journey back to England. By the following evening, the pot would be safely stashed in the various barns and warehouses that had been rented around the country.

Stuart's two yachts continued up the loch to establish their alibi by celebrating New Year's Eve noisily in Fort William. The operation had been successfully completed.

'Let's get smashed,' Tom said.

The soldiers were back in their dorm and busy opening the three cases of whisky. We hadn't even bothered to change the labels: no time and no energy. 'Tell them Bruichladdich is Norwegian for bat's piss,' Howard said. He was already digging into a bale of pot. 'Fell off the back of a lorry,' he explained with a grin. Tom and I grinned back and the three of us took deep drags on the joint of freshly delivered Colombian.

'We did it, lads,' Howard said, and for the first time in days we started to relax. Howard smokes joints all the time. He always has done, ever since I've known him. I don't, not since I became a father. Unless I'm totally relaxed and secure, smoking dope just makes me anxious and paranoid, terrified something bad will happen to my daughters and I won't be able to protect them. But that night, knowing that everything had gone according to plan and that the project was finished, I plunged my hand into the bale of Colombian pot and rolled myself a giant joint. Everything was over and I could finally unwind.

We had also given the soldiers a bale to smoke and after a while in a spirit of mellow camaraderie, we decided to join them in their dorm.

This is possibly the first documented account of what happens when otherwise healthy men, in good physical shape, who are never exposed to meat, are subjected to intense physical activity followed by copious amounts of single-malt Scotch whisky and Colombian marijuana all within a short period of time.

When we entered the dorm, they were all naked.

'We're going swimming,' Vinnie told us. 'Get your fucking clothes off and join us.'

'Where?' I asked.

'In the fucking fjord,' Vinnie said. 'We're gonna catch us some fucking Norwegian salmon.'

Obviously, their strong vegetarian principles did not extend to fish. 'Concentrated omega acids,' Billy explained. I thought that was what he said but his Bronx accent was so thick he could have been asking if I wanted to go canoeing.

Empty bottles of whisky littered the floor and broken pieces of the Colombian pot covered every surface. The mood in the room was electric and hostile. All the mellowness we'd anticipated had long since departed. 'Wassupwitcha?' Vinnie shouted. 'You fucking faggots or what? Get your clothes off!'

Slowly, we removed our clothes. Scotland in July is cold compared with southern England or France, where I spent most of my time. In December, it is much colder. When we all moved outside into the night air, I was reminded just how close we were to the Arctic Circle.

Male shrinkage is sufficiently documented these days for me not to labour the details. Let me just say that, as a result of the cold night air, my own scrotum had retreated so far back into my body that I had a lump in my throat. Whatever penis remained was no larger than a nun's clitoris. As we charged into the night emitting manly cries, dashing bravely towards the fjord to challenge the icy waters, there was not one waving willy between us.

This could explain the delayed reaction of the Highlanders. They must have driven to the castle as soon as the pub closed. Perhaps, inflamed with whisky and hints about the presence of foreign actresses from the bailie, they had driven to the castle with plans to scale the walls, or at least peep through the windows at the stiff nipples. Confronted with the sudden apparition of a dozen naked, white-skinned and apparently desexed New York thugs chanting what they believed were Norwegian war cries, the good citizens of Inverness-shire stood their ground for less than a minute before they fled in total disarray. They piled into their cars and turned clumsily on the gravel driveway. The light snow on the ground made everything muddy. Their visions of foreign actresses had been for ever destroyed by the sight of naked squaddies.

'Commies!' Tom yelled. 'Commie soldiers! Come on, men, back to the castle!'

'The irony is,' I told Howard as he stood beside me watching the retreating tail lights of the cars, 'the Celts always fought naked and that put the fear of God into the Roman legions.'

'Shut the fuck up, will you?' Howard said. 'And get these fucking morons back indoors and roll them some joints before something else goes wrong!' In fact, something else did go wrong that night, but I'll come to that later.

First thing in the morning, we shipped Tom and the soldiers south to Glasgow, where they caught the first plane to Norway and on back to New York. Howard and I did some forensic cleaning after they left and drove to Glasgow in the afternoon. None of us saw the bailie again.

The actors all arrived two days later as promised, with no idea of what had preceded them. The gloomy countess wandered around the shores of the loch and along the battlements of the castle. Unfortunately, neither she nor her faithful maid ever exposed their breasts or even removed their tops. The film met with mild success and won second prize at a minor festival in Belgium. The prize, unfortunately, was for directing, not for the script.

Peter Whitehead, the director, said that he had been impressed with the hospitality they had received from the locals on the set. 'Could not have been nicer,' he told us. 'Especially the bailie. He was always making sure we had enough blankets and insisted on guiding us whenever we wanted to shoot in the hills or in the woods.'

'What about shooting on the shore?' Howard asked.

'The bailie insisted it would be too cold for the girls.'

In the end, our precautions were all for nothing. Stuart's team had accidentally dropped several bales of pot into the sea during the transfer and they started washing up along the coast. By pure coincidence, Paul McCartney, a founder member of a popular singing group, owned a Scottish estate nearby and had recently been busted for pot in Japan. The national and international press drew its own conclusions and the story followed a different direction. Since that time, I have been unable to listen to 'Norwegian Wood' without thinking about that Scottish adventure.

There were no further repercussions – not immediately, anyway – though I did hear a rumour that the Drug Enforcement Administration office in Oslo had been placed on special alert.

6

COPS

It is embarrassing to admit, but I've always liked policemen. I understand that this could undermine my status as a racketeer – not enough, unfortunately, to influence a court of appeals into reversing my conviction – but nevertheless it is true.

I was named Patrick after my maternal grandfather, who, as a policeman in Northern Ireland, was murdered in the line of duty before I was born. After his release from prison, one of the killers achieved a certain eminence in the IRA and by the late '60s and early '70s he was often quoted in the press. My mother was in and out of hospital at the time, engaged in a long-drawn-out battle with cancer. Sitting in her hospital ward and listening to her father's killer speaking self-righteously on the television news was obviously hard for her and it was painful for me to observe.

This was during the time when Howard and I were working with Jim 'The Fox' McCann to import Pakistani hashish into the Irish Republic, with Jim using his supposed links to the IRA to get the hash through customs. Who knows what was true, how genuine Jim's IRA connections were. They always disclaimed him in later years. With the Fox, nothing was real and everything was possible. But the hashish was real and that was all that mattered at the time.

'So you'd like to kill the auld cunt, would you?' Jim said, nodding approvingly. 'I know what Dublin pub he drinks in,' he confided. 'I can put you there with a gun in your hand.' For several months after that, he and I practised target shooting with large, evil-looking guns at the farm in Paradise. Even Jim acknowledged that I became a fairly decent shot. I still do not know what motivated him to help in this scheme to assassinate my grandfather's killer, whether he wished to get rid of a man whom he saw as a headline-grabbing rival or to trap me into some international scandal. Jim's motives were always Byzantine. I was blinded by my Irish blood, trapped in some romantic fantasy of taking revenge on behalf of my mother.

It was Howard who finally talked sense into me. 'She's in hospital and dying. The last thing she needs is to see her eldest son shot by the IRA like her father or thrown into prison for murder. You know better than to listen to fucking Jim!' I grudgingly accepted the wisdom of what Howard said but nevertheless regretted not making that final romantic gesture for my mother.

My mother's brother, like her father, was a policeman. He was always my mother's big hero and whenever I did something wrong or behaved badly, I was always compared unfavourably with him. When I had a difficult decision to make, I would always wonder what my uncle would do. When I started openly expressing doubts about the existence of God at the age of 11, my mother would always say that her brother and Winston Churchill were God-fearing men and ask who was I to think myself better than them (Churchill was my mother's other great hero). Those two men became and remain two of my own big heroes, along with Teddy Roosevelt and Nelson Mandela. I soon learned, of course, that Churchill was an atheist. However, I didn't know that back then, as a child, and I assumed I was the only person who did not believe in God.

I first started questioning my religion in 1955, when I was about nine years old and stricken with polio. Eleven people in Stevenage got polio that summer and one by one the other ten died. Salk's vaccine was distributed in the USA that same year but was not introduced into England until a year or so later, too late for me. I was completely paralysed on one side of my body, though I can't remember now which side, and spent some months in an iron lung and some years off school and bedridden. My Irish relatives would fly over to visit my sickbed and would recite the rosary and tell me how God wanted me to join him in heaven and sit at his side. Obviously, they wished me nothing but a full recovery but I could not help reflecting that if I was going to die, they might reasonably wish, after what was in those days a major journey, that it should happen during their visit, so that I could benefit from their prayers. They also talked rather ominously about sin and the importance of a full repentance. I knew nothing of sex in those days or even of masturbation, which was big with Catholics, and although I was no angel, I could not help feeling slightly inadequate in terms of sin.

Altogether, the whole business of God's will seemed unfair. When you cannot move a limb and have nothing to do all day except think about your mortality, it does not take long to move from questioning the justice of God's will to questioning the very existence of God himself. If I was ever to get well, I could obviously expect no assistance from the Almighty. It had been made very clear by my Catholic relatives that my recovery was not part of His plan. The doctors looked fairly gloomy as well and I always thought I could see surprise on their faces when they entered the room – as though my continuing existence insulted their professional prognosis.

I finally made the decision that the only person who could make me better was me. Instead of passively accepting the wisdom of my elders and trusting in a benign Providence, I would have to choose to get better, embrace life and fight for my own recovery with no outside assistance. It was a fateful moment and a decision that has affected my life and my philosophy ever since.

'I don't need you,' I told Him. 'I don't believe in you.'

Within days, I was twitching my limbs and within weeks I was able to stand, albeit shakily, on my own two feet. Within a couple of months, I was walking. 'It's a miracle!' they all said. 'Praise be to God for showing His divine mercy.' I was still young but already wise enough to say nothing of my conversion and I pretended to accept my recovery as a sign of God's munificence.

I tested my atheism a few years later, as a teenager, when I went alone to the middle of the school rugby field at midnight during a furious thunderstorm. 'Strike me down, you hairy old bastard!' I shouted at the heavens. 'No one will know. This is just between you and me.' But nothing happened and I walked home soaked to the bone.

COPS

I remember, I remember
The fir trees dark and high;
I used to think their slender tops
Were close against the sky;
It was a childish ignorance,
But now 'tis little joy
To know I'm farther off from heav'n
Than when I was a boy.

Thomas Hood

Some years later, when my mother had forced me to go to confession after some transgression, I told the priest the story of recovering from polio after questioning and then rejecting the existence of God. The priest was a Jesuit and he barely flinched: 'Well, obviously Our Divine Lord could not let you die in a state of mortal sin. You have to continue living until you can find God in your heart again.' I never have found him; maybe that's why I've reached my seventh decade and am still going strong.

I love the religious music of Bach and Palestrina. I adore the cathedrals of Europe and experience a profound inner peace within their lofty vaults. As Albert Einstein said, 'I am a deeply religious non-believer.' I certainly have a love of nature and feel profoundly moved even in my own garden looking at the rich profusion of growing things. To quote Einstein again, 'I believe in Spinoza's God, who reveals himself in the orderly harmony of what exists, not in a God who concerns himself with the fates and actions of human beings.' My garden is full of Buddhas, but I detest all organised religion with a passion and firmly believe that the priests, mullahs and rabbis should be placed in the arena and fed to the lions. This loathing increases daily as I see the dark forces of fundamentalism and intolerance growing ever stronger.

But I do not have this same hatred for cops that I have for preachers. Not even the ones who have arrested me over the years. They had their job to do and they always did it well and professionally. Even my nemesis, Craig Lovato from the DEA, turned out to be a decent guy and a man of his word. Their job was to catch me and my job was to not get caught. Sometimes they won and sometimes I did.

The policemen who followed the trail of blood and arrested me for being drunk and disorderly in Staffordshire were doing their job and following police procedures. They were right to arrest me; I was drunk and had been very disorderly before I passed out. Their boss the chief constable holds an even warmer place in my heart, as he was the man who denied mother's request that I be flogged.

I'm not saying that policemen never had the power to terrify me, especially foreign policemen, but I've always found them to be decent human beings at heart. There was the time when my family and I were living in France and I had to leave in rather a hurry. Scotland Yard had phoned to inform their colleagues in Paris that they wanted to question me about several suitcases of money they had discovered in my London house. It would appear that I had not completed the requisite VAT forms and they wished to discuss this, along with other matters. Alerted by a telephone call from a friend in London, I grabbed my family and we left our home about ten minutes before the local police surrounded the house.

Very little had happened in my village in Périgord since the Hundred Years War, so policemen digging machine-gun emplacements and observation posts in my neighbours' fields around the house generated quite a lot of excitement. The senior investigators from Paris arrived a couple of days later and installed themselves in the local hotel in Beaumont. Luckily, the owner was a friend of mine and would spend the evening in his bar drinking with them. Many of the Parisian policemen had never been to Périgord before and were completely overwhelmed by the food. Our local cuisine is famed for the foie gras with truffles and the omelettes made with cèpe mushrooms, which appear only in autumn, after the rains of late summer. 'This Monsieur Lane is a major criminal,' they confided to my friend. 'We have found cheque books and bank accounts in his house from 18 different countries. We cannot abandon the search. We must continue to return here every year until we have caught him. Tell me again when the cèpe season begins? Ah, yes. We shall be back again.'

Although our friends and neighbours were shocked and horrified to learn of my criminal background, they all remained loyal. As many later explained, the intrigue reminded them of the German occupation, when they had clandestinely supported the Maquis, who hid out in the region's thick woods and hidden caves. While encouraging the police from London and Paris to stay and spend their money on good food and wine, they gave out no information and kept me updated by phone on each stage of the investigation. Several officers did return in subsequent years but their half-hearted pretence at pursuing an investigation fooled nobody, except possibly the Parisian clerk who authorised their expense accounts.

As the police were receiving a warm welcome in Beaumont, we were in a couchette on the midnight express from Bordeaux to Madrid, hoping to reach the Spanish border before Interpol put out a general alert for me. What we did not know was that Spanish railway tracks were a different size from French ones and that there would therefore be a several-hour delay at the border while the axles on each railway carriage were lengthened to match the Spanish tracks. We had already handed over our passports, ostensibly so that our sleep would not be disturbed during the night. There was nothing we could do but hold hands nervously and wait.

Sleep was the last thing on our minds as we sat in the small cabin, listening to the sound of workmen adjusting the wheels of the train. The two children were both asleep in their bunks but sleep would be impossible for me and Jude until we had finally left France and reached the safety of Spain. Spain did not have an extradition treaty with Britain, which is why English gangsters and bank robbers traditionally retired to the sunny Spanish coast.

Eventually, the sound of hammering stopped and the train started to move again. We clenched our hands and looked at each other. Perhaps we were safe. The train stopped again and we heard movement in the corridor outside our cabin. There was the harsh sound of a foreign language.

Suddenly, the door flew open and three Guardias Civiles jammed the doorway. Franco was still in power and the Guardia, with their strange hats, symbolised all the Fascist excesses of his rule. All three policemen carried sub-machine guns.

'Stand up, you miserable pigs,' their leader said in Spanish. 'We've got you surrounded. Put your hands in the air. You will rot in prison until you die.'

I clasped my wife. 'What?' I murmured, looking at him in despair.

The policeman stood back. 'S'cuse, señor,' he said in English. 'You no spik Spanish. I say, "Welcome to Spain, please enjoy your visit in our beautiful country."' He handed me our passports, made a formal bow to my wife and closed the door.

French border police are equally daunting. A few years before we fled France, when my first child was just three months old, we went camping in the Pyrenees. Our home was no more than a four-hour drive from San Sebastián and the Spanish border, and we loved the scenic beauty of the French Pyrenees. We had followed a rutted path through some woods and found ourselves in a remote valley, a meadow surrounded on all sides by woods and mountain peaks. A fast-flowing stream, bubbling over rocks, ran through the centre of the valley. We pitched our tent and that night we cooked a chicken on a spit over an open fire while we counted the shooting stars in the clear sky above. We had found paradise.

The next morning, we washed ourselves naked in the cold waters of the stream. Peggy lay on her back amidst the buttercups and wild flowers that filled the meadow. She made contented cooing noises as she grasped for the waving petals and butterflies. Jude, naked in the clear water of the stream, looked like some beautiful, pagan woodland elf; I wanted to reach for her. But as I watched, I saw her body slowly stiffen and her hands move urgently to cover herself. I turned and saw five dark figures emerge from the treeline. They all carried guns.

I recognised them immediately: they were CRS, a division of the French police responsible for riot control and border patrol. I had seen them in action in May 1968 in Paris, when I had joined an invasion of the Sorbonne during the student protests. They had frightened me then; they scared the life out of me now.

'Where are you from?' their leader asked.

'Périgord. The Dordogne,' I answered. They could see the 24 number plate, signifying the area we'd come from, on the back of our Citroën 2CV.

'But you are English,' he replied aggressively, while his companions didn't bother to disguise their interest in Jude's state of undress.

In an isolated valley like this, with two foreigners and no witnesses, they could do whatever they pleased. This was the Basque Country, close to the Spanish frontier, and if anything happened it could be blamed on the local terrorists.

'Where in the Dordogne?' he persisted.

'Molières,' I told him.

'Molières?' he repeated slowly.

'Near Cadouin and Beaumont,' I added.

There was a pause while he digested the information.

'So you know Robert Lacoste?' he asked.

'He's my neighbour.'

'He's my cousin,' he replied, and reached forward to shake my hand.

The cop waved at his men dismissively and they turned away. 'Please, madam,' he said to Jude, 'you may dress in your tent.'

He saw Peggy lying in the grass making happy gurgling noises. 'You have a princess,' he said. 'Tell Robert that Fabrice says hello.'

Swiftly, he followed his companions into the woods, where they vanished and the sound of their movement slowly faded. But our little valley was no longer ours; it had been violated and we left a few hours later.

From that day on whenever Fabrice visited his cousin Robert, he would stop by our house in Molières. Jude was always somewhat uncomfortable but I enjoyed his company and the bottle of wine he always brought. As I've said, I like cops.

Whenever I saw a cop, I always thought of my grandfather and my uncles. So it was quite natural when a uniformed cop appeared at the door of our rented Scottish castle after midnight during the biggest dope deal we had ever attempted (this was the something else going wrong that Howard had anticipated) that Howard should instruct Tom: 'Get Patrick to deal with him.'

Not only was the cop wearing a uniform, it was a full dress uniform with rows of campaign ribbons, silver buttons and a very important-looking hat. He introduced himself rather apologetically. He was a high-ranking officer, and indeed I would later discover that he was one of the more senior policemen in Scotland.

'Apparently, I've run out of petrol,' he explained. He had obviously been doing the New Year's Eve thing, attending some bigwig banquet in Fort William with other local dignitaries and now, slightly the worse for wear, found himself stranded in the middle of nowhere without petrol. 'I saw the lights from the road,' he explained contritely. 'I wondered if you might have some spare petrol to get me home.'

Poor man. The dignity of his position in jeopardy, out of petrol, he had stumbled into the largest smuggling operation ever attempted in the British Isles. Or had he really stumbled? His eyes were darting around while he spoke to me, trying to see beyond me into the house.

'Maybe it's a trick,' Howard hissed when I went indoors to consult with the others.

'I say let's just whack him,' Tom said.

As I've explained, ever since my first child was born I have been uncomfortable smoking pot unless I'm in a totally controlled environment and I know my children are safe. Earlier that evening, however, I'd felt sufficiently relaxed to smoke pot with Howard and Tom. After seeing Dutch Nik and his colleagues drive off into the night with our 20 tons of Colombian pot, we'd competed to see who could roll and consume the biggest joints. As a consequence, when I stood in front of the bemedalled policeman I was plunged into an extreme of drug-induced panic. It was not the usual pot paranoia; in fact, paranoia had nothing to do with it. Paranoia is based upon irrational panic. There was nothing irrational about my fears; they were firmly grounded in reality. I had ten drug-crazed New York marines in the back room working through their third case of Scotch whisky, I had kilos of Colombian pot lying everywhere and, for all I knew, several carloads of sex-crazed local farmers skulking in the gorse and heather of the surrounding glens, waiting to spy on naked French actresses.

'Give him some petrol,' Howard whispered, ignoring Tom, who was wandering around naked and striking karate poses. 'Have him drive you to the pub to collect your car so that you can sound him out. Chat to him. Get a sense of what's going on.'

Easy for Howard to say. His brain was not fragmenting into random, brightly coloured patterns and nobody was asking him to socialise with the local Gestapo.

'I still say we whack him,' Tom insisted, glaring fiercely at the door.

Howard pulled deeply on his joint. 'Want a hit for the road?' he asked.

I shook my head as I walked out into the cold, dark Scottish night to join the policeman. 'No, thanks. Not right now. Maybe later.'

I am over 6 ft tall but the policeman towered above me. Together, we walked around the side of the house to where some barns opened onto the stable yard. The night was clear and the bright moon cast long shadows as we crunched across the gravel.

'It's a braw bonnie night,' said the policeman.

'What does he mean?' I asked myself desperately. 'He's trying to trick me.' I decided to say nothing and gradually felt my self-confidence return as I recognised that by remaining silent I had outmanoeuvred the wily Scot. In the distance, I heard the sound of glass being smashed and yells of male bonhomie as the marines finished yet another bottle of whisky. The cunning policeman pretended not to hear. Was there no end to his trickery?

We entered the barn and I used my flashlight to locate a can of petrol. Silently, I thanked Howard for making sure we had enough supplies for any sort of emergency.

'It's a full can,' the policeman said as he picked it up. 'That's perfect. That'll get me all the way home.' He offered me a five-pound note. 'Here,' he said, 'I cannae possibly thank you enough.'

I shook my head, refusing his money. 'I'll walk you to your car,' I said gruffly. I wanted to see if he was alone or if there was a column of armed police vehicles awaiting his signal to storm the castle.

'That's very kind of you, man,' he said as I led the way across the courtyard towards the main road. Suddenly, he grabbed my arm. It was the moment I'd been waiting for and I spun around to confront him. The karate practice sessions I'd been doing with Tom were paying off and I felt lithe and vigilant. The marijuana-induced sluggishness had vanished. My hands dropped to my sides in case he tried to slip cuffs on them and my knees were slightly bent and flexed. Coldly alert, my body prepared its defence, ready to roll into a ball away from the threat. From the corner of my eye, I saw an area of dark shadows and swiftly calculated how effectively I could dart and weave my way there if he started shooting. For a drug bust on this scale, it was quite likely that the police would be armed. There was a nervousness about the man that I'd noticed when I first saw him at the door. He'd have an itchy trigger finger. The nervous ones are the most dangerous.

He thrust an arm towards me, palm outstretched. I flinched backwards but he was only directing me towards his car, an old Vauxhall. 'It's my son's,' he explained apologetically as we approached it. 'Don't like to use the official car if I'm drinking.' He filled the tank and handed me back the empty can. 'I can't thank you enough,' he said. 'Anything I can ever do, just let me know.'

'Well, actually,' I said, 'I wonder if you could give me a lift down the road to The Highlander?'

'Bit late for the pub,' he said. 'They'll be closed by now. You're not in London, you know.' He grinned at me. 'We're law-abiding folk up here. Though I wouldn't mind a wee dram myself.'

'No, no,' I explained in my best good-citizen voice, 'I left my car there this evening. Had a bit too much to drink and asked a friend to drive me home.'

'Good man,' he said approvingly as we both got in the front. I moved some magazines to make room on the seat. A copy of *Fly Fishing* and two copies of *Penthouse*.

'My son's car,' he repeated.

I finally relaxed. However devious the police mind might be, it would never, surely, conduct a major raid in a beaten-up borrowed Vauxhall with dirty magazines lying around in it. The road was deserted and there was no sign of reinforcements.

As we approached The Highlander, he finally broke the silence. 'The young ladies from France,' he began, 'would they have arrived yet?'

'You know the bailie?'

'Aye, I do,' he replied. 'You know, if there's anything we can do to assist with the film, if you need security when you're filming your outdoor scenes, we'd be very happy to help.'

'That's very kind,' I told him. 'That's certainly reassuring to know.'
'It's the least I can do,' he said.

As I stood outside The Highlander and watched the policeman's tail lights vanish into the night, I felt pleased that he was already high up in the force. To have uncovered the largest drug-smuggling operation in British history would have ensured instant promotion for somebody lower in the police hierarchy but this guy was near the top. To have wandered, blissfully unaware, through the heart of the conspiracy while hoping for a glimpse of a naked French actress would not harm his career. I was relieved for him. As I said before, I like cops.

But the cop I remember most vividly is the young policeman who bled to death in my arms. When I came home from college to my parents' house in Barnet during the Christmas and Easter vacations, I always got a holiday job as an orderly at the local hospital. Barnet General Hospital serviced a large region of north London, from the Watford Bypass in the north almost to Hampstead in the south. The Watford Bypass was a fast section of road at the southern end of the M1 motorway from Birmingham and was the scene of endless accidents and car wrecks. There were no speed limits in those days and no safety belts. I don't recall any specific laws against drinking in the car and, of course, everybody was busy lighting up cigarettes or stubbing them out while they drove. Road deaths were simply part of daily life. Easter was the busiest time for Barnet General in terms of traffic accidents. Half the population of the city would hit the road for the bank holiday and then all converge on the Watford Bypass when returning to London. Ambulances and police cars would deliver an endless supply of maimed and bleeding bodies to our accident and emergency department and we would find places for them in beds, in corridors and on the floors. Sometimes we would deliver them straight to the morgue.

It was one of those jobs that you either quit in horror at the end of your first day or else you stick with because the pay is so good. During the night shifts, I spent a lot of time drinking tea with policemen while we tried hard not to think about the latest mangled wreck we had just wheeled into surgery. I found policemen often had a certain resigned calmness, a weary cynicism tempered with a quiet decency.

If Easter was the busy time for car wrecks at Barnet General, the week of Christmas and New Year was the season for suicides. For whatever reason, it is during times of public festivities, when families gather together, that the burden of 'that perilous stuff which weighs upon the heart' becomes too great to bear. In the hospital, the doctors, the nurses and the policemen all knew to anticipate the arrival of suicides when Christmas carols began to be heard in the streets. Strange that such an intimate and unique act for the individual should be so predictable to the professionals.

Finchley in those days was a large north London suburb of drab apartment blocks, grim pubs and lonely hearts. A lot of single people lived in Finchley, young people who had come to London to make their fortunes and follow their dreams. They were secretaries and clerks, policemen and nurses, government workers, people who could not afford to live closer to the centre of the city or further out in the green suburbs. And so they crowded together in their lonely flats, separated by thin partitions and private sorrows. Finchley could have been the answer to Paul McCartney's question in 'Eleanor Rigby': it was where all the lonely people came from, and where they all belonged.

At Christmas, we got a lot of business from Finchley. Again, the police and the ambulance crews would deliver us their broken wares. The messiest ones were the 'Northern Liners'. Barnet and Finchley were served by the London Underground's Northern Line, which, appropriately enough, is coloured black on the Tube map. Early in the morning, setting out for another day in a dead-end job, a young secretary would throw herself in the path of the train. Or late at night, after some solitary beers at an anonymous pub, a clerk would wait for the rush of air along the tunnel and the rumble of the train bursting into the station before leaping off the platform. They always went straight to the morgue, where some young policeman would have to sort through the bits and pieces looking for ID and the address of somebody to notify.

'What colour are the eyes?' one rookie policeman once asked me, his own eyes determinedly focused on his pencil and notebook, ignoring the decapitated corpse.

'Let me see.' I lifted the head away from the body. 'Brown,' I said as he rushed out of the morgue to throw up in his helmet.

Lying down in the kitchen with a bottle of gin and your head on a pillow in the gas oven was very popular. People would fill the meter with a few shilling coins prior to lying down so that the gas would not run out before the job was done. They were easy to recognise; there was a bluish swelling to their bodies. They were usually no more than a few hours dead; neighbours, alerted by the smell of gas, would quickly phone the police, whose sad task was to deliver the corpses to me.

The ones who overdosed on pills were often not discovered for several days, or even weeks. Again, it was only the smell that alerted the neighbours. This was partly a consequence of the English tradition of not 'interfering' and our national horror of 'making a scene'. Neighbours would 'mind their own business' even if they suspected the solitary anguish beyond the thin walls of the next-door flat.

The policeman they delivered one Saturday morning was still alive. He had swallowed a bottle of painkillers washed down with Bulmers cider. Luckily, a suspicious friend had broken down the door and found him. There was no time to lose and he had to be operated on immediately, right there in accident and emergency. It was 9 a.m. on a crisp, bright January morning and I had just arrived to start my shift. I'd been hoping to have a cup of tea with a pretty young nurse whom I'd been observing all week.

The doctors could not give him any anaesthetic because of all the painkillers he had swallowed, so my job was to sit on his chest with my knees on his upper arms, my hands clutching his and sometimes my forehead pressed down to force his head back onto the pillow as he struggled against me. Behind my back, the doctors started to cut open his stomach.

I was about 19 years old and he was 25. He was a man while I was a boy. He was a good-looking guy, extremely fit and well built, and it was all I could do to hold him to the bed. We struggled for what seemed like hours while he screamed and shouted between fits of calm during which he told me his story.

A few years earlier, soon after joining the police force, he had saved a small girl from a burning house. He had shielded her body as he carried her through the flames and the girl had emerged unscathed. The policeman, however, had sustained third-degree burns all over his upper arms and back. He had spent months in the burns unit and even after he was released and returned to duty, the skin of his upper body and back was scarred, horribly disfigured. We had cut his shirt off him when he'd arrived and his back was not a pretty sight.

Though he had dated girls since his accident, he had not had sex again. He felt he could never undress in front of a woman. 'I'm a monster. No woman could ever go to bed with me,' he told me. In another quiet moment of lucidity, he said, 'I can never marry or have children.' That was why he had decided to end it all and swallow the painkillers, which he had been saving for months.

I told him that a woman would see his scars as a badge of courage and would love him for it. 'That's 'cause you're a bloke,' he said, with all the wisdom of his 25 years. 'Women are different. They want beauty.'

At this point, I need to digress into the public-service part of this book. If you, gentle reader, should ever decide to commit suicide, do not do it with an overdose of pills. You do not drift peacefully away while the drugs do their work. It's not the drugs that kill you; it's the calcium in the pills. The calcium forms a mass on the inside of the stomach and bursts the walls. You die an agonising death while your digestive acids attack your vital organs. You also throw up a lot of blood until eventually you choke.

The nurse whom I had planned to share my breakfast with used a damp cloth to wipe the blood off my face whenever the policeman threw up. He told me a lot of things while we struggled in our strange intimacy, many of them sad and some of them banal in their ordinariness. We had both played fly-half in our school rugby teams and we discussed things associated with that, between bouts of screaming.

There were sounds of exasperation behind me as the doctors worked desperately to save him, but gradually I felt the struggle subside and the muscles in my arms relaxed as he calmed down and lay still. I leaned forward and held him tightly until eventually they lifted me off him. It was not yet noon when they pronounced him dead.

I looked down at my shirt and jeans, which were solid with blood. I pulled them off and stood trancelike and naked while my little nurse found an old hospital gown to wrap me in. I walked home in the gown and my mother made me a large mug of tea. She asked if I wanted some lunch and I shook my head. I quit my job and never returned to the hospital, not even to collect my final pay cheque.

At the time, I thought of the young policeman as a mature adult. As the years have passed and I've grown older, he has remained 25 years old; now that I am 62, I can see that he too was just a young boy. I've never forgotten him but I never knew his name. He's always been just the young policeman – like my grandfather, Patrick, who died before his time.

|7|

A GAY TIME IN CALIFORNIA

My father had a simple philosophy concerning children. Considering that he had six of them, I fully understand that for him it was a case of the simpler the philosophy the better. When he saw me 'fussing', as he termed it, over my firstborn, Peggy, and being attentive to her every whim, he felt compelled to share that philosophy with me. 'Children innately crave attention,' he confided, 'and it is the duty of parents to deny them it. You make sure they are properly fed and that they are well clothed and protected but you must always resist their unhealthy demands for attention.'

I was in my late 20s when he told me this and I immediately gained an insight into our relationship. I realised I had been trying to win his approval and attention all my life and had assumed that it was only the demands of my five siblings that had distracted his interest. Now I understood that it was a conscious decision on my father's part to resist all my 'unhealthy' demands. For many years, I had strived to be a 'good boy' and win his approval by excelling in everything I attempted. When that hadn't worked, I'd started being a 'bad boy' and rebelling against his rules and values. Being bad was no more successful than being good but it was much more fun.

One evening, when I was home from university for the Christmas vacation, my father and I stood together in the kitchen doing the dishes after a family meal. I wanted to somehow break through and make contact with him. I wanted him to notice me. I realise now, of course, that I just wanted his attention.

'Dad, I'm homosexual,' I suddenly blurted. 'I've been this way for years but I can't keep it secret any more!'

'Oh,' he said, 'well, I don't think you should tell your mother. It would only upset her. And it would set a very bad example for the children. You know that George copies everything you do.'

My brother George not only copied me, he exceeded me. Whatever I did, he took to extremes, far surpassing me. The idea of George becoming gay did not bear thinking about!

My father and I never mentioned the matter again. With hindsight, I suspect that he was aware of what I was doing and never believed a word I said. And, of course, he was right. I just wanted to shock him and get his attention.

Just for the record, I am not gay and even at school never had any homosexual experiences – not that there's anything wrong with being gay, of course. I just love women's smooth, soft bodies too much and hate rough, hairy legs. But I would have performed fellatio on the Pope to make my father notice me.

* * *

I was still working at Price, Waterhouse & Co. when I first started running errands for Graham Plinston in 1969. During the day, I balanced books wearing my bowler hat and in the evenings I plotted international dope deals at Graham's kitchen table. We were doing a lot of work with some Californians at that time. The Americans would buy VW camper vans in Germany and then drive them across Europe to Turkey. Sometimes, perhaps not trusting my friend Mohamed in Istanbul, or wary of his sharp knife, they would drive down to Lebanon's Bekaa Valley, where Graham's contacts would fill their secret compartments with hashish. They also bought BMW 2002s and loaded those up with hash in the same way. The BMWs carried less hashish, of course, but were faster and more fun to drive. The vehicles would then be driven to somewhere innocuous like Holland or Denmark and shipped back to the US.

Consequently, there was a constant stream of Californians passing through London during this period. They would either be on their way to Germany to buy a van or returning from Holland after shipping home their loaded vehicle. They were usually bored and would expect Graham and me to entertain them. Without exception, the Californians were tall, lanky and blond. Most of them were part of an organisation called the Brotherhood of Eternal Love, of which our Californian contact Ernie Combs was a founding member. The Brotherhood, based in Laguna Beach, were evangelical about psychedelic drugs; their guru was Timothy Leary. When they were not actively engaged in doing dope deals they spent all their time, as far as I could gather, surfing. Surfing was what they lived for and all they wanted to talk about. As a consequence, they found London, indeed Europe, to be very boring. 'There's no waves, dude. What do you do for fun?'

They did not like the English habit of smoking joints. They found it disgusting that we mixed our hashish with tobacco. 'That shit will kill you, dude,' they would say with that disdainful puritan vigour that Americans have made their own. They all smoked 'spliffs' which were just marijuana strands, no tobacco. They were difficult to hold and tended to burn your fingers. Call me old-fashioned if you will but I preferred a proper English three-paper joint with a cardboard filter. I never did take to spliffs.

The Brotherhood of Eternal Love also shared a vague New Age philosophy of spiritual mumbo-jumbo, which they preached at any and every opportunity. Graham and I had studied philosophy and comparative religion at university and Howard had studied philosophy and logical positivism. Listening to the lectures of these blond surfers while keeping a straight face was part of the price we paid for a life of crime.

It was Ernie who organised the movement of blond surfers and Lebanese hash around the world. He was a mythic figure in the Brotherhood and his name, seldom mentioned openly, was always spoken with awe. He was the son of a Californian oil tycoon whose family had sold their Anaheim farmland to Walt Disney for the construction of Disneyland. Ernie's father apparently gave him oil wells for each birthday: one oil well on his first birthday, two on his second, three on his third and so forth. Sometime during his teens, resentful of all the oil wells, Ernie vowed to his father that he didn't need any more handouts and was going to make a bigger fortune than his father had ever dreamed of. By the time Graham first met him, doing a deal in Lebanon, Ernie was well on his way to achieving his goal, and Graham recognised that Ernie and his millions represented a whole new way of conducting business.

Although he came to Europe a couple of times, Ernie did not like anything he saw and preferred to stay in California. 'Too small and uptight, man,' was his final assessment of European culture and he never wavered from that opinion in all the 30 years that I knew him. Ernie preferred to send his Brotherhood people to Europe while he pulled the strings from his house in Laguna Beach or his Nevada cabin near Lake Tahoe. Consequently, we had all these Californians whom we could not relate to expecting to be entertained by a bunch of English faggots who spent the greater part of their time in the pub drinking Guinness. Most of the Californians did not drink alcohol. 'That shit will kill you, man,' they would say.

They didn't like pubs: too much beer, no ice, too many cigarettes, too few chairs, no carpets and no soy bean salads. 'How can you eat those sausages, dude? They're, like, dead pigs or something. That's what Jews eat.' A slight pause and then, 'OK, that's what Jews don't eat, man. Anyway, they're totally disgusting.' Neither did they understand why we were not surrounded at all times by a bevy of interchangeable blonde surfer chicks. We never did have a good answer for that question and that was where all our fancy university training left us with no good rejoinder.

Occasionally, one of the surfer dudes would bring his 'old lady' for the trip and sometimes he would leave her in London with us while he did 'the business' over on the Continent. While entertaining these busty blonde bimbos, we fluctuated wildly between feelings of overpowering lust and overwhelming boredom. Luckily, we soon discovered that most of them, unlike our English girlfriends, had no concept of angst, remorse or even of personal relationships and were as happy as we were to indulge in mindless, guilt-free and very energetic sex.

Looking after Ernie's Californian boys was an increasing strain. Not only were they demanding and intellectually vapid, they would use our office phone to speak to their girlfriends back home – and even to their dogs. In the 1970s, calls to the US were very expensive, logistically challenging and involved international operators. It was therefore disconcerting to walk into your house and find a blond surfer dude using your phone.

A typical conversation might go: 'Hey! Watcha say, girl? . . . Yeah, it's me, Randy. Yes, princess, I'll be home soon and we'll go run on the beach.' He turned, his eyes wild with excitement: 'She recognised my voice, dude. She knows that it's me!' It was only after being offered the phone to say hello and hearing heavy panting noises at the other end that I realised that either my house guest was calling his dog in California or his girlfriend took the concept of phone sex far too literally.

One afternoon, Ernie called to say that his right-hand man, Val Johnson, was staying overnight in London on his way home to Laguna Beach. Could we look after him? Graham's girlfriend, Mandy, was visiting friends, so he needed to stay at home with his two-year-old son, Sam. He asked me to do the honours and 'entertain Val'. Val was very important for the future of our relationship with the Californians; he had the ability to either cut off or increase the amount of funding we received. It was important that he enjoyed his short visit to London.

Apart from the Hilton on Park Lane, next to the Playboy Club, most of the American chain hotels were located out by Heathrow airport in a dreary and alien part of London with no clubs, few pubs and certainly nowhere to surf. However, Ernie's boys did not like to stay in hotels that were not part of a recognised American chain, so I drove out to the Hounslow Marriott to visit Val Johnson in his little piece of the USA.

Val was lying on his bed watching television when I entered and indeed he remained on the bed watching television for the duration of my visit. He had just flown back from Beirut and was still wearing the short-hair wig that all the Brotherhood sported when they took part in foreign missions. They would tuck their long, blond surfer-dude hair under a brown, insurance-underwriter-style wig so that they looked like straight, normal guys. Unfortunately, there was always at least one long strand of blond hair hanging below the wig, which proclaimed the wearer to be a Californian dope dealer on a mission.

My main recreational activity at this time was hanging out in pubs, drinking pints of beer and hoping some girl without a bra would ask me to fondle her. I had no idea what important Californian dope dealers liked to do in their free time.

'Would you like to go to the bar?' I asked him half-heartedly, imagining the empty sterility of a midweek airport-hotel lounge bar at 9.30 p.m.

'I've got a minibar up here,' he muttered, 'but it's got no Tab.'

'What's Tab?' I asked, hoping it would be some exotic form of tequila, which I understood was popular with certain Californian hipsters.

'It's like a sugar-free Coke, man,' he explained, 'but they use saccharin instead of NutraSweet.'

Only during the discussion of Tab did Val raise his eyes away from the TV set or the Zenith ultrasonic remote-control unit with which he was flashing from channel to channel without leaving the bed. I had never seen a TV remote before and was fascinated.

'This is a piece of crap,' he finally exclaimed. 'It can only pick up three stations.' He turned and looked at me. 'What the fuck do you guys do around here? There's no beach and no TV worth shit. All I've been able to find is *Gunsmoke*, except you guys call it *Gun Law*. I mean, how fucked up is that?' He flipped the channel to a scene of grim-looking men on horses. 'Anyway,' he moaned, 'I've already seen that episode a bunch of times.'

I managed to last maybe another hour in Val's company. I poured myself a gin and tonic from the minibar and persuaded Val to have a Diet Pepsi. I suggested going for a meal, going for a drink – I even offered to drive him around London and show him the sights: 'Buckingham Palace by moonlight,' I suggested lamely.

Val wanted none of it and angrily bounced between BBC1, BBC2 and ITV. 'Even the fucking commercials are crap,' he observed. Finally, feeling I had more than performed my social duties and having got him to confirm there was nothing more he wanted, I made my excuses and left.

That was the beginning of my reputation among the Californians as a flaming English faggot. Apparently, Val thought I was trying to seduce him and told Ernie he had barely survived the evening with his honour intact.

My final day at Price, Waterhouse & Co. came not long after that odd evening and it was both sudden and unexpected. As the summer months drew to a close, most of the Californians were returning to Western Europe and wanting to ship their dope-laden vehicles stateside. Graham and I were charged with organising the logistics and the endless paperwork and we needed to be in regular contact with Ernie. When he was in Laguna Beach, we could at least call him direct in the evening (West Coast time). During the day, he would be out surfing; in the early evening, he would still be mellow (but not yet too stoned to conduct business). As winter approached, however, he tended to spend more time at his cabin in Nevada and then he became extremely difficult to reach. We would have to call his 'phone guy', Danny, to tell him we needed to talk to Ernie urgently. Danny would say, 'OK, man,' and then we would have to wait for several hours beside the phone until Ernie finally called us back.

Graham was becoming increasingly irritated by this communication problem. None of the Californians had Ernie's phone number in Nevada, so all contact between them and him was relayed through the office in Warwick Place above our carpet shop. Some of the complications with the shipments of various BMWs and VW campers were becoming quite complex and a face-to-face discussion with Ernie was required. Unfortunately, because of his previous legal problems on the Swiss–German border, Graham was unable to get a visa for travel to the USA. Michael Durani was using his diplomatic contacts to work behind the scenes but for the moment Graham could not cross the Atlantic.

'Patrick,' he said, 'you're going to have to fly out and explain all these issues to Ernie. You've got to impress on him the importance of a far more responsive telephone call-back arrangement.' I was excited by the idea of flying to California but was well aware that I was still employed as a chartered accountant with Price, Waterhouse & Co. I wore a bowler hat every morning as I read my copy of *The Times*, travelling to Bank Station on the Northern Line – the black line on the map. 'Make a decision, Patrick,' Graham said. 'Are you a chartered accountant or a dope smuggler? You can't be both for ever. You have to choose.'

My girlfriend, Jude, who was to become my wife and the mother of my children many years later, had not liked the direction my life was taking and had already posed similar questions. After hearing my equivocal and evasive answers too many times, she had decided to leave me. I was footloose and fancy free, so I decided to give Graham a definitive reply. The following morning, I walked into Edward Welsh's office and told him I was leaving PW.

'That's terrible news, Patrick,' Edward said. Having hired me three years previously, he had always taken a friendly interest in my progress within the firm. 'What are you going to do?'

'Some friends have set up a company in France, sir,' I said. 'They want me to help manage the financial side.'

'Well, that sounds intriguing. What sort of business is it, if I may ask?'

'Canoeing, sir,' I said. 'We'll be organising canoeing trips down the Dordogne River for tourists. We believe that recreational investment is the wave of the future. Rather like plastics, sir.'

Edward's eyes gleamed. 'That sounds like a splendid idea,' he said. 'Wish I was a bit younger myself and I'd be tempted to join you. Canoeing, eh? I remember now, you've always been fond of canoeing.'

I left the PW office in Old Jewry and walked down to the middle of Blackfriars Bridge. To my left, I could see the mock-Gothic majesty of Tower Bridge; to my right the river curved south towards Westminster and the Houses of Parliament. I was aware that this was a decisive moment in my life and I recalled standing on the school rugby pitch at midnight, shaking my fist defiantly at God during a thunderstorm. Slowly, I removed my bowler hat and, copying the new American fad of Frisbee throwing, I launched it out over the black, murky waters of the Thames. The black bowler floated for a while in the middle of the wide, deep river and then it sank into the darkness of the future.

Ten years later, another life would end at that very same spot. In 1982, Roberto Calvi, banker to the Masons, the Vatican and the Mafia, was found hanging by his neck underneath the bridge, his pockets weighed down with masonry and foreign currency. Members of the secretive Masonic lodge to which he belonged were called 'black friars', like the bridge, and they were based on the Swiss–Italian border, where Jude and I were living at the time of his murder. All this, of course, was still in the future, which, like my submerged bowler hat, was now impossible to see.

I walked briskly from the bridge and hailed a cab. 'Heathrow,' I said. 'Please take me to the airport.' Within a few hours, I was on my way to Los Angeles, California. I was no longer a chartered accountant. I was a professional smuggler at last.

I was very proud of the way that, after landing in Los Angeles at 6 p.m. local time, I was able to ignore my jet lag, hire a car, negotiate the extraordinarily complex Orange County freeway system and somehow find myself a couple of hours later on the main drag of Laguna Beach, California.

I parked my car outside a bar on the main street, planning to gather my wits before calling Ernie and announcing my arrival. I needed to wind down before meeting our Californian boss.

After the bright sunshine, the interior of the room was dark. I made my way to the bar and ordered a martini, 'straight up with an olive, please'. Ordering a martini as soon as I arrived in America was a ritual of mine. I never drank them anywhere else and even in the USA usually had one only on my first day. But to me a martini was the quintessential American drink and I did not feel I had arrived in the States until I had sipped one. Previously, I had always entered the US through New York and every New York barman knows how to make a martini – it's a matter of local pride. In Laguna Beach in the '70s, however, there was little demand for martinis and the barman not only did not have the proper glass but kept wanting to add ice and half the fruit bowl. It was not the best martini I have ever had but it was wet and cold and it hit the spot. I started to relax.

'Are you from England?' asked the man at the next bar stool. 'My name's Archie and my father was in England during the war. He loved it. Absolutely adored it!'

In addition to my English accent, I had come straight from the PW office and was still dressed in a three-piece pinstripe suit and carrying a battered leather briefcase. Even without the bowler hat, I must have looked like a caricature of a City gent. I explained that I had just driven from LA airport and had only been in the country a couple of hours.

Americans are famous for their hospitality, and were even friendlier in those more innocent days when there were fewer foreign tourists. I was quickly surrounded by half the bar. People were asking about England and about my flight, while others told me about Laguna Beach and local places I absolutely had to visit. Everybody wanted to buy me drinks and invite me to their home to meet their friends. I was quite overwhelmed by the warmth and kindness of all my new chums. It was more than an hour and certainly more than a few drinks before I excused myself to call Ernie from the phone outside the men's room. A crowd of friendly patrons even escorted me to the toilet and left me alone only after I'd explained that I needed to call a friend. 'We'll wait for you at the bar,' they promised.

Ernie answered the phone and was delighted to hear that I was already in Laguna Beach. 'That's great. I thought I would have to drive to LA and find you. Most Europeans can't handle the freeway system. Where are you? I'll drive down and get you.'

'Just give me the address of your house and I'll drive myself.'

'No, we're up in the hills. It's hard to find. Tell me where you are. It'll only take five minutes.'

I read the address on the book of matches I'd taken from the bar. 'It's a place called the Pink Poodle,' I said.

'The Pink Poodle?' Ernie repeated.

'Yes, do you know it? It's a nice place. The people are really friendly.'

'I bet they are,' Ernie said. There was a pause while he spoke to someone in the room with him. 'Listen, why don't you book into the Ramada Inn, just two blocks down the street? That way you can get rested and then we'll collect you in the morning.'

I put down the phone feeling slightly uneasy. There had been a distinct change in Ernie's manner and I sensed that I had done something wrong. I returned to my friends at the bar feeling thoughtful as I replayed the conversation in my mind. But it was hard to think clearly, as everyone wanted to talk to me and buy me drinks. It was probably at about this time that I realised there were no women in the bar, even though, on the small dance floor at the back of the room, I saw a few couples swaying together. Archie saw me watching the dancers. 'Would you like to dance?' he offered shyly.

I had never been in a gay bar before. I didn't even know they existed. When you first arrive in a new place, you are so overwhelmed by the differences in everything you see, from street signs to the size of the cars or the way people dress and speak, that you do not catch the social clues that would be more obvious back home. Hastily, I finished my drink, left some money on the bar, grabbed my briefcase and mumbled something about jet lag. Ignoring the shrill protests of Archie and his friends, I quickly left the bar and drove to the Ramada Inn.

Ernie collected me in the morning and I followed him to his large timber-frame house, built on stilts, overlooking Laguna Beach and the Pacific Ocean. Val Johnson was there waiting for us and made some crack about the Pink Poodle. Flustered, I mumbled some excuses about post-arrival cultural blindness but I could tell that Val was not convinced. The problem was that to many American men all Englishmen are faggots by definition. It's not just the funny way we speak or the fact that we don't all wear baseball caps and understand the rules of football; it's also our strange humour, the things we laugh at. If you add to that his interpretation of my behaviour in his London hotel bedroom and my visit to the Pink Poodle, it's easy to see why Val was convinced I was as bent as a seven-dollar bill. What's more, nothing would ever change his mind.

Tall and blond like all the other Californians, Ernie had broad shoulders and a barrel chest. Unlike the others he had thinning hair, an unkempt mountain-man beard and humourous eyes behind thick glasses. He was always, unquestionably, the boss.

We spent the next few hours discussing business. I summarised the various shipment problems with the VW vans and BMWs in Rotterdam and we looked through the paperwork. I also gave Ernie the air waybill numbers of various shipments coming direct from Pakistan, which Michael Durani and Shemsi were arranging, and offered him an overview of Graham and Howard's plans to import directly into the US.

'That's enough work for today,' Ernie suddenly announced. 'Let's go and play with some toys.' I remained friends with Ernie for the next 30 years and the pattern never changed: a few hours work at most and then we'd go and play with his new toys. Ernie's toys were usually fast, noisy, dangerous, consumed large amounts of fuel and were always expensive.

That first afternoon, we drove a four-wheel-drive all-terrain vehicle through the desert canyons behind Laguna Beach. Puffing on Colombian spliffs, we roared up impossible slopes and skidded down dangerous inclines in a cloud of dust. I was still suffering from jet lag and hungover from my excesses at the Pink Poodle, and my heart, stomach, mouth and sphincter all fought for control of my bodily functions. 'Well, we sure had some fun, didn't we?' Ernie beamed when we finally returned to the house. 'Tomorrow we'll go dirt-bike riding.'

In subsequent years, Ernie was the first kid on the block to have a water bike for speeding across the waves off his houses on Malibu Beach or a snowmobile for roaring across the stillness of the Sierra snows behind his houses on Lake Tahoe. On the tennis courts of his houses in Beverly Hills and Bel Air, he had ball machines that could pump tennis balls over the net faster than I could hit them. At his condo in Miami, he kept a cigarette boat and at his Manhattan townhouse he had a couple of Harley-Davidson bikes. As for his collection of luxury German cars, let me just quote him by saying 'there's always a bunch'. Over the years, I would return from my visits to Ernie with bumps and bruises and the occasional broken bone.

I moved into Ernie's house for the rest of my stay and he lent me a set of clothes so that I could change out of my suit. 'You look like a fucking Fed, man,' Ernie said. 'Gives me the shivers.'

I spent the next few days driving around Laguna in one of Ernie's Mercedes visiting various members of the Brotherhood in their spacious but walled and well-guarded compounds. They were all keen to repay the hospitality extended to them in London. I was finally able to meet their various girlfriends and dogs, and, by listening to the panting, tell which was which. Without exception, the girls were blonde with large breasts and the dogs were Afghan wolfhounds specially trained to attack whenever they smelled gun oil. 'All cops smell of gun oil, dude,' was the only explanation required. Otherwise the dogs, like their owners, were large, friendly and boisterous.

Most days involved surfing. While the others searched for the big waves offshore, I paddled around and wobbled on my big board close to the beach. None of this did anything to improve the reputation of my manhood and Val Johnson looked increasingly contemptuous.

Then Ernie left for Nevada on business and I was charged with looking after one of Ernie's girlfriends, Barbi. They were both very proud that Hugh Hefner also had a girlfriend called Barbi who lived with him in the Playboy Mansion. 'But she has bigger boobs,' Barbi told me. 'She's had them done. Do you think I should have mine done?'

'I think they look very fine as they are,' I told her, not quite knowing where to look but aware that my natural reserve probably reinforced my growing reputation as an English fag.

Barbi had a three-year-old daughter from a previous relationship and I was surprised when she put her in the back of the Porsche one evening as we set off to a party at Val's house. 'She can sleep in the back seat,' Barbi assured me. 'I'll leave one of the windows slightly opened.' Having grown up looking after my younger siblings, I was slightly appalled by this arrangement but I was too excited about the party to feel guilty as we left the car and the kid in the street. I had never been to a Californian party before but I'd seen many images of them in *Playboy*. Giddy with anticipation, I wondered if I should have packed a toga. Barbi's breasts had never before looked so tantalising and accessible, and I pictured them bobbing on the waters of a jacuzzi.

The reality, as is so often the case in America, was somewhat different. Barbi and I were the only guests. We spent the evening with Val and his girlfriend smoking spliffs and watching Val's home-made surfer movies. Val had hired his own cameraman to film him riding the waves. He considered himself an excellent surfer and often thought about turning pro. 'The business would suffer, though,' he explained, while his girlfriend clung proudly to him like a flowering vine. 'I've got responsibilities, dude. Ernie relies on me.'

There was nothing to drink in the house except Tab and iced tea.

Deciding he was dealing with an alcoholic, Val eventually managed to find a quart of sweet cooking sherry that his parents had left at Christmas. It was disgusting; I barely managed to finish the bottle.

Not only did we have to watch endless shots of Val standing on his board or being knocked over by a large wave, we also had to listen to his running commentary as he explained every shot in detail and replayed each experience for us.

'Do you ever go canoeing, Val?' I finally asked him, if only to keep myself awake.

'What's that?' he asked suspiciously. 'Is that some Brit thing?'

'Well, we don't have big waves in England,' I explained, 'so we make do with what we can.'

I've been to many parties in California since that evening but never in my life have I had such a gnarly time. I knew my friends in London were waiting to hear stories of wild nights and I could not wait to tell them all about it.

Barbi and I left the party to find that the baby had not been kidnapped and the car had not been stolen. 'Ernie would have been mad if it had been stolen,' Barbi told me. 'That's why I wasn't sure about parking it in the street.'

The following day, I flew to Reno, Nevada, to join Ernie at his cabin in the mountains. I was told to rent a four-wheel drive at the airport and was given directions to Ernie's place on Lake Tahoe.

Having left all my borrowed clothes in Malibu, I was once more wearing my three-piece pinstripe and, like Cary Grant standing in a prairie wearing a business suit in *North by Northwest*, I felt conspicuously out of place. Determined to finally put my respectable English past behind me, I stopped the car when I saw a Western clothing store out in the boonies near Carson City. In a scene worthy of Hitchcock, a traditional English City gent disappears inside a store in the middle of the desert and 20 minutes later a cowboy emerges, in jeans, high-heeled pointed boots, a shirt with pearl buttons, a leather waistcoat and a large white Stetson. After three years with Price, Waterhouse & Co., I was ready for a new uniform.

As the road climbed into the mountains, early snow was already falling and the pine forests grew thicker and closer to the road. I switched on the heater in the car.

Ernie's cabin was about the size of a small English manor house, built from wood and with high cathedral ceilings. After he recovered from the sight of my new wardrobe, Ernie grilled us some steaks the size of a small English cow and we washed them down with a bottle of Jack Daniel's. Ernie was much more tolerant about alcohol than most of his friends.

It was a civilised evening in front of a blazing wood fire and we chatted in that companionable way that men do the whole world over after consuming red meat, most of a bottle of bourbon and several spliffs. I told him of Graham's concerns about the breakdown in communication and explained that much time was often lost while we waited for Ernie to return his phone calls. Ernie nodded and looked thoughtful but said nothing.

Around 9 p.m., we were interrupted by Danny, the phone guy, who had driven over from his house. 'That English guy just called,' he said. 'Sounds pretty pissed. Says he can't get ahold of you.'

Ernie raised his eyebrows at me and grinned. 'Better call him back right away,' he said.

Ernie insisted I borrow a thick fur-lined parka and we climbed into one of his monstrous four-wheel-drive trucks. There had been a storm while we were eating and the snow was now thick. 'Good job I've got snow tyres,' Ernie said as we followed the lights of Danny's truck down the bumpy mountain track.

After 20 minutes, Danny pulled to the right along a narrow snow-covered track towards his house. With a farewell flick of the powerful headlights to high beam, we continued further, into the dark forest. 'We don't use Danny's phone for outgoing,' Ernie explained. 'Creates a pattern the cops can track. I always use a variety of different phones to return calls. I prefer using casinos but tonight we're going to use the nearest public phone available.'

We continued up into the mountains. The swirl of snow against the windscreen wipers became thicker and the trees crowded closer to the narrow road. Eventually, we reached a clearing in the forest and Ernie stopped the truck with the headlights full-beam on a giant sequoia tree. The tree was about the size of Post Office Tower in London, but taller.

As we got out of the car, the cold and swirling snow immediately stung our faces. I envied Ernie's thick beard. He led me to the base of the tree and showed me the metal spikes that would enable us to climb it. We pulled ourselves painfully above the comforting lights from the truck into an unknown darkness redolent of pine needles and fresh snow. Finally, we reached a telephone inside a protective plastic dome. 'It's way above the snowline,' Ernie explained, 'for use in emergencies.'

While I clung desperately to the metal supports, Ernie deposited several dollars' worth of quarters into the meter and then asked the international operator to connect him to Graham's number in London. 'Here,' Ernie said, handing me the phone, from which came the comforting sound of an English telephone ringing, 'explain to the little cocksucker why there's a communication delay.'

I was sorry to leave the West Coast. I had a lot of fun riding snowmobiles with Ernie through the mountains of Nevada and discovered the secret of what he referred to as his 'other business' – it was gambling in the casinos of Reno.

However, I had a meeting organised with some financial people on Wall Street, so, reluctantly, I took a red-eye flight from Las Vegas to New York. Ernie drove me to the airport in a brand-new Mercedes he had bought with his winnings from a long game of craps in the casino the night before. 'Hey, we had some fun, didn't we?' he said. 'Even if you are English.'

I'd been in New York just a few hours when Ernie called to say that he wanted to send some money to our Zeitgeist account in Switzerland in order to test my new Wall Street connections. 'My courier's flying over tomorrow and will meet you in the bar of your hotel,' he told me.

On Graham's advice, I had taken a suite at the Plaza, on Fifth Avenue, in case I needed to entertain these new Wall Street bankers. The next evening, at the appointed time of six, I waited in the Oak Bar, looking out over Central Park. That's my favourite time to be in a bar. It's the magic hour, poised between the duties of the working day and the responsibilities of the home. The happy hour. The bar was filling rapidly with people on their way home from the office and the noise level was increasing as the room became more crowded. I commanded two stools next to the bar and fought off any invaders. I had no idea how I was to recognise Ernie's courier nor how he was to recognise me. I assumed it would be somebody I already knew.

'Patrick? Hi, I'm Angie.' A petite and very beautiful girl with long black hair perched herself on the stool next to mine. 'What are you drinking? Fancy tequilas?'

'How did you recognise me?' I asked.

'Ernie said you would either be dressed as a cowboy or wearing a three-piece suit.' Having spent the day on Wall Street, I was in my suit. 'He also said you had a large nose.' She pulled out some cigarettes and ordered the barman to give us a couple of shots of tequila. 'I hope you don't mind but I had my bags sent up to your room.'

I'd never actually drunk tequila before and was fascinated when Angie explained the whole ritual of making a little pile of salt on the back of the hand, dipping the tongue in, taking a shot of tequila and then sucking on a lemon. We tossed them back simultaneously. 'Wow!' she said. 'That hit the spot. Let's do two more.'

I'd always enjoyed sipping whisky and, to a lesser extent, brandy, but that's a slow and sensuous process, accompanied by good conversation or maudlin reflections. Tequila was a whole new ball game. As soon as one shot was finished, Angie ordered another. The business with the salt and lemon slowed the process a little, but not much. It also had potential for causing confusion. At one point, after the fifth or sixth shot, Angie snorted the white powder up her nostril, forgetting it was salt. Tequila is not a drink that encourages reflective conversation.

I don't believe we can have remained at the Oak Bar for more than an hour. The next thing I knew, I was waking up next to Angie, both of us fully dressed, on the king-size bed in my suite. My head was throbbing and the bedside clock showed midnight. I had no idea how we'd got there. Either the two of us had crawled out of the bar on our hands and knees, through the Palm Court and past the portrait of Eloise, or, more likely, the hotel staff had carried the two of us out to the service elevator and dumped us on the bed in my room.

'Wow!' said Angie, sitting up and looking around. 'Let's order some champagne from room service and have a shower.'

We spent the next 24 hours in my suite. We spent some of it on the bed, some on the floor, some on the table, a lot of it in the shower and I vaguely recall imaginative use of a plush red-velvet ottoman and footstool. At one point, I remember us leaning out the window of the 58th floor, overlooking Central Park, and shouting, 'Yes! Oh, Yes!' in unison.

I also remember Angie shouting, 'Fuck me in the ass!'

'What? Do you mean in the bottom?' I asked primly.

'Isn't that what you like?'

'Well, I don't know. I've never done it before.'

On the second morning, I woke up and found she had gone. There was no note and no explanation. But she had left me $100,000 in grubby ten- and twenty-dollar bills in a large suitcase. It wasn't a Hartmann.

I took the cash to my new Wall Street contacts, Nicholas Deak and Juan Dejesus of Deak-Perera, near the World Trade Center and arranged to have it transferred to the Zeitgeist account in Switzerland. After completing the paperwork – of which there was remarkably little – we all took the elevator to have lunch at the Windows on the World restaurant on the 107th floor of the North Tower. Lunching with two major Wall Street bankers at one of the most prestigious financial restaurants in the world was not sufficient to stop me from thinking about the previous night of wanton abandon.

Nicholas and Juan opened up a new world of financial opportunities of which Howard, Graham and I had never dreamed. Unfortunately, I was so distracted by the world of shameless sexual possibilities to which Angie had introduced me that I barely listened to them as they talked.

I later found out that Angie was a hooker whom Ernie had hired to discover if I was gay or not. Ernie was a friend of Hollywood madam Alex Adams, who later wrote a memoir, *Madam 90210*, and Angie was part of her stable of call girls, along with Heidi Fleiss. Val and Ernie had wagered a large sum on Angie's report. Ernie was meticulous in his research and he always liked to be sure. Trusting a hooker with

$100,000 on a cross-country flight was a worthwhile investment as far as he was concerned. As he explained to me later, 'We can't have faggots in the organisation. It's bad for morale. We need to be able to depend on each other.' I'm not sure what the criteria were but apparently I passed muster. Angie gave me the official seal of approval and thereafter I was accepted as a regular guy. Ernie would often add, when he introduced me to somebody, 'He's English, but he's not a fag.' Val Johnson, however, was never convinced.

I never saw Angie again but many years later Val and I found ourselves on trial together in a Florida courtroom. A number of us were accused of several federal racketeering and conspiracy charges and we all faced possible life terms. Ernie and I were being held in a federal prison in Miami but Val was free on bond. He leaned towards me one day in the courtroom while we were waiting for the jury and said, 'How's prison? Meet any of your old friends from the Pink Poodle?'

I was found guilty by that Florida jury on all counts. Val Johnson was found not guilty. As he walked jauntily from the courtroom, he turned to me, grinned and then made an obscene gesture with his tongue. If there really is any justice in the universe, one of these days Val Johnson is going to get the sharp end of a surfboard up his bottom. Or maybe a canoe.

The guilty verdict made front-page headlines all over the world, so at least I finally managed to get my father's attention.

8

BETWEEN A ROCK AND A TRUFFLE

Whenever we went on excursions in the family car, which was often, my father always made meticulous plans. He would make long lists of things we needed to take with us and create a detailed itinerary of our journey, with projected times of arrival for each place we would visit. Obviously, with so many children, normally including one in nappies, such careful planning was essential.

The 1950s and '60s were the age of the family motor holiday in England, and my father was determined to explore the British Isles and share the experience with his children. Lunch would involve picnics along the route and at night we would camp in a large tent in some muddy field. With six children, restaurants and hotels were out of the question. Looking back, I am amazed at the fortitude with which my parents undertook these expeditions and touched by the love they must have felt for their unruly brood to even contemplate regularly repeating them.

My father's written itinerary usually started with '8 a.m. – depart house', which would be followed by hourly indications of interesting places that we would pass or visit. There would be suggestions of scenic spots that we could reach by noon for the midday picnic and he would have consulted the *AA Guide* for suitable camping places. The day would be planned with the precision of a military manoeuvre.

Of course, by the time the breakfast things had been washed, the baby had been changed and George or Judy had been located at a friend's house, we would never, ever depart earlier than 10 a.m. Then there would be the roadworks along the A41 or the four-car pile-up outside of Bletchley or the fact that Judy needed to pee 'so bad' we had to drive off the main road to find somewhere suitable. Or we would get lost because Natasha or I misread the map.

I suspect that is why my father so enjoyed that first trip up the M1 to Birmingham and back. The new motorway really was predictable. There were no diversions, so the journey could all be calculated in advance, and after the first trip he included the Watford Gap service station in any itinerary for travel on the M1.

'8 a.m. – depart house.

9.45 a.m. – stop at Watford Gap.'

Other than that Birmingham trip, not once on all the hundreds of family trips we made over the years did we succeed in following the itinerary. We always ended up somewhere different from where we had planned and had fun doing something that wasn't on the schedule.

Even our packing lists were inadequate. Either we needed something that wasn't on the list or the car was overloaded with things we had no use for. Most of the time, either Natasha or I simply forgot to pack something that was clearly listed and which it was our duty to tick off and pack.

'That was Tasha's job, Daddy. She said she'd packed it.'

'No, I didn't. Mummy, Patrick's lying again!'

'Shut up the two of you or I'll bang your heads together!'

'Liar!'

'No, I'm not.'

'Yes, you are.'

And, of course, there was the endless shoving and fighting on the back seat as the space got smaller with the addition of each new child.

'Mummy! George keeps sticking his bogeys on me.'

'You little liar!'

My mother's arm would sweep across the back seat, striking whichever child was too slow to duck. 'George, stop picking your nose!'

My parents devised a game called Legs in order to keep us amused on these journeys. The game involved taking it in turns to spot the next pub sign and count the legs. The One-Legged Pirate, though not brilliant, was, obviously, one point better than the King's Head or the Queen's Arms, while the Duke of Salisbury produced a more respectable score of two. The Cricketers was one of the most sought-after signs because a cricket team had eleven players, which meant a score of twenty-two legs. The Coach and Horses was always a little controversial.

'That's sixteen because there're always four horses with a coach.'

'Could be two horses.'

'Look at the sign! Are you blind? Look at the sign – there's four horses.'

'There are four horses,' my father corrected from the driver's seat.

'What, Daddy?'

'Four horses are plural. So you say "there are" not "there is".'

'Well, it's gone now. I can't see it.'

'"They're gone" not "it's gone". Didn't you hear what Daddy just said?'

'Mummy, Natasha's cheating again.'

'No, I'm not.'

'Anyway, what about the coachman? You have to have a coachman, so that means eighteen. Nah nah nee nah nah!'

'And passengers,' suggested George, supporting his brother. 'There must be passengers. Suppose it was a lady with two little dogs?' He paused to calculate.

'Or a one-legged pirate,' said Judy, supporting the girls' side.

'Well, he'd have a parrot, wouldn't he? So that's three more legs.'

The Fox and Hounds produced even more bickering, as far as I can recall. The exact definition of a pack of hounds could continue for miles.

Yet despite all the back-seat fighting, the fact that nothing ever went according to plan and the itinerary becoming inaccurate before we even left the house, my father continued to make his meticulous schedules and his detailed lists for all the time I lived at home. I imagine he did so all his life. Fifty years later, I can still picture his small, neat notations written with his precious Parker pen: '8 a.m. – depart house.'

If his objective was simply to execute a well-planned and organised expedition, then he failed miserably, time and again. But if his goal was to create enjoyable outings for his impossibly boisterous family, then he succeeded brilliantly. After 60 years, some of my happiest memories are of picnics in the New Forest or the Forest of Dean, of muddy camping sites below Harlech Castle or beside the Solent. We watched gliders landing at Luton airport when it was still a grass field and we went punting along the River Cam past my father's old Cambridge haunts.

It is because of my parents' determined perseverance against all the odds that I have such an abiding love for the English countryside and retain so many happy family memories. My own children grew up in France and America, and it was always a regret of mine that neither country offers pub signs with which to entertain the family on a road trip. I am eternally grateful to my parents for many things, and the family outings remain high on the list.

* * *

One consequence of growing up with such meticulous planning is that I never plan anything. I have a deep-seated belief in Murphy's Law and prefer to maintain the flexibility of the unpredictable. It can be no coincidence that the Oxford thesis of my brother-in-law Howard Marks, business partner in my life of crime, was on the theory of chaos.

In the early '70s, we all drove BMW 2002tiis. Unlike Mustangs, Porsches and E-Type Jaguars, which were obviously fast and sporty, these BMWs had a box-like anonymity and were quite unknown outside of Germany. They were, however, as fast as the other, more flashy cars and totally discreet: the perfect driving machine for a dope dealer. The person who first designed these cars and gave them the pedestrian name Bavarian Motor Works had obviously never planned or even imagined that they should eventually define all that was hip. Nor, it must be said, can Adolf Hitler ever have imagined that his VW 'People's Car' would become the favourite mode of transport for long-haired hippies and peaceniks. All of which is to say that I do not believe we can ever predict the future, however precise our plans and however detailed our schedules.

I was not so crass, after one of our periodic separations, as to offer Jude a BMW to win back her affections as my girlfriend, but I did buy her a bright-orange VW Beetle with a large duck painted on it. I secretly arranged with her boss at Sussex University for him to give her two weeks' holiday. When she arrived at the office on her birthday, I was ready to spring my surprise. We took the noon ferry from Newhaven to Dieppe and meandered through the French countryside for a fortnight. Sometimes we slept in small inns and sometimes under the star-filled heavens. There were no lists, no schedules and no itinerary; the objective was to get lost. We headed south in a general manner but would always take whatever road seemed more minor or secondary than the other. We had no goal other than to enjoy wherever we happened to find ourselves, wherever that might be. My father did eventually disown me, but some years later and for other reasons. Had he been aware of the unplanned manner in which we conducted our tour of France, I'm sure he would have done it much sooner.

Eventually we found ourselves in a remote valley in Périgord, not far from the Dordogne River, beside a deserted old mill set in a long meadow filled with buttercups, poppies and butterflies. Périgord reminded me of the lost England of my childhood. Small villages, unchanged for centuries, lay nestled between gently rounded hills covered in ancient forests of oaks and chestnut. It reminded me of the Nutwood of Rupert Bear as much as of the Granchester of Rupert Brooke.

We removed our clothes and lay in the long grass enjoying the spring sunshine. Lunch was our usual: a fresh baguette split down the middle and spread with a whole Camembert, fresh chopped garlic, sliced tomato and country cured ham. The whole thing was washed down with a litre of red, *vin ordinaire* from the bottle. Not far away, we could hear a stream gurgling over rocks; there was the lazy hum of bumblebees and in the background the interminable chorus of cicadas. We drifted happily into sleep.

We were rudely awoken by a cross little man wearing a crumpled beret and carrying a stick. '*Eh, alors, que faites-vous ici?*'

He was asking us what we thought we were doing. He was no taller than Jude and his face was brown from the sun and wrinkled like a walnut. Hastily, we covered ourselves and explained that we were having lunch and admiring the beauty of the valley and the peacefulness of the old mill.

'Oh, so you like it, do you?'

'We love it. It's such a shame that nobody lives here any more.'

'Do you want to buy it?' he asked.

The concept of purchasing a property in France, or even in England, was far too wild and exotic even to contemplate.

'I don't know. How much is it?'

He paused for a moment thoughtfully and then said, 'Two million.'

I knew enough about the French to understand that he was talking old francs. Two million old francs, or twenty thousand new francs, was the equivalent of about fifteen hundred pounds in today's money. I had just completed my first Irish hash deal and had the cash to spare.

'OK,' I said.

He pointed scornfully at the remains of the bread and cheese. '*Ça n'est pas un déjeuner, ça! Suivez-moi.*'

We dressed as quickly and modestly as we could and followed the strange little man down to the stream, crossing over to the other side. After climbing through a grove of walnut trees for about five minutes, we arrived at his farmhouse, where he introduced us to his wife and ordered her to make lunch.

Monsieur Ferdinand Carrière and his wife Paulia were ageless. They look no different today from when we first met them 37 years ago. He must be in his 90s now but he still has the energy and the curiosity of a teenage boy.

Lunch consisted of a rich country soup made from vegetables and cured ham. This was followed by a pâté de maison followed by foie gras with truffles and a long discussion in which we assured them that no, we'd never had foie gras or truffles before and had no idea what they were. All we knew was that we wanted more. It was sublime. Though appalled by our ignorance of food, they were delighted with our enthusiasm.

I can't remember everything we ate at that first Périgordian meal; there was a lot to remember. There was a cèpe omelette, there was steak, lots of fresh vegetables from the garden and a delicious salad. Each of the many courses had its own wine and we finished the meal with plums soaked in eau de vie, followed by Armagnac with coffee.

'That is a proper lunch,' Monsieur Carrière finally pronounced, just in case we hadn't noticed. During the long, lazy meal, we learned a little about our new neighbours: that their family had lived there for as long as written records had existed and that they had three grown children who had since left home. Monsieur and Madame Carrière, on the other hand, learned everything there was to know about Jude and me – with the exception of our DNA code, which was not available in 1971.

After finally rising from the table, Monsieur Carrière, apparently none the worse for wear, set off to milk the cows, plough the fields and complete the rest of his farm work, while Jude and I staggered down the hill to our car and a deep sleep. The plan was to meet at the lawyer's office in the nearby town of Beaumont the following day to complete the purchase of the old mill.

In addition to Monsieur Carrière and the *notaire*, the next day's meeting also included Monsieur Georges Rouchon, who actually owned the property, and Monsieur Besse, a neighbour. There was a lot of animated discussion and waving of arms, interrupted by regular consultations of the map. They were no longer speaking French, having switched to the local patois, *langue d'oc*, meaning 'language of yes', '*oc*' being the dialect's word for 'yes'. This old Provençal language, which had been suppressed by the Inquisition in the thirteenth century during the Albigensian Crusade and effectively outlawed in the sixteenth century by the Edict of Villers-Cotterêts, was still the everyday language of the people of Périgord. This was the language used by the local people in the marketplace and in their homes when there were no outsiders around. This was the language they used during the German occupation and the language they used to discuss prices when selling wine and truffles to wealthy Parisians or property to a couple of English hippies.

After a few hours, everybody seemed happy. Monsieur Rouchon and I signed all three copies of a twenty-three-page document containing many stamps and official markings. We all went to Marboutie's, the local café in the main square, and drank toasts to each other in Ricard. After the others left, Jude and I remained in the café for lunch while I mused on the strange sensation of being the owner of a French mill. I had never owned property anywhere before and now I owned a house and land – with a stream – in the south of France.

Despite all his meticulous research and planning, I reflected, my father could never have found and purchased such a treasure. His research would have taken him somewhere already commercialised, somewhere more ordinary and more expensive. By allowing fate to guide me and refusing to make any plans, I had chanced upon this small rural gem at a ridiculously low price and was now going to bring life to this forgotten corner of the world. There had been no economic activity or outside influence on this corner of France since the Hundred Years War in the fourteenth and fifteenth centuries. Had I not stumbled across it the previous day, I mused, it might have continued sleeping undisturbed, like the beautiful princess in the forest, for a few centuries more.

Of course, I was totally wrong. As I was to discover later, it was not me, the international sophisticate, who brought life to this sleepy little place; it was the land itself, teeming with activity, that gave life to me. The mill had always been there and so had the village, Molières, and all the people who lived there. I was, by comparison, transient and unimportant.

* * *

I made a similar mistake a few years later, again with the arrogance and ignorance of an outsider, when I made plans concerning a part of the world I knew nothing about. Graham and I shared the city boy's attitude that if a place was not an urban centre like London, New York or Paris, then it could not be important and one could make complex plans without ever considering the local realities. A prior experience involving a yacht race from Guam to Hawaii should have made me wiser about this but obviously I had learned nothing.

This time, the unimportant piece of land was a rock in the Mediterranean, just a few miles from the entrance to Heraklion harbour, off the island of Crete. We found the rock by studying a detailed map of Crete and its surrounding waters. Not much more than an acre in size, it was too small to have a name but ideal for our purposes.

One of Graham's contacts had commissioned a large luxury yacht that was secretly capable of travelling at twice its officially registered speed. The plan was to schedule a journey from Cyprus to Crete, which would normally take a couple of days, but to make a high-speed and unrecorded detour to the coast of Lebanon to pick up a load of hash before arriving in Crete at the officially scheduled time of arrival the following morning. Just before entering Heraklion harbour and reporting to the customs inspectors, the crew of the yacht would hide all the hash on the rock for the night, returning to collect it the next day after having cleared customs. Eventually, the hash would be sailed to the Greek mainland and delivered to Dutch Nik and his merry men for onward delivery with no further inspections. Nik planned to deliver the hash to our contact at Transatlantic Sounds, who handled logistics and sound equipment for major rock groups on world tours. Emerson, Lake and Palmer were on their Someone Get Me a Ladder world tour at the time and, unknown to the band, the hash would be loaded into their speakers and sound equipment when they performed in Athens. Using an ATA carnet, which allows containers to pass through customs without inspection, the band's equipment would then be shipped to California for the next leg of the tour and Ernie would arrange to have the hash discreetly unloaded in Los Angeles.

My father would have approved of this scheme. It involved maps, detailed plans, stopwatches, precise plotting and carefully calculated times of arrival.

The first stage of the project went precisely according to plan and the initial report was good. The yacht arrived in Heraklion harbour exactly on time and was given a clean bill of health. Indeed, the head of customs was so enamoured with the boat that he was given a short ride around the harbour and out past the rock.

An international phone call to London the following day brought us the bad news.

'It's not there.'

'What do you mean?'

'It's not there.'

'It's not there?'

'Right. We went to get it and it wasn't there.'

'It wasn't there?'

'No.'

'Where it was before?'

'Right. It's not there any more. It's all gone.'

'It's all gone?'

'Gone. It's not there.'

Back in the Warwick Castle, we debated what to do. How could 350 kg of hash vanish from a deserted rock in the middle of nowhere? There were no houses or fields or anything on the rock. We had studied the place on all the most up-to-date nautical maps. 'It's just a fucking rock, for God's sake,' we said. 'James must have got drunk and screwed up.'

James was an old college friend who had been sent to Crete to liaise with the boat's captain and report back to us. We were confident of his honesty but we all agreed, as we ordered another round of Guinness, that he did tend to drink rather a lot.

I flew to Heraklion the next day and met James in a bar near the harbour. He expanded on the story. The boat had arrived at the rock late in the afternoon and the hash had been unloaded and hidden under a pile of stones and shale. The yacht had then continued into Heraklion and cleared customs that same day. The following morning, they had returned to the rock and found the hash gone.

'Of course, they remember where they put it?' I asked.

'Yes. The stones and shale were all there. They'd been thrown around a bit but they were still there. Somebody's taken it!'

We spent the next few days making discreet enquiries. James and his girlfriend had been on the island a couple of weeks and knew most of the dope smokers. None of them were aware of any fresh Lebanese hashish. I rented a car and drove to the other side of the island, where a large colony of international hippies congregated on a beautiful nudist beach. I spent the next few days among the beautiful nude people and smoked a lot of dope with a lot of girls but never picked up a hint of any new source of Lebanese hash.

Back in Heraklion, James and I sat in the bar and scratched our heads.

'Take me to the rock,' I finally said.

The captain of the yacht had been spooked by the whole mystery and did not want to meet with me. He stayed in port and mixed only with local officials and respectable people. However, he did loan me one of his crewmen, who accompanied us out to the rock in a rented boat. He showed me exactly where they had landed and where they had hidden the hash.

'Leave me here,' I told James. 'Come and get me in the morning. I want to spend the night on the rock.'

Of course, it was obvious in hindsight. If we could sit in faraway London and select this obscure rock as a perfect smuggling spot, then local people were even more likely to see its potential.

The first visitor arrived soon after dark. I had not brought any warm clothes and was wearing only shorts, flip-flops, a T-shirt and an extra shirt that James had given me when he left. I was starting to feel the cold night air when I was alerted by the creak of oars to the fact that I wasn't alone. Somebody had rowed silently from the mainland and was moored near our own landing spot. I peeped through the rocks and saw the silhouette of somebody in a rowing boat sitting absolutely still and silent. After maybe 30 minutes there was a flash of light from out at sea and an answering flash from my mysterious companion. The soft sound of an outboard motor signalled the arrival of a rubber dinghy.

I guessed, from what I could see of the size and shape of the goods they unloaded into the rowing boat, that they were cigarette smugglers. It was a traditional occupation in that part of the world and as good an explanation as I could think of. However, they had used the rock only as a convenient meeting place; nobody had actually wandered around the island in such a way as to accidentally stumble over our cache.

My next visitor did step ashore, however. Two men arrived in a large wooden boat with an outboard motor. These were not smugglers and there was nothing stealthy about them. The motor was noisy and they conducted a conversation as though they were on separate fishing boats in a raging storm. They also had about a dozen goats on the boat. As soon as the boat hit land, the goats jumped to the shore and raced to the top of the rock, bleating loudly. The two men followed, lugging large plastic containers.

The place was really a small island. It was about an acre in size and there were high bits and low bits. There were lots of cliffs, a small inlet and even some low shoreline. There was not much vegetation – some stubborn and prickly bushes, which even the goats ignored – and there was a lot of bird shit.

There was also a small cave-like hollow in which I crouched until my visitors had departed. While the men remained, doing whatever they were doing, at the highest point of the island, the goats strutted all over the place, bleating and chewing their beards. I was sure that, had the animals seen me, they would have alerted the men to my presence through some sort of mysterious Greek goatherd telepathy. Possibly it was the goats that had found the hash. They might simply have eaten it all. No wonder they were so keen to leap ashore!

Finally, my visitors departed and I climbed up to see what they had been doing. At the summit of the rock, on the side facing away from the mainland, a spring of clear water bubbled out of the rock face down into a pool and from there splashed to the sea. Who knows upon what barren field my goat farmers spent their days, or how primitive and sad their lives might be compared with that of a BMW-driving London hipster – but they knew where to find water. The history of the human race, let alone the history of the Mediterranean and the Middle East, concerns the discovery and control of fresh water. Wars, dynasties and empires have revolved around that basic resource. My anonymous little rock, with its freshwater stream, would have been known and treasured by goatherds and sponge fishermen since the

Phoenicians. This damned rock was probably mentioned by Homer!

I realised then that if my rock had a source of fresh water, we had probably picked the Greek equivalent of Piccadilly Circus to conduct our surreptitious dope deal. By midnight, I had fully understood and digested the moral of the story. I was cold, shivering and humiliated. Our dope could have been lifted by any combination of smugglers, fishermen and goatherds who regarded our 'secret' hiding place as their front room.

Although the goats had wandered off, I remained huddled in my little cave. I was protected from the wind and gradually warmed up slightly but I was still unnerved by the unexpected activity I had discovered in this barren spot. I thought of *The Tempest*:

> Be not afeard; the isle is full of noises,
> Sounds and sweet airs, that give delight and hurt not.
> Sometimes a thousand twangling instruments
> Will hum about mine ears, and sometime voices
> That, if I then had waked after long sleep,
> Will make me sleep again: and then, in dreaming,
> The clouds methought would open and show riches
> Ready to drop upon me that, when I waked,
> I cried to dream again.

But none of my philosophical reflections prepared me for what happened next.

I had been aware of strange noises, 'sounds and sweet airs', which I had interpreted as the soft crash of the waves and the sighing of the wind. I sat on my heels, swaying rhythmically backwards and forwards, with my arms clutched around my knees, trying to keep warm and mentally practising my explanation to Howard and Graham of how they should interpret the abject failure of this whole project within the context of European history. 'Odysseus lost his whole crew. Turned into swine. At least you started off with swine. Ha ha!' I always like to add a little humour, especially when I deliver bad news. It was one of my ways of attracting and also distracting my father's attention.

While I silently struggled to place the loss of a whole shipment of dope within a European tradition of mythic dimensions, I started to realise that I was no longer alone on the island. Peeping over the ledge above my little cave, I noticed that some of the black rocks were moving and I heard the faint static sound of walkie-talkies. Then I became aware of another sound: the dull thump-thump of a helicopter growing steadily louder until it hovered directly overhead.

By now, I was terrified and cowered back inside my cave. I had no idea what I had stumbled into but I didn't want any part of it. I wanted to go home. Although I wasn't exactly an innocent bystander, I was, like Warren Zevon in his song 'Lawyers, Guns and Money', caught between a rock and a hard place, and I too desperately wanted somebody to get me out of this! The noise and the down-draught from the blades were overwhelming. Cautiously, I peeped out from my refuge and saw that the frogmen, which was what they appeared to be, were scaling a rope ladder that had been lowered to the rock. Eventually, they were all aboard, the ladder was pulled up and the helicopter tilted out to sea and vanished as quickly as it had arrived. Like Prometheus, I was alone on my rock again with nothing but my fevered thoughts to keep me company.

When James collected me in the morning, I told him to take me straight to the airport. I also suggested he collect his girlfriend and that they both leave the island as soon as possible. 'Something is happening and I don't know what it is but this is not a good place to be. Let's get the hell out!'

Heraklion airport was crawling with armed troops and Athens airport was even worse. There had been an anti-government revolt by Athens University law students in February, a couple of months earlier, and we knew that the governing junta was nervous. However, the level of security now was intense. At passport control, I was subjected to close questioning about my visit before I was allowed to board the plane.

It was only when I returned to London that I discovered there had been an abortive coup against the 'Regime of the Colonels' by the Greek navy the previous day. The coup was brutally suppressed by the junta and a naval destroyer, the *Velos*, defected to Italy. What role my little rock had played in the drama and which side those frogmen were on, I still have no idea. I retain a sense of guilt: what if the coup only failed because the naval officers were all stoned on Lebanese hash? We never did find out what happened to our hidden stash. It was either the Greek navy or the goats.

Neither Howard nor Graham believed my story and to this day they insist that I spent all my time in a bar with James drinking ouzo.

* * *

Just as I turned out to be a walk-on figure in the story of the Greek rock, despite all our careful planning, so too was I only a minor figure in the drama of the French mill. I did not learn the full story till many years later, after I had left London and moved to Molières, where I married Jude and we raised our children.

Three families owned land in the long valley that stretches north of Molières towards the Dordogne River: the Carrières, the Besses and the Rouchons. Old man Rouchon actually owned the mill and the other two families owned a patchwork of land in the vicinity. The three families had owned their little parcels for centuries and they knew every blade of grass and every inch of their respective territories. The problem was that the division of the patchwork of small landholdings among them was haphazard; it would have made much more sense for them to swap the land around and divide it so that they had three larger contiguous properties. However, this was impossible to do without somebody losing an inch here or a millimetre there, and so the pattern of fields got more complex with each generation and each dynastic marriage.

Rouchon's son Georges, on the other hand, could not wait to sell all the family holdings. His dream was to relocate to Beaumont and enjoy the more sophisticated pleasures that a larger market town could offer. But the father refused to sell any land and kept Georges on a very tight rein. Ever since his wife had died, many years previously, old man Rouchon had become ever more morose and despondent, and from time to time he would try to kill himself. His suicide attempts were well known around the region; he was always saved at the last moment by an alert neighbour. For example, Madame Besse just happened to be passing the well a few seconds after Rouchon had thrown himself down it and was able to call her sons to haul him out. Another time, Ferdinand Carrière heard sobbing sounds as he passed the Rouchons' front door and was able to grab the shotgun, though Rouchon's big toe was still jammed in the trigger guard.

Finally, however, old man Rouchon succeeded. Early one morning, he climbed onto a bicycle in his barn and put his head into the noose of a rope hanging from a large oak beam. When he heard somebody approaching, he kicked away the bicycle and slowly choked to death. Whoever was coming must have turned away at the last moment. The body was not found until 10.00 a.m. and Ferdinand Carrière did not learn the news until noon.

Two hours later, walking past the old Rouchon mill, Monsieur Carrière found a young English couple enjoying a siesta in the long grass and buttercups of the meadow. Suddenly, he saw a way to resolve the situation to the benefit of all. He could not believe it when the Englishman agreed to buy the mill for two million. That was a ridiculous price to pay for an old abandoned piece of property. It was just a figure he had made up on the spur of the moment. Two million old francs would keep Georges Rouchon happy for a long, long time. More importantly, by involving an ignorant Englishman in the complex land deal, they would be able to divide up the various small properties into three decent-sized lots, with the Rouchon property being used to make up any shortfall.

I was happy. I ended up with a property that stretched from the road as far as the stream and which was neatly rectangular in shape. Monsieur Besse and Monsieur Carrière were happy because they were able to rearrange their properties without losing face or giving away so much as a blade of grass. Georges Rouchon was very happy because he had two million francs with which to start his new life in Beaumont.

Whatever I might have originally planned when I collected Jude for her surprise trip to the French countryside, I could never have calculated that Monsieur Rouchon would climb onto his bicycle for his final ride on the day we arrived. Nor, when we planned our trip to Crete, could we have predicted an attempted *coup d'état* by the Greek navy. That is why, unlike my father, I seldom make detailed plans and I never, ever begin '8 a.m. – depart house'.

9

A DOG'S LIFE

Many online bank accounts and credit card companies ask for the name of your first pet as a security question. I suppose the theory is that that's something you never forget. Mine was a dog called Spud, a golden cocker spaniel with long ears and a nervous disposition. He was a small puppy when I got him and I was about seven years old. He was my best friend, even better than Natasha, because he was a boy. My brother George was a boy, of course, but he didn't count because he was still a baby in his pram. Spud and I did everything together. When I came home from school, he would be waiting for me and I could hear his tail thumping as I approached the back door. If my mother saw me coming, she would open the door and Spud would come bounding along the driveway, jumping up and licking my face. At weekends and during the school holidays, the two of us would set off in the mornings and not return till the evening, exhausted and dirty but always happy and filled with stories of the adventures we had shared. Sometimes we let Natasha come with us, even though she was a girl and couldn't run as fast, but usually it was just me and Spud.

Stevenage was just a modest Hertfordshire village in those days. They had started building the 'new town' but it was still separated from the 'old town' by fields and woods. These days, of course, it is a vast urban sprawl and most traces of the old town, including our house, have long been demolished. We weren't allowed to play with the children from the new town because they had all come from the slums in London and they were 'common' and didn't speak properly.

In any event, Spud and I didn't need anyone else; we were a team and had each other.

Although it was a small, sleepy town with only one main road, that road happened to be the busiest in the country. The Great North Road, or A1, followed the route of a Roman road and ran the full length of England, connecting London to Edinburgh. This was long before they built the M1 motorway with its six wide lanes connecting London to Birmingham. In some parts of the country, the A1 had been widened to four lanes, two in each direction, but where it ran past our house in Stevenage there were just two lanes and it was always busy. Among all the values drummed into us as children – don't tell lies, don't say bad words, always say 'please' and 'thank you', don't hit girls (especially not down there), don't talk with your mouth full – the most important rule was never, ever cross the road without an adult.

The problem was that we lived on the eastern side of the Great North Road, which was the side where the new town was being built. Each week, more woods were cut down and more fields levelled to make room for the new estates that were spreading widely in all directions. The ancient woods of oak and chestnut trees, the pristine meadows, the fields of cows and the streams filled with trout and pike were on the west, the forbidden side of the road.

During the long summer holidays, when school became a distant memory and the endlessly sunny days stretched far into the future, Spud and I would be out of bed at dawn, ready for adventure. We would not return home till late evening when the sun was setting, or perhaps earlier if the hunger for Heinz baked beans with Welsh rarebit proved too strong.

About ten minutes south of our house, on the same side of the road, were the Six Hills, where Spud and I usually started our adventures. If I was to be gone for the day, my mother would make me a sandwich and pack it with an apple and some dog biscuits for Spud inside a large handkerchief, which she would tie to my special stick. With my lunch over my shoulder and my best friend by my side, I would walk along the 'safe side' of the Great North Road till we reached the Six Hills. These were round barrows, old Anglo-Saxon burial mounds, and probably no more than twenty feet high, but to an imaginative seven year old and a small puppy they were like the Alps.

We would climb our special hill, the tallest one, where there was a large hollow hidden by some bushes, and sit in our Secret Cave to plan the day's adventure. The first step was usually to eat whatever my mother had packed in the handkerchief. Spud would eat his biscuits and I would eat my sandwich. Sometimes I would save the apple for later but usually our lunch would all be eaten before 9.30 or 10 a.m. My rationale for eating lunch so quickly was that I would then have the handkerchief available for carrying home all the gold. It was always my plan to dig deeper into the hill from our cave. I was certain that underground there were large caverns in which long-dead Saxon kings in suits of chain mail lay stretched upon their shields, holding their long, glittering swords and surrounded by gold. In the bright sunlight, walking along the busy A1, it was easy to imagine entering a cavern and heaping gold coins into the handkerchief while Spud watched my back. The kings, after all, were long dead and their flesh had rotted.

In the darkness of our cave, however, hidden in the shadow of the bushes, smelling the dampness of the earth as I dug it away with a spoon, the plan seemed less appealing. It would be dark inside the cavern and I had not brought any candles. Besides, I had no matches; my mother would not let any of us touch them. Even if I had had a candle, I could picture the cold glittering eyes of the dead kings following my every move as I crept through those haunted halls to steal their gold.

'Come on, Spud,' I'd say. 'Let's go to the castle instead. We'll get the gold another day.' After checking there were no crumbs left, Spud would follow me out from behind the bushes into the bright morning sunshine, where no dead things with thin blue lips and cold cruel eyes could pursue us. He'd bark excitedly as I rolled through the long grass and down the hill to the entrance of our Secret Tunnel. This was our biggest secret. The few times I had brought Natasha, she had been blindfolded en route to the entrance and had solemnly sworn never to reveal our secret on pain of an excruciatingly savage and blood-soaked death. At the foot of one of the Six Hills, there was a large culvert or drainage pipe that led under the Great North Road to the other, prohibited side. It was large enough for a seven-year-old boy to walk through just slightly stooped over and for a puppy to scamper through with his long ears flying behind him, back and forth from one end of the tunnel to the other, excited to be off on another adventure in the forbidden world.

There were very few houses on the other side of the Great North Road, just fields and woods. This is where I would come in the autumn to collect conkers from the ancient chestnut trees, my secret source for some of the best conkers ever seen at school. Spud loved the woods and while I hunted through the fallen leaves for the deep mahogany glow of a freshly fallen conker, he would be snuffling through the same leaves for the scent of rabbit. But the real goal in the forbidden land on the far side of the road was the haunted castle. After crossing several fields and meadows and following a track that only we knew through the dark wood, Spud and I would eventually emerge from the trees and gaze across a lake at Knebworth House.

It had been a Saxon castle long before the Norman Conquest and is even listed in the Domesday Book. In 1490, it became the home of the Lytton family, who continue to own it more than 500 years later. Each generation added to the design of the building, none more so than Sir Edward Bulmer-Lytton, the novelist, most famous for being the first to use the opening line 'It was a dark and stormy night'. As a result, the Gothic extravagances of Knebworth House were everything that a romantically inclined young boy needed to inflame his imagination. There were tall towers with crenellated battlements, turrets, spires and gargoyles. It's been many years since I last saw the place, but in my memory there is even a drawbridge and a moat surrounding a medieval keep and a soaring donjon tower.

For more than 20 years, since the mid-'70s, Knebworth House has enjoyed a new lease of life as a venue for rock concerts. The Rolling Stones, Queen, Led Zeppelin and Pink Floyd have drawn thousands of fans to Knebworth but back in the '50s the house was all but abandoned. The gardens were untended and overgrown, many of the windows were broken, tiles were missing from the mansard roofs and all the walls were dense and overrun with ivy. The Lytton family lived in London and nobody inhabited the castle except an elderly caretaker, who would shout and chase us whenever we were spotted.

It was a haunted, magical place, and Spud and I found many unlocked doors and broken windows into which we could climb, allowing us to wander unseen through the empty halls and dark passageways. More than 50 years later, I often walk through those same cobwebbed rooms and climb those mysterious stairways in my dreams. Sometimes I was scared; strange noises in the dark would startle me. But as long as Spud was by my side, I knew I was safe.

Halfway between Knebworth House and the Great North Road was a sinister area of quarries and gravel pits, which we normally avoided. The pits were flooded with dark, muddy water, creating a series of lakes, and I had no idea how deep they were. There was little vegetation but for lonely clumps of sedge and thistle; there were no fish and consequently no birds to be seen or heard. It was a desolate place and if anything bad happened to Spud and me there, it could be weeks or even months before we were found. Nonetheless, we did go there sometimes because it was a good place to play with my model sailing boat. That was where I met the nice fisherman.

Spud saw him first and started growling. He was a large, fat man with thick glasses and he just appeared suddenly from nowhere. Possibly he had been watching us. He asked what we were doing and I explained that this was our secret lake where we tested my sailing boats.

'So your mummy and daddy don't know where you are?' I shook my head, worried I would be in trouble for playing at the lake. The man smiled and assured me that it would remain our secret. 'Do you like fishing?' he asked me.

I nodded excitedly. 'Be quiet, Spud,' I said. He continued to growl.

'I know a wonderful fishing spot near here,' the man said. 'It's a secret spot and nobody else knows about it. The water is crystal clear, not like here, and the trout are so big you can just lay your hand in the water and tickle them.' I looked surprised. 'That's how you catch them,' he explained. 'You tickle them on the tummy and then you just pull them onto the bank. Would you like me to teach you?' I nodded enthusiastically. 'I bet your mummy would be pleased if you brought home a couple of large trout for her to cook for dinner.'

I glowed inwardly at the idea. I hated eating fish but knew my mother would be very pleased and my father extremely impressed if I returned home with a couple of fresh trout. Natasha would be speechless with envy. We arranged to meet at the same place the next day and I promised to keep it a secret and not tell anyone. That way it would be more of a surprise when I brought the trout home with me. 'And don't bring your dog with you,' the man added. 'Dogs frighten the fish, especially when they growl all the time like yours does.' I promised to leave Spud at home.

Mothers, of course, have an instinct for that sort of thing. Maybe it was because I was leaving the house the next morning without Spud; maybe it was my shifty demeanour. Whatever it was, she knew that I was 'up to something'. It did not take her long to get the full story out of me: 'But, Mummy, he's such a nice man and he's going to teach me how to tickle trout.' Later that morning, a policeman came to the house. He was very polite and asked me all sorts of questions. He seemed to know the lakes where I'd met my friend.

'But there's no trout streams near there,' he told me. 'Nothing till you reach Knebworth House.'

'Nobody knows about it,' I explained patiently. 'It's a secret spot.'

I don't know what happened to the man. My parents didn't say much about it. I was worried that I'd got him into trouble. Maybe he was a poacher, I thought. I wanted to be a poacher, if I couldn't be a smuggler. One of my favourite books was *John Macnab* by John Buchan, which describes a big poaching adventure in Scotland. I was cross with Spud for growling at my friend and getting us all into trouble. That was Spud's problem; my mother said he was highly strung. He was usually friendly but he did growl at people sometimes and he used to bite them, too. In fact, that was how I finally lost him.

I can't remember what I did to provoke him but one day Spud bit me on the wrist so badly that he drew a lot of blood and I had to go to the hospital for shots. More than half a century later, I still have faint scars to remind me of my first friend. When I returned from the hospital the next day, Spud was gone.

'One of the men at Daddy's office has a friend who's a farmer,' my mother explained. 'The farmer was looking for another dog to help guard his sheep and when he heard about Spud he asked if he could buy him. Look, he gave us £20 and we're going to open you your own bank account and put the money in. It's a lovely farm. We visited it yesterday and Spud loved it. There are big, wide sunny fields of springy grass, and he ran round and round with the other dog, chasing each other. They were having so much fun. His tongue was hanging out and his ears were flying behind him. We'll take you to visit one day, when your arm is better. And look, I've made you your favourite, apple crumble, for tea. Would you like a little slice now, before Natasha sees you?'

Of course, we never did go to visit Spud's farm. I never asked to go and my mother never mentioned it again. I don't know if I ever really believed her; I just accepted what she told me, as I couldn't face the implications of the alternative. Even today, a bit of me believes in Spud's farm. And now my mother has gone to play with him as well.

I took Natasha to visit Knebworth House with me but it wasn't the same. When we crossed the field of cows, she got scared and we had to climb a tree until they lumbered off again. Spud would have chased them away. At Knebworth, Natasha kept talking about the princess of the castle and pretty dresses and fairy coaches and other silly things. Spud never talked. He just wagged his tail, and growled when there was danger.

I've since learned that parents often tell their children about the 'lovely farm' where their pets have been sent. Jude and I certainly continued the tradition with our own kids, and some day we will visit the farm where gerbils, hamsters and tortoises chase each other happily around a lake teeming with hundreds of goldfish. I suspect that most children don't believe these stories any more than I did but pretend to do so, even to themselves, because sometimes the truth is just too hard to bear.

Sometimes, though, the story turns out to be true. When we lived in Molières, our neighbours, Monsieur and Madame Carrière, were given a baby lamb whose mother had died in childbirth. The Carrières were no strangers to the blood-red claw of nature; they raised and slaughtered chickens, ducks and geese, and Ferdinand was in great demand for killing pigs. But they did not raise sheep. The baby lamb spent the winter in their warm kitchen and Madame Carrière fed it milk from the bottle, like a baby, three times a day. Christened Titou, the baby lamb had the run of the house with the dogs and when spring arrived Titou joined the others in chasing around the farm and barking at the postman when he came to deliver mail. Titou obviously thought of himself as a dog. Whatever the dogs did, Titou copied; he lifted his leg to pee and even pretended to help Ferdinand as he hunted for truffles in the woods.

Within a couple of years, Titou was no longer a cute little lamb but a large, fully grown sheep, ready for slaughter. The Carrières, however, could see him only as their baby lamb and, despite the neighbours' protestations, continued to treat him as a household pet. Titou, like the dog he believed himself to be, chased cars and roamed the countryside. We lived on the other side of the valley, about a kilometre from the Carrières, and Titou would often come visiting, hoping for some free food. Jude always had something cooking in the kitchen and Titou would follow the smell. We once had some smart visitors from London, already unused to country living, when our elegant late-night dinner party was interrupted by a loud knocking at the door. Jude opened it and this very large sheep walked in, went straight to the table and helped himself to some bread. I held out my glass and he slurped down some wine. Our guests were impressed. 'He only likes red,' I explained.

Unfortunately, white wine was not all he disliked. With the exceptions of Madame Carrière and Jude, Titou did not like women. He would chase them and knock them off their bikes, he would butt their buttocks with his very hard head and growing horns. The women of the neighbouring farms were terrified of him and when Titou appeared in the village, Monsieur Ferandon, the mayor, would have to phone Ferdinand to come and collect him. The social pressure to convert Titou to mutton was increasing daily and people in other villages like Cadouin and St Avit Seigneur were openly scornful of the folks of Molières being terrorised by a sheep.

And then the miracle happened. A sheep farmer from near Cadouin heard the story being told at the Thursday market and offered Carrière 15 baskets of walnuts in return for Titou. A deal was struck, the walnuts were delivered, and Carrière and I helped the farmer load Titou into the back of his truck. Ferdinand and I visited the farm and checked regularly but everything was above board. Titou had been put out to stud. The lone male in a flock of some 40 ewes, he had job security for the rest of his happy and energetic life. He finally decided that life as a sheep was better than life as a dog.

One of the dogs that ran with Titou was our own, called Dog. It was our way of teaching our neighbours a little bit of English and they would all delight in saying 'Allo, Dog' whenever he appeared. He was a black mutt, mostly collie, with a white chest. We got him from the animal pound in Bergerac. It was love at first sight; he bounded into our life as he bounded into our car when we collected him, immediately after which he promptly threw up. Jude was six months pregnant and we had decided that looking after a dog would improve our parenting skills. Certainly, during the three months he was an 'only child', Dog became the beloved centre of our lives.

Peggy was born at three in the morning and, after leaving mother and child sleeping at the clinic in Bergerac, I drove back to Le Moulin and sat up all night in front of the fire with Dog and a bottle of Armagnac. Together, we shared that metamorphosis by which a boy becomes a father. For all men, there is a moment of truth when the implications and responsibilities of being a father are suddenly revealed. I think women spend most of their lives acquiring and assimilating that knowledge about parenthood, so they are already prepared when the moment comes. Men, however, never give it a moment's thought until the midwife places the soft, fresh little gurgling thing in their arms. Then suddenly, overnight, they must put childish things aside and learn the meaning of fatherhood. So Dog and I stared manfully into the flames and made solemn vows to become better and more responsible; we promised to prove worthy of Peggy.

Dog certainly lived up to his vows. He never expressed any jealousy about this new, smelly, noisy intruder, who deprived him so much of our loving attention. He quickly became Peggy's big brother and guardian, watching over her and alerting us whenever she needed anything. As she grew older and stronger, he patiently allowed her to pull his tail and his ears, never growling even when she hurt him. As she learned to walk, she would totter around the fields looking for blackberries in the hedges, Dog always at her side. We never needed to worry about Peggy because we knew that Dog was looking after her.

But the rest of the time, Dog was a dog. Unlike the Great North Road, the road that ran past our home down the hill from Molières probably bore no more than ten cars or trucks per day. Dog chased them all. He would leap into the road, seconds after a vehicle passed, barking wildly and chasing it, snarling at the tyres, until it turned the bend in the road, no longer a threat to the family. We also had cyclists on our road, little old men in berets riding their bikes or plump farmers' wives, their large bottoms overflowing the seats of their mopeds. Dog had a special hiding place on a tree stump beside the road; hidden by branches, he was at about the same height as the bike rider's face. Motionless until the unwary cyclist was close beside him, he would suddenly plunge his head through the branches and release a loud bark mere inches from their ear. Often, they would fall off in surprise and we would have to rush out with profuse apologies and a small glass of red wine to ease any hurt feelings. Eventually, most people learned to ride past our house on the other side of the road.

But Dog's greatest love was lady dogs. We noticed that there were periods when he would vanish for days on end. When he returned, he would be both famished and exhausted, his body lean and a haunted restlessness about his eyes, a glitter that reminded me of Coleridge's Ancient Mariner. We would feed him up and nurse him and then he would be off again for a few more days. Often when he came back he was limping or bleeding from some new scar. Obviously, he had been fighting, but where and why? And then, one day, he returned with a strand of barbed wire tied around his tail and some tin cans clattering behind him. We asked the Carrières if they could think of any explanation.

'*Ah*,' said Ferdinand, his eyes twinkling, '*il galope.*'

'*Ah, oui*,' Madame agreed. 'He's chasing the girls.'

Apparently, Dog had earned quite a reputation throughout the region, for five or more miles in all directions. Not a female dog was safe from him and no male dog could compete. He would jump over fences, dig under fences or just sit outside the farm door and howl if a female was in heat. One farmer confined his bitch inside his new barn, built with cement floors and freshly cut timber walls. In the space of two nights, Dog clawed his way through the solid oak doors in order to satisfy his romantic desires. 'He's a French dog,' everyone agreed, 'certainly not English.'

Tying barbed wire around a dog's tail was a way of warning its owners: 'Next time he comes around, we'll shoot him.' We did our best to curb his enthusiasm and tried keeping him indoors when we recognised the fires of true love in his eyes, but the call of nature was too strong and Dog continued to 'gallop' until the end. Dog was part of our lives for more than three years. He was still with us when Bridie was born and she too benefited from his warm protection. But his daily duel with fast-moving vehicles proved his undoing. Despite his most ferocious barking, a large truck failed to stop and Dog was killed instantly, his big heart crushed. I told Peggy about the farm where Dog and Spud were able to chase sheep all day long but I don't know if she believed me.

Not all my encounters with dogs have been so loving. In fact, I had an experience on a Pacific island that instilled an abiding fear of large dogs that has never left me. In the early 1970s, Michael Durani's partner in Karachi, Shemsi, managed to purchase an exclusive Japanese auto dealership on the island of Guam in the Mariana Islands. Richard Nixon was still President, the Vietnam War was in full swing and there was a large military base on the island, Andersen Air Force Base, which provided a good market for Shemsi's cheap Japanese cars. Moving automobiles and parts between Asia and Guam provided Shemsi with many opportunities to move large amounts of hash onto the island as well. Guam is an unincorporated territory of the United States in the far Pacific: 'Where America's Day Begins'. Although physically far removed from the mainland, indeed twice as far away as Hawaii, it is still part of the US as far as passport and customs controls are concerned. Any flight or shipment coming from Guam did not have to clear US customs again, which was why Shemsi was anxious to develop a presence on the island.

In addition to priding himself on his surfing abilities, Ernie's sidekick Val Johnson also fancied himself as an accomplished yachtsman. He decided we should organise a transoceanic yacht race from Agana in Guam to Honolulu in Hawaii. We would enter five yachts of our own to compete in the race, load them with Shemsi's hashish before leaving Guam and unload when we reached Hawaii. After a long life of stupid ideas and ill-conceived plans, I would put this one near the top of the list. Nevertheless, I was as stoned as everyone else when Val proposed it and I agreed to fly to Guam and locate a suitable beach for loading the hash onto the yachts.

Except for hordes of Japanese honeymooners moving around in large organised groups, there were few tourists on Guam in those days. There were probably lots of CIA spooks and Soviet spies, since Andersen was the base from which all the B-52 bombing raids were organised and where Kissinger and Nixon based their incursions into Cambodia and Laos. It was important, therefore, to be discreet and keep a low profile. At the airport, I rented a large, bright-red LT-1 Corvette. I didn't want one of Shemsi's cheap Japanese cars and, besides, the moment I saw my first 'Vette I fell in love. It was the only Corvette on the island and wherever I went people stared at me and asked questions. It attracted attention partly because of its colour and exotic styling but also because I was never able to get it beyond second gear and as a result had to keep revving the engine to stop it from stalling. All the roads in Guam are built from volcanic rock and there is some quality in the lava that makes them extremely slippery. At any speed above 15 mph, cars simply slip off the road. When the roads are wet, the safe speed drops to 10 mph. The clock on my Corvette went to 180 mph but I doubt that I ever managed to reach 18. The car was great for meeting girls, though, so I didn't bother to change it.

At least my cover story was fairly solid, even though I knew less about yachts than I knew about ladies' underwear.

'So what yachts will be racing?'

'Oh, sailing yachts.'

'Sure, but what class?'

'Oh, high-class yachts. Only the best.'

'Like the America's Cup?'

'Oh, more like the English Cup or the French Cup. As I say, this is going to be a top-class event.'

There is not much to see on Guam and after a couple of days, even at 15 mph, I had driven around the whole island. After making friends with a couple of female officers, I was even able to drive them around the military base in my Corvette and watch the B-52s lumbering ponderously towards take-off, though nobody would say where they were going: military secret. Most of the island was covered in dense jungle, so dense that a few months before my arrival the authorities had found a Japanese soldier from the Second World War. Refusing to surrender in 1945, he had retreated into the jungle and remained there for 25 years, not knowing the war was over. That's pretty dense. Except where it entered the occasional fishing village, the road that circled the island seldom touched the coast. Between the road and any potential hashish-loading beaches there was a good mile of Jap-infested jungle. Val Johnson's plan was beginning to reveal some of its flaws.

By studying the map and climbing a few trees to look over the thick canopy, I was finally able to identify a promising bay below me on the coast. I drove out early one morning and parked the bright-red Corvette as discreetly as was possible just off the road. Armed with a machete, which I'd bought at a hardware store, I descended the slope towards the sea. I doubt the distance was more than a mile but it took several hours of hard work before I arrived on the beach. I emerged from the treeline scratched and bloody from my exertions but delighted at what I found. It was an image of paradise. A large bay, perhaps two miles in diameter, was surrounded by jungle-clad slopes. The place was entirely hidden from the rest of the world. The water was clearly deep enough for several yachts to anchor safely and the whole bay was edged with pristine white sand. It was like a photograph from an exotic travel brochure. I took off my clothes and entered the sea. The water was warm and crystal clear. I swam out and could see brightly coloured fish darting in rainbow shoals beneath me. However, I also felt a strong current, possibly pulling me towards the entrance to the bay, so I struggled back to shore. I am not a strong swimmer and have always had a fear of drowning.

I'd brought lunch with me, including a bottle of now warm beer, and I settled down to enjoy it. This was the perfect spot to effect the transfer. Using one of his motorboats, Shemsi could ship the crates of hashish to the beach in the morning and then the yachts could load up in the afternoon. No prying eyes would see a thing. I felt pleased with myself and had a roll of photos on my camera to prove it. I could report back to Ernie: Mission Accomplished.

Glancing along the beach, I saw three figures approaching, perhaps a mile away. Hastily, I pulled on my shorts and finished my lunch. I realised gradually that two of the figures, ahead of the third, were dogs – large dogs – and they were running purposefully towards me along the sand. Feeling slightly foolish but increasingly nervous, I walked towards the sea. As the dogs got closer, I waded further away from the shore. They continued to canter in my direction and I could see now how large they were, how powerful their muscles, how sharp their teeth. I don't know what breed they were, possibly Wild Tibetan Wolfhounds, but they certainly put the fear of God into me.

The dogs both stopped at the water's edge at the sound of a whistle. The third figure was approaching and I saw he was a young boy, maybe ten years old. He had thick black hair hanging in a dark fringe and a solemn face. He whistled again and both dogs turned and ran to join him. Gratefully, I moved back towards the shore. 'Thank goodness you came,' I smiled. 'I was beginning to get nervous. Those are big dogs.'

As I stepped out of the water, the boy whistled again. The dogs leaped to their feet and rushed snarling towards me. I retreated quickly into the water. The dogs did not stop at the edge this time but continued to pursue me into the sea. I was out of my depth when the boy whistled again and the dogs returned to his side. I moved towards the shore and regained my footing. This time, I stayed in the water while I tried to establish contact. 'Are they your dogs?' I began stupidly. 'What are their names?'

The boy said nothing, his eyes expressionless beneath his fringe. He whistled once more and the dogs leaped into action. Again, I retreated beyond my depth and this time I felt the current tugging at me, pulling me towards the wide indifference of the Pacific Ocean. The dogs had shown that they were perfectly capable of swimming and snarling at the same time; it was only the boy's whistle that kept them from ripping open my throat.

It is true that children get bored easily but it is equally true that they can continue repeating the same routine for hours if it amuses them, far beyond the boredom threshold of any adult. I was not exactly bored but as the sun moved slowly across the sky and the afternoon wore on, my sense of discomfort grew alarmingly. Not only was I very frightened, I was increasingly weary. My whole body ached and my ability to fight the current when out of my depth was growing weaker. I had swallowed a lot of seawater and was feeling nauseated.

The boy was neatly dressed in a clean, long-sleeved white shirt and pressed trousers. He even wore shoes. The dogs, too, when I could take my eyes from their slavering jaws, looked well groomed and healthy. There must be a respectable family house that I had not seen further along the coastline – hidden among the trees, overlooking the bay, able to observe the comings and goings of strange yachts.

'Are your parents here?' I asked the boy in a cheery, adult-sounding voice. A whistle, forcing a hasty retreat, was my only answer.

As the sun began to sink, he must have got bored at last. Maybe it was time for his supper or possibly he was returning home to watch *The Brady Bunch* on the TV in his bedroom. Gathering up all my clothes, my machete and my camera, containing the evidence of my discovery, he moved away along the beach, the dogs trotting silently beside him. He never looked back and neither did they but I remained in the water till they'd vanished in the distance, small figures swallowed up by the fast-gathering dusk.

I dashed across the beach dressed only in my shorts, shoeless and shirtless, and plunged into the jungle. As the boy had taken my machete, I had to claw my way through the undergrowth, unable in the thickening gloom to find the path by which I had descended. Night arrives quickly in the tropics; it's as if a light has been switched off. I was struggling in the dark, unable to see where I was going, stubbing my toes and stumbling over twined roots and fallen tree trunks; branches and sinewy creepers lashed at my eyes. It was not just the harsh shriek of a howler monkey, inches from my face, that finally changed my mind; it was the memory of what I had read on the plane. I turned around and returned to the beach; better to spend the night here in the open with the dogs than to stumble through snake-infested jungles crawling with vengeful remnants of the Japanese Imperial Army.

Most people have some bad memory that allows them to look back and say, 'That was the most awful night ever.' But I confidently assert that nobody's was ever as awful as my night on the beach in Guam. For a start, it was too noisy to even think of sleeping. The jungle was a cacophony of howls and shrieks from the monkeys, roars and growls from who knows what and the slithering sounds of long, cold-blooded things that hiss and coil themselves around warm-blooded breathing things. I was also convinced I could hear ominous orders being shouted in Japanese. The only sound missing was the sound of birds.

The zoology of Guam used to be noted for three unusual features: there was a proliferation of colourful and exotic birds, a total absence of snakes and a remarkable lack of spiders. I don't know why there were no native snakes (perhaps St Patrick had passed through on his way to Ireland) but the result was that birds were able to thrive and multiply with no serious predators. The birds' main diet was spiders and, although plentiful, the spiders tended to keep a low profile. As I had read on the plane crossing the Pacific from Hawaii, all this changed at the end of the Second World War. In order to rebuild the island after the devastation of the Japanese occupation, boatloads of timber were imported from Malaysia. Among the stowaways on the boats was a colony of Malaysian brown tree snakes (*Boiga irregularis*). One of the favourite delicacies of these snakes are birds, and the birds of Guam, having developed no protective defence against snakes, were easy prey. The problem was compounded by the tree snakes' preference for nocturnal hunting; they attacked while the birds of Guam were all vulnerably fast asleep in the trees. Within a couple of decades, there were hardly any birds left in Guam – just hungry, nocturnally hunting tree snakes. It was my recollection of this bit of trivia that made me decide to leave the forest and spend the night on the beach.

Nature is arbitrary in her blessings and, while it was obviously bad news for the birds, the arrival of the snakes proved extremely good news for the spiders. Without any major threats to their existence, the spiders of Guam abandoned their low profile and multiplied. I did not read about the spiders' resurgence on the plane; I discovered it for myself on the beach. They were all over me. I don't know why they were on the beach – perhaps for the same reason that I was, to avoid the tree snakes – but, whatever the reason, they were crawling all over me. The more I smacked and squashed them on my flesh, the more fiercely they bit. I still do not know what species of spider they were but the infections remained with me for years and were finally diagnosed by the University of London's School of Hygiene and Tropical Medicine. In cold weather, the red marks of their bites still reappear.

Quickly, I removed my shorts because the spiders had climbed the legs and were swarming inside. With a depressing sense of déjà vu, I ran into the sea. The water got rid of the spiders but exposed me to fresh horrors. The waxing moon cast a sepulchral light across the whole of the bay, creating shadows and shapes upon the waters and a waxen glow across the vast expanse of white sand. My imagination went into panicked overdrive and I recalled *The Rime of the Ancient Mariner*:

> The very deep did rot: O Christ!
> That ever this should be!
> Yea, slimy things did crawl with legs
> Upon the slimy sea.

There were things in the water; unseen things that wrapped about my ankles, things that brushed against my horribly delicate and vulnerable private parts, pale and formless things that rode upon the waves towards my face. Struggling against the current, I returned to the beach and the spiders. The night was spent slapping at the spiders as I ran from one end of the beach to the other in terrified exhaustion. I had not eaten since noon and, surrounded by water, I had nothing to drink. I was delirious and hallucinating in the moonlight; images of large dogs racing along the sand drove me back into the sea and dark shapes with probing tentacles groping from the waves made me retreat up the beach towards the shadows of the jungle, filled with harsh cries and the gleam of watchful oriental eyes.

Eventually, I just collapsed exhausted in the shallows, letting the gentle rhythm of the waves wash over me and protect me from the remorseless spiders until the sun rose like a red festering boil above the entrance to the bay. As soon as there was enough light for me to retrieve my shorts and car keys, I headed into the jungle. The last thing I wanted was another encounter with the dogs during their morning constitutional. It was hours before I reached the safety of my red Corvette, dressed only in torn wet shorts, my flesh ripped and bloody from my ascent through the tangled vines and undergrowth. I took the next flight out of Guam and returned, defeated, to Ernie's house above Laguna Beach.

Much to my relief, I discovered that Val Johnson had decided to cancel the whole yacht-race operation. 'The Newport Beach Yacht Club, man, they're like a bunch of fucking Nazis. I think Nixon's a member. I can't deal with them. It ain't worth it.' Apologising for the fact that my trip had all been for nothing, Ernie explained that the strategy had changed. Shemsi was now planning to ship his Japanese cars to the US mainland direct from Guam. That way we could load more dope into the containers than we could ever get onto a yacht. 'God knows what we're going to do with the cars, though. Who the hell would ever buy a fucking Japanese car?' He looked at my still-torn flesh. 'Doesn't look like a nice place to go anyway,' he said. Val was even less sympathetic: 'Been in a cat fight at the Pink Poodle?' he asked with a smirk.

I just shrugged and muttered something about hostile Japanese jungle fighters. My reputation with Val Johnson as a 'nancy boy' was already bad enough, so I most certainly did not tell anybody that I'd been driven off the island by a ten-year-old boy and his pet dogs. Nor did I mention picking up uniformed military officers in my red Corvette.

* * *

When I was still a teenager in the 1960s, England was gradually discarding all its old colonies. The school atlas that I had been raised with showed the world still coloured pink, 'the Empire upon which the sun never set'. Following the debacle at Suez, however, our world became smaller and the expats of Rhodesia and Kenya started to return to the mother country. They tended to settle on the south coast of England, in places like Torquay, Bournemouth and Brighton, where they grumbled about creeping socialism and the difficulty of getting decent servants. The men were easy to recognise with their clipped military-style moustaches, their cavalry twill trousers and their brown suede Hush Puppies. I would see them walking along the seafront in Brighton, with their stout and disapproving wives, and always walking a pair of fluffy little lapdogs.

'Please,' I would beseech my friends, 'please kill me if I ever become like that.' Of course, it was an empty rhetorical statement. None of us, with our long hair, leather jackets and torn jeans, could imagine ever reaching middle age, let alone wearing cavalry twill trousers – or owning a lapdog. In my particular case, I could not even imagine growing a military or any other type of moustache, despite all my best efforts. So it was with a sense of great discomfort that I finally agreed, in later years, to let my two daughters have a white poodle.

I refused to walk him or even acknowledge his existence. His name was Sam and they got him at the Miami dog pound. He was old and flea-ridden when he arrived, and we had him for about two years. Who knows what life he had led before arriving in our home? I doubt it was a happy one. Jude and the girls loved him but I always held back. He was incontinent and gradually losing his eyesight but worst of all he was a lapdog. I owned a smoked-salmon factory at the time, in a rough part of Miami where the only dogs were pit bulls with spiked collars and thick chains. The girls were sometimes, against their will, forced to visit the factory if Jude and I were working late, and Peggy and Bridie often wanted to bring Sam. I always refused; I had my image to consider.

Nevertheless, Sam did benefit from the factory since the only food we could afford at the time was Norwegian salmon, which I imported by the container-load. Gradually, during the two years that Sam lived with us enjoying a diet of nothing but salmon, he turned pink. The pigment in the salmon slowly but surely took over his hair follicles until the only white things remaining on Sam were the cataracts on his eyes. Bad enough for Val Johnson to see me walking a poodle – but a pink poodle was going too far!

Eventually, Sam's blindness and general ill health could not be ignored; he stumbled endlessly around the house and kept falling into the swimming pool. It was commonly agreed that he needed to be 'put down' and that this was 'the father's job'. It was only on the drive to the vet, alone in the car with Sam, that I realised that he was part of our family and how much I had come to love him. He nuzzled trustingly against me as I drove and I remembered all the good things about him: his gentleness, his loyal affection and the joy he had given my daughters. I carried him into the vet's office and handed him over. 'Would you like to be with him at the end?' the vet asked.

The last time I visited my mother in hospital she was asleep and the nurse asked if she should wake her. 'No,' I said, 'let her sleep.' I was on my way to Le Moulin in France and had only three hours to catch the cross-Channel ferry at Newhaven. It seemed cruel to wake her for just a brief visit. I could spend time with her on my return the following week. 'Just tell her I was here,' I told the nurse, 'and I'll see her next week.' She died later that night and a message from my father was waiting for me when I arrived the following morning at Marboutie's café for breakfast.

Obviously, not waking my mother and saying goodbye is the biggest regret of my life. But I don't feel the guilt about my mother that I do about Sam. I didn't abandon my mother, I just wanted her to have some rest; sleep was difficult towards the end. Sam I abandoned. I handed him over to the vet and turned away. He died alone in the hands of strangers and I can never forgive myself. I told the girls, 'We will never have another dog.'

I stuck to my guns for several years and refused the endless entreaties from my wife and daughters to get a new dog. They are dirty, smelly and they pee everywhere, I said. They bark all the time, they need walking and they crap all over the lawn, if not inside the house. But eventually, after my eldest daughter got married and moved to Paris,

I bought Jude a little white Maltese lapdog to fill the void in her heart. 'Here,' I said gruffly, 'it's yours. You train it, you walk it. I want nothing to do with it – and it sleeps in the kitchen.'

Of course, within a matter of days, I was a lost soul, completely enamoured of Frodo's soft white hair and penetrating black eyes, and I would go nowhere without him. The following Christmas, I bought a second Maltese, Miki, and the two of them have slept in bed with Jude and me for the past six years. Our friends think we have become a very sad old couple, as the two of us talk endlessly about 'the boys', Miki and Frodo. They run our lives; in fact, one or another of them was sitting on my lap throughout the writing of this book.

Unfortunately, Miki has always been weak. He has a problem with his liver that often causes dementia. The first time it happened, we rushed him to the Miami Animal Hospital and spent the night anxiously waiting. I bought a packet of Marlboro from an all-night gas station across the road and after a 15-year break Jude and I started smoking again. I had an extremely important meeting the following morning at the university where I worked. There was a major strategy conflict under discussion between the vice president, the dean and all the associate deans. My role was to capitalise on my corporate background and represent the voice of practical common sense, to be firm, mature and masculine. I apologised for arriving late and explained that I had just brought Miki home from the hospital. 'I had no idea,' I told them, 'that a silly little lapdog could generate such emotion.' As I spoke, I felt my eyes grow hot and my voice began to choke. In front of that room full of people, sitting around the conference table in their dark suits, I broke down and began to sob uncontrollably. All the repressed sorrow and painful memories, including those relating to the long slow death of my mother, that my English upbringing never allowed me to express came flooding out at the thought of a stupid little sick dog and his black and desperate eyes.

In Miami, there was a very flamboyant gay couple who lived a couple of blocks from us and we often ran into each other when I was walking the dogs in the evening. They had a pair of Maltese puppies too, their fur always neatly combed and tied up with colourful ribbons on their heads. We would stand together in a happy little group on the corner of the golf course, earnestly discussing and comparing our pretty white lapdogs. If he had seen me, Val Johnson would have felt truly vindicated. As surly teenagers in their black punk outfits with their multiple facial piercings walked scornfully past our little group, I was often tempted to shout loudly that at least I wasn't wearing cavalry twill trousers and I didn't have a moustache.

When I was finally arrested and sent to prison in 1988, one of the first people to take me under his wing and show me the ropes was an elderly bookie from Miami Beach. John was in his late 60s and had been a professional criminal, in and out of jail all his life. With thin, lank hair in a combover and a grey, heavily lined face, this was a man whose entire life had been spent in dark pool halls and smoke-filled bars. For many years, he had worked closely with Lucky Luciano's partner Meyer Lansky, one of the founding members of the National Crime Syndicate. After returning to the USA from Israel in 1972, Lansky spent the remaining decade of his life in semi-retirement with his wife Teddy in Miami Beach, from where he continued to oversee his gambling empire. John was one of Lansky's local sidekicks and loved to tell stories about the good old days on the Beach before Lansky's death in 1983.

One of my favourite stories involved a meeting with a delegation from one of the New Jersey families in The Forge restaurant on Miami Beach. Apparently, the meeting was not progressing too well and one of the young punks got exasperated with Lansky. 'This is all bullshit!' he said. 'We don't have to listen to this. Shit, he ain't Sicilian. He ain't even Italian. He's a fucking Jew.'

An embarrassed hush fell over the table, not because of political correctness but because Lansky was still one of the most powerful racketeers in America.

'So he's Jewish,' somebody said. 'So what?'

'So what?' the young punk continued. 'The fucking Jews, they killed Jesus. They fucking murdered him.'

Lansky finally took the cigar from his mouth. 'I don't know nothing about Jesus,' he rasped in his thick New York accent, 'but if the Jews whacked him, he musta had it coming to him.' Slowly, he blew a smoke ring and rose from the table. The meeting was over.

When Lansky had private business to discuss, he would call John over to his house and they would walk Lansky's dog along the quiet tree-lined streets of Hibiscus Drive. Lansky often said that walking his beloved dog Bruiser was one of the few remaining joys of his life. I don't know if the FBI ever thought of trying 'Bruiser' as a security code when they were attempting to locate the millions of dollars that Lansky left hidden in Swiss banks after he died. Certainly a better bet than 'Jesus'.

I asked John what Lansky's house was like, but he'd never been inside: 'Teddy wouldn't let him talk business in the house. Anyway, the fucking Feds had it wired.' So they would walk the quiet streets, heads close together, discussing the finer details of Lansky's international criminal empire, guarded all the while by an alert Bruiser.

'What sort of dog was he?' I asked. 'What was he like?'

'Fucking thing never stopped pissing and yapping,' John grumbled. 'No wonder the fucking Feds couldn't hear nothing, with all that yapping.'

'So what breed was he?' I persisted.

'A lapdog,' he said with disgust. 'It was a fucking shih-tzu. I felt like a goddamn faggot.'

Although the federal government officially classified me as a racketeer I always felt something of a fraud. I constantly worried that somebody would challenge me, saying, 'You're not a proper racketeer. You're just a plump middle-aged ponce.' However, Meyer Lansky is recognised as the quintessential American racketeer, and so, as I walked Frodo and Miki around the streets of Miami, I knew I was walking in his footsteps – a true racketeer at last.

1|0

PHONES

In 1973, the US DEA discovered a large and embarrassing consignment of containers filled with Pakistani hashish in Las Vegas. As a result, I had to leave London rather suddenly and move to Le Moulin in Molières. Our whole organisation had been destroyed, we were all on the run and the telephone was our only means of communication.

The nearest phone to my house was at Café Marboutie in Beaumont, a 20-minute drive away. It was an old-fashioned model with a separate earpiece and speaking tube, and it was located very close to the bar's only toilet, which, equally old-fashioned, consisted of a simple hole in the cement floor. Because the floor flooded each time the chain was pulled, making a phone call could be a very wet and messy business. The operator would phone back after the call was completed and tell M. Marboutie how much to charge me. Most of the people I called were either pot smugglers or fugitives but the concept of privacy was unknown. *Le patron*, René Marboutie, had a record of everybody I had called and knew exactly how long I had been speaking for. The nice thing about French village life, though, is that anything outside the village is of no interest. The outer limit of Marboutie's world was Bergerac, a 30-minute drive away, so he was completely indifferent to my phone records.

Today's criminals just don't know how lucky they are. When I was a young racketeer in the last century, we did not have emails, the Internet or online money transfers. We didn't have mobile phones or even faxes. Our international calls were made through live operators from public phone booths. There was no FedEx, there were no electronic money-counting machines and suitcases didn't even have wheels. Most communication was handwritten and even Nigerian letters were delivered in an envelope with a proper stamp. The practised eye could easily recognise a real racketeer in those days: arms elongated from the weight of heavy suitcases, thumbs calloused from counting banknotes and pockets bulging with small change for the phone booths. Today's racketeers have got it made.

I can remember when we didn't even have a phone in the house. In the early 1950s, we were living in Wales when my grandmother was dying in Ireland. In order to maintain contact with her family and, in the end, to arrange her visit to Belfast for the funeral, my mother used the phone in the corner shop at the end of the street. That was the only public phone in the area, the one that everybody used. Obviously, the owner of the corner shop listened to all the conversations and knew everything that happened in the neighbourhood. My mother always brought home a little bit of gossip with her groceries.

The lack of privacy continued even after we got a telephone installed when we moved to Stevenage in the mid-'50s. Although we had our own phone, it was a 'party line', which meant we shared the same number with another family close by. When the telephone rang, both parties would pick up, not knowing who the call was for. Mrs Clegg, who had no children, would sit by her phone all day in her dressing gown and grab it at the first ring.

'She's got nothing else to do,' grumbled my mother, who had three children and more on the way. 'She just sits there and listens to all our secrets.'

My mother was always trying to persuade my father to phone home from his office and pretend to be a Russian spy or an IRA terrorist plotting a bomb attack on the local police station.

'That'll teach her,' she would say. 'She'll go rushing down to the police station in that silly robe with her pink rollers in her hair.' She laughed gleefully at the thought. 'The police will lock her up for being mad – or tell her to stop eavesdropping on her neighbours. Go on, Ken. Please do it. It'll be such fun.'

'Don't be stupid, Peggy,' my father replied. 'We'd just get into trouble. And, anyway, you shouldn't say things like that in front of Patrick. You'll put ideas in the boy's head.'

In 1960, we moved to Barnet in north London, where we finally had our own phone with no intrusive neighbours to listen to our secrets. As was normal in those days, there was only one phone in the house, located in the hallway at the foot of the stairs, near the front door. It was large, heavy and black, made of Bakelite at a time when the smart money was moving into plastics. There was no rotary dial, just a round disc with the telephone number, BARNET 0457. You would pick up the receiver and wait for the operator to ask, 'What number please?'

Telephone operators in those days, like BBC radio announcers, were selected because of their good speaking voices. There were no regional accents and no working-class slang. You felt that you were dealing with a respectable, upper-middle-class person with proper English standards and you responded accordingly. I saw my parents unconsciously arranging their hair, straightening their backs and clearing their throats before picking up the telephone to make a call; they were on their best behaviour.

Initially, only my parents were allowed to use the phone and we children were forbidden to touch it. I remember once, when my parents were out, my sister Natasha and I tried to telephone one of our school friends. 'Do your parents know you are using the telephone?' the operator asked us in a very disapproving tone of voice. 'Have they given you permission?' Hastily, we replaced the handset in its cradle and hoped the operator wouldn't tell our parents.

As I eased into my teenage years, friends started to phone me at home and so I was allowed to use the telephone when they called. My father did not really approve of this but my mother persuaded him that it was all related to school homework. Most of the conversations consisted of mumbled grunts as I stood in the front hall aware that my whole family was trying to listen. One evening, the inevitable happened and a girl called asking to speak to me. It is quite extraordinary how fast sensitive news can travel within a family, certainly faster than a virus attack in a computer network. Within seconds of my mother saying, 'It's for you, Patrick. She says her name is Paula,' I was aware that Natasha was standing at the top of the stairs listening intently. George and Judy had been playing loudly in the back garden but I could now see them hiding behind the coat-rack down the hallway, giggling. I could see my mother's shadow; she was standing just inside the kitchen doorway.

My father chose that moment to return home and, as he came through the front door, a look of mild annoyance passed over his face when he saw me on the phone.

'Hello, son,' he said. 'Problem with homework?'

'No, no problem, Daddy,' I mumbled, my ears burning a bright red.

'It's his girlfriend,' Natasha announced importantly, coming down the stairs. 'Her name's Paula and she's his girlfriend.'

I had already muttered my excuses to Paula and put the phone down.

'You little liar!' I yelled at Natasha. 'She's not my girlfriend.'

George and Judy had joined us by this point and were dancing around me shouting, 'Patrick's got a girlfriend, Patrick's got a girlfriend.'

'Well, if she's your girlfriend, you should bring her over so that we can meet her,' my mother said brightly. 'Why don't you invite her for tea?'

My whole face was red now and I wished the telephone had never been invented. 'She's not my girlfriend,' I insisted. 'She's just somebody I know from church.'

My parents looked at each other knowingly. After years of having to be dragged to church for Mass, in the past several weeks I had suddenly changed. I would be ready on time each Sunday morning, standing at the front door, neatly groomed and telling my siblings to 'hurry up or we'll be late'.

More than 45 years later, I can still clearly remember the first time I saw Paula Derham walking up the aisle after receiving Communion. I had never seen anyone so beautiful, so elegant, so feminine and sophisticated. I stood awkwardly in the back row of the church with a huge erection, terrified that the priest would see it throbbing beneath my Sunday suit and denounce me to the congregation.

I started to live for Sunday mornings, when I would next see the mysterious blonde girl at Mass and then follow her as she walked home with her equally elegant mother and impossibly dignified father. All my hatred of the Catholic Church vanished at the sight of this devoted and devout family. The only time I have ever wavered in my atheism was under Paula's spell. I found out where she lived, I discovered her name and then, one magical Saturday evening, I finally met her at a party given by one of my school friends. I was with the other boys, drinking warm beer or sweet white wine out of coffee mugs, looking cool and hip in my cheap sunglasses and my black plastic jacket, when suddenly I saw her. Sitting on the landing, halfway up the stairs, with her blonde hair cascading over her face, she was strumming a guitar and softly singing Joan Baez's 'John Riley':

> Well, if he's in some battle slain,
> I will go and mourn all on his grave,
> And if he's drowned in the deep salt sea
> I'll be true to his memory.
>
> And if he's found another love,
> And he and his love both married be,
> I'll wish them health and happiness
> Where they dwell across the sea.

I had never heard anything so spiritually moving or heartbreakingly sad in all my 14 years. When I saw that Paula was wearing black stockings and knee-high black boots under a denim miniskirt, I knew that I was in love. I knew that this was not some youthful infatuation or the sort of gross indecency that other boys boasted and sniggered about at school. This was a deeply mystical passion and it was eternal. She and I were fated to spend the rest of our lives together. To have Paula call me on the telephone was one of the most exciting and fulfilling moments of my whole life, and to have my family listen in and jeer at me was one of the most dispiriting.

I had recently seen the movie *Billy Liar*. Paula was the spitting image of Julie Christie in the film, exuding the same sense of untamed beauty and unattainable freedom. Like Christie, Paula, in her short, flouncing skirt, was a ray of bright sunshine, moving through the dark, bourgeois shadows of north London suburbia. Billy Liar, played by Tom Courtenay, was a fantasist, retreating to his imaginary world. Whenever he felt frustrated, he would picture himself as a storm trooper with a machine gun. His stifling family, the boys who bullied him at school and his boring colleagues at work would all shudder spasmodically and fall lifelessly to the ground, spurting blood, as Billy's bullets ripped them to pieces.

Standing at the foot of the stairs, my hand still resting on the heavy Bakelite handset as though it were a warm gun barrel, I stared wordlessly at my brothers and sisters and my parents. Their bullet-riddled bodies continued to twitch for a short while on the blood-soaked carpet but finally they lay still.

'I'm going to finish my homework,' I said.

Upstairs, I locked the door of my room and put 'Barbara Allen' by Joan Baez on the turntable. It was one of Paula's favourite songs:

> So slowly, slowly she got up
> And slowly she drew nigh him,
> And the only words to him did say,
> 'Young man, I think you're dying.'

Paula had only called to ask for the address of one of my friends. She had also wanted to know if he already had a girlfriend.

> When he was dead and laid in grave,
> She heard the death bells knelling,
> And every stroke to her did say,
> 'Hard-hearted Paula Derham.'

By the late '60s, nearly all phones had a rotary dial so that you could call direct in most large towns. In the countryside, however, and for international calls, you still needed the operator. One good thing about the relative scarcity of private phones was that public phone boxes could be found everywhere and usually in good working order. Howard and

I gradually compiled a database of the numbers of strategically placed public booths all over the British Isles, in town centres, at railway stations and in airports. When I say 'database', I unfortunately do not mean it in the sense of some easily accessible list or spreadsheet that could be stored on a laptop or PDA. By 'database', I mean handwritten notations scrawled on the back of an envelope or maybe on a wet beer mat from a local pub. From time to time, these rough scrawls from the field would be updated onto a master list, typed on an IBM Selectric typewriter, using carbon paper to create extra copies. Howard and I were always at the cutting edge.

Our list of phone numbers eventually became international and started to include airport booths in Frankfurt and New York, as well as major railway terminals such as Zurich and Amsterdam. Just as some women are irresistibly drawn to shoe-shop windows, so Howard was drawn to public phone booths. He found it hard to walk past one without using it and he certainly never passed a useful-seeming one without writing down its number and location.

We even devised a simple code for exchanging these numbers over the phone and for the next 20 years the code remained unbroken. It really was simple: 0 = 0, 1 = 9, 2 = 8, 3 = 7, 4 = 6, 5 = 5, 6 = 4, 7 = 3, 8 = 2, 9 = 1. So the phone number 702 385 1281 would become 308 725 9829. I suspect the authorities never cracked it because it was too basic. But the advantage of such a simple code was that we could translate it instantly in our heads, even when we were drunk or stoned.

It is hard to imagine such an archaic system being used these days, when every teenage street-corner hood has a disposable mobile phone and access to encrypted algorithms. But somehow our system worked and we maintained a network of stoned hippies all around the globe exchanging complex information from one public phone box to another. These weren't just in airports and railway stations: many were located in pubs and bars, and one was halfway up a giant sequoia above the snowline near Lake Tahoe.

International calls remained a problem for many years. They were very expensive and time-consuming, and they required an operator. By the early '70s, when we had our oriental carpet shop with working phones on every floor, I was inundated with Californian dope smugglers calling their girlfriends and dogs back home. Ironically, even though we were well equipped with phones, we continued to conduct business from the public phone next door in the Warwick Castle pub. It wasn't a matter of being discreet; it just so happened that that was where we spent most of our time.

Perhaps the most sophisticated users of telephones were the Afghanis. Graham Plinston and I spent a lot of time in the money market in Kabul when we did business in Afghanistan. The walled Sarai Shahzada market was a warren of small rooms and stalls on three levels, covering a couple of square miles in the centre of the city. It was located next to the river and the Blue Mosque, within walking distance of the gold and silver markets. I had received my financial training on Lombard Street in the heart of the City and later I was to work closely with sophisticated currency exchanges on Wall Street, but I have never found anywhere in the world to be as informed and efficient as the Kabul money market. Equipped with just an abacus and an old Bakelite telephone, a little bearded ageless man in a turban could quote you the latest exchange rates for Australian dollars, Lebanese pounds or Pakistani rupees and then transfer your money anywhere in the world.

Graham and I would spend hours sitting cross-legged on a carpet in one of the small stalls, drinking endless cups of green tea, staring at the black Bakelite telephone sitting on a pile of carpets in the middle of the room. Eventually, the phone would ring and the owner of the stall would answer in rapid-fire Farsi or Pashto. Sometimes there were problems and he would replace the receiver with a frown but more often the phone call would end with nods and smiles and calls for yet more tea. This meant that Michael Durani had visited the stall-owner's cousin in Birmingham or Leicester and given him a suitcase or two filled with sterling or US dollars. Sometimes the cousin in England would want to hold on to the Hartmann suitcases and Michael would object or insist on increasing the amount of our credit in Kabul. There would be intense negotiations over the phone but in the end they would be resolved in another round of green tea and smiles.

With just a simple old-fashioned black telephone and a handshake, Graham and I would thus have access to, say, £30,000 in cash, or even in gold sovereigns, to give to Big Dave for the purchase of carpets and best-quality hashish for export to Europe. This *hawalah* system of transferring money around the globe was as old as Kabul itself. Far more venerable than the European banking system of the Lombard money changers and the great Rothschild family of financiers, the Kabul money market survived the Russian invasion and the Taliban. The dealers now use satellite phones and laptop computers but the piles of carpets, the bundles of cash and the endless cups of tea – all that, I am sure, remains unchanged.

* * *

Moving to the French countryside in the wake of that Las Vegas bust was much more of a culture shock than doing business in Afghanistan. When I moved into Le Moulin, my three top priorities were to organise the installation of running water, electricity and a telephone.

The first two were swiftly accomplished. EDF, the electrical company, erected an ugly twenty-foot concrete post next to my twelfth-century mill. They then attached a 240-volt cable with an electrical meter and left me to get on with it. So I became an electrician, and within a few months and after many electrical burns and shocks, the whole building was wired. Almost 40 years later, the wiring I installed remains in place and still functions.

A water main was installed by the Commune of Molières, running underground all the way from the village. Over the next few months, I also became a plumber and installed a kitchen and a bathroom with running water. Jude and I were to be married in June and we had about 50 guests arriving from England. Our major goal, therefore, was to have a proper flushing toilet before the guests arrived. Installing a septic tank and running the water lines was a mammoth task and I only completed it the day before the visitors came. Having lived through a harsh winter with no running water and no toilet, we were terribly excited. During the three-day party that followed the wedding, whenever anybody asked us how we felt now that we were married, we both had the same response: 'Fabulous! Amazing! You just pull the chain and it all flushes away.'

Installing a phone was a different matter. The only phone in Molières was in the mayor's house and I always felt I was intruding in Monsieur Ferandon's private life when I used it. I would therefore drive to Marboutie's to make my phone calls outside the overflowing lavatory.

Like most official business, an application for a telephone had to go through the appropriate government office in Périgueux, the capital of the Dordogne. This was a two-hour drive from Molières and necessitated sitting in grey and draughty government offices and completing endless forms in triplicate. It took about five visits before the application was finally completed, with all the required stamps and signatures, and I was officially added to the waiting list for a telephone.

I was then informed that the wait would be seven years. I couldn't believe it. I was outraged. As soon as I returned to Molières, I stormed up to see Monsieur Ferandon for his advice.

'Ouf! Ils exagèrent,' he shrugged. Then he took the official papers from me and shook his head sadly as he read through them. 'Il faut au moins neuf ans,' he said. 'It will be at least nine years. Your neighbour Monsieur Carrière, he applied seven years ago and last year they told him it would be at least another five.'

Jude and I were devastated. We loved Molières and wanted to start a new life there and raise children. But there was no way we could survive without a telephone. Sadly, we resigned ourselves to moving back to civilisation. And then a miracle happened.

It was commonly accepted in the early '70s that France had the worst phone system in the developed world. Even the French acknowledged this. Government engineers had therefore developed a technologically advanced system that would change everything and make France a telecommunications leader overnight. Needing to quietly test the system, the ministers in Paris decided to install it in the most remote and backward part of the country so that any mistakes or disasters could be kept under control.

Within weeks of my conversation with the mayor, during which

I had told him that I would not accept this state of affairs and that I would return to Périgueux and complain, yellow PTT (Postes, Télégraphes et Téléphones) vans, marked 'Direction Générale des Télécommunications', were all over the village. Within a matter of weeks, not only did every household in Molières have a telephone, we had the newest and most efficient phone service in Europe. To say the mayor was impressed is an understatement. For ever after, he was convinced that I was a man of power and influence, and, of course, I modestly did nothing to disabuse him of this belief.

Ferdinand Carrière had applied for a telephone only for his wife's sake. Paulia missed her daughters, who both lived in Pau, in the foothills of the Pyrenees. Having a telephone would enable them to stay in contact but old man Carrière felt that no good would come of it. With instant communication, bad news would travel too fast, affecting people before they had time to prepare themselves. News, he felt, should travel at a slower, more natural pace. Telephones would just destroy the natural rhythms.

I still vividly remember his description of receiving the news of the end of the First World War. Several times a year, I would help Carrière in the fields. The hay had been cut, tied and bundled, and my job was to lift the heavy bales with a pitchfork and hoist them onto the trailer behind his tractor. Later, we would unload the trailer and store the bales in his barn. One year, we were standing in the middle of the meadow looking down on the valley and I could see in the distance where my daughter Peggy was lying in her cradle, just outside the front door of the mill.

We were both sweating from our labour, taking slugs of red wine from a bottle and chewing crusty bread with cloves of garlic. 'This is where I heard about the end of the war,' he said, pointing to the spot where we were standing. 'I'll never forget it.'

He told me that he had been a young boy, helping his father with the harvest, just as I was helping him now. When peace was officially declared, the bells of Notre-Dame in Paris were rung by order of the government. Within the radius of the sound of the great cathedral's bells, other church bells were rung as the signal was taken up. Slowly but surely, across the whole breadth of France, from one parish to the next, the pealing bells spread the news, and from city to town to village the sound travelled until even the smallest hamlet knew that the nightmare was finally finished.

'I've got sharp ears,' he told me. 'I told my papa I could hear the big bell in Beaumont de Périgord, but he didn't believe me.' Carrière smiled at the memory, as though he could hear the bells ringing again. 'But then we heard the bells of the Abbaye de St Avit Seigneur and he lifted me up above his head and said, "You're right, the war is over." ' Then the two of them had thrown aside their tools and run to Molières to join the other men at the church, ringing the bells.

Even with a telephone installed at Le Moulin, international racketeering was very difficult following the bust. Ernie Combs had gone into deep hiding, Graham had fled to Ireland and Howard was being hunted not only by Interpol and Scotland Yard but also by every newspaper in England. Always good copy for the press, Howard played up his IRA and British intelligence connections and threw in a few hints about the Mafia as well. The British media loved it all and kept the story alive. We were described as 'the University Egghead Gang' and Howard was always referred to as 'Mr Mystery'. Maintaining contact and planning new deals was quite challenging for a while.

In the meantime, Jude and I settled into married life in France. Our wedding took place in the Molières church where old Carrière had helped ring the bells to proclaim the end of war. My first daughter was born a year later, in 1974. We grew our own food and I supported us by painting scenes of Périgordian rural life, which we sold at local fairs to rich tourists from Paris and Bordeaux. Life was simple and we were blissfully happy. We also raised snails, and on our wedding certificate my profession is recorded as 'heliciculturist', which means 'snail rancher'.

France at that time was a net importer of snails, mainly from the Middle East and Eastern Europe. The French habit of using pesticides everywhere had killed off the snail population and by the time we moved to France they were only to be found in cemeteries – giving rise to the false rumour that snails feasted on dead flesh! The French government was encouraging research into the raising and farming of snails, so Jude and I set up the Société d'Élevage des Escargots du Sud-Ouest. We travelled all over south-west France, meeting with other snail farmers and exchanging information and techniques. I actually became quite an authority and the Ministry of Agriculture was in constant communication. My daughter Peggy had a whole collection of toy snails and Jude started writing a book called *365 Ways to Cook Snails*. As a newly married couple, Jude and I would get out of bed at dawn to observe the snails having sex. Being hermaphrodites, snails have both male and female genitals in the same opening, and copulation could take several hours while they languidly poked and pricked each other as the sun rose. We had no television in those days and had to make our own entertainment.

Eventually, Monsieur Besse's herd of cows broke into our property, trampling our fences and breeding pens, and all the snails escaped, galloping off into the night. Oddly enough, after I became a fugitive several years later and moved to California, I continued to receive mail from the French government on the subject of snails. Interpol had been unable to track me down but the French Ministry of Agriculture apparently had no problem.

During this period, I was also researching tax havens and international banking regulations. Today, of course, I could discover everything I needed in just a couple of days Googling. But in the '70s, there was no easy way of getting the information I wanted. Packing a pregnant Jude, baby Peggy and Dog into an old Renault van, I set off on a camping tour of Europe's financial capitals.

We visited Switzerland, Austria, Liechtenstein, Luxembourg and Germany. We would pitch our tent in a remote field and then drive to the business district in the morning. I would change into a smart suit and visit the local banks and attorneys' offices, accumulating information about each country's fiscal regulations. Jude would wait in the van, shooting me baleful looks as I walked shiftily past if one of the people I was visiting offered to take me to lunch. Gradually, I built up a network of useful contacts and opened bank accounts in most of the more fiscally accommodating European capitals.

Howard and I had re-established contact following our hasty departures from England and he financed a research trip to the Caribbean, where, again, I made useful acquaintances on many of the different islands. After that, Howard and I controlled offshore corporations and bank accounts in about 20 different tax havens in the Caribbean, Europe and the Far East.

By the time my second daughter, Bridie, was born in 1977, my international tax-consulting business had expanded to the stage where our communication needs had outgrown what Molières could offer, and so we moved to Campione.

Campione d'Italia is a small part of Italy on Lake Lugano that is totally surrounded by Swiss territory. As a result, the Italian authorities are unable to visit Campione officially without crossing neutral Swiss jurisdiction. At the same time, the Swiss authorities are unable to enter the enclave because it is sovereign Italian territory. Consequently, the laws of each country are difficult to enforce in Campione and, more importantly, there are no taxes. Living in Campione has all the advantages of living in Switzerland: everything is clean and efficient and runs like clockwork, including the phone service. At the same time, the food, the music and the relaxed way of life are entirely Italian. It is the perfect tax haven.

My sister Judy, Howard and their children lived in an apartment close to ours. Myfanwy was the same age as Peggy, and Amber had been born a few days after Bridie. The British press at the time were running front-page stories about Howard almost daily. Some claimed that he had been kidnapped by the Mafia and was being held in Italy, others that he was being guarded by MI6 while he carried out undercover operations against the IRA. Howard and I would sit at a lakeside table drinking Campari sodas while we read the latest newspaper reports. In the winter, we would all go skiing in the mountains behind the town and in the summer we would take all the children to the beach on Lake Lugano. The lake was surrounded by rustic little tavernas where we would enjoy long, lazy Sunday lunches of fresh Italian food while the children played along the shore. Campione was more than a fiscal paradise; it was Paradise itself.

Our apartment was on the side of an Alp, overlooking the lake, across from the Swiss town of Lugano. The phone service was excellent, the postal service was first class and the train service, south to Milan or north to Zurich, was modern, comfortable and always on time. I loved Campione and would live there still, but Jude hated it. In the two years we lived there, she did not make a single friend. Even the nuns at the local school were unfriendly and Peggy, who learned to speak fluent Italian, was always in trouble for undressing her Barbie doll. Jude and I were forever being summoned to Mother Superior's office for a lecture about Peggy's naked Barbies.

Every morning, Jude would walk Peggy down the hill to school and every afternoon she'd walk back to collect her. Each day, she saw the same mothers collecting their own children and every day she would say, '*Buon giorno, signora.*' Her friendly greetings were always ignored. The problem was that Campione was mainly inhabited by Mafia dons who had moved north to avoid all the crime in Italy, or by sinister people with German accents who had quietly installed themselves there at the end of the Second World War. Nobody was really friendly except the Mafia dons themselves. Whenever we walked Bridie in her pushchair past an outdoor café, dark-suited men in sunglasses would move aside so that the old men sitting at the table could admire her. '*Che bella bambina!*' they would rasp as they tickled her chubby cheeks. 'She must have Italian blood in her,' they would suggest, meaningfully. Even at that tender age, Bridie had perfected the cold hard stare of the Las Vegas pit boss and would regard them balefully from behind her long lashes. Even the Sicilian dons and their consiglieri would wilt under Bridie's disdainful gaze.

None of this improved Jude's feelings about Campione. I, however, was delighted. I had a phone in every room and could call Hong Kong and New York without needing an international operator. Howard and I could take a ferry across the lake to Lugano and transfer money from my Swiss bank account to anywhere in the world. For major transactions needing more discretion, I could take the train to visit my private bank in Zurich. Reading the *International Herald Tribune*, I would eat a delicious Italian meal served on bone china while the Alps glided silently past my window. Best of all, I had a state-of-the-art Swiss telex machine.

A telex machine was a sort of large electric typewriter that punched holes into a roll of paper tape at the same time as it typed the letters onto a sheet of paper. After typing your message, you fed the tape into the machine, dialled the number of your correspondent and then your message would be typed out at the other end. This was how banks communicated with each other in those days and how they transferred millions of dollars around the globe. I controlled cash reserves in various Swiss banks for Howard, Ernie and others. Through Deak-Perera, I had arrangements with and telex codes for correspondent banks in most of the world's major cities and thus I was able to send instructions to have money moved anywhere it was needed within hours. If a bank needed to communicate with me, they could simply send a telex to the machine in the bedroom and immediately, day or night, the typewriter keys would start clattering, the hole punch would start hammering and the message would print out for me to read. I loved it! I felt I was in communications heaven. When the telex would start clattering at three in the morning, I would excitedly leap out of bed to stand over it and tear off the message. 'It's the Hong Kong bank,' I'd say disbelievingly. 'They're sending a transfer to my account in Geneva.'

Jude hated my business. She disliked the questionable legality of it, the secrecy of it and the uncertainty of it. She disliked Campione, she disliked the uptight nuns at Peggy's Catholic school and she disliked the lack of friends and a social life. But more than anything else, Jude hated the noisy, clattering telex machine in our bedroom!

So we packed up our home in Campione and moved to Ireland.

By 1979, the Irish punt had broken free of its relationship with the English pound and Ireland was a member of the European Monetary System. With an excellent, modern phone system, and located between the US and the European mainland, Ireland looked like the perfect spot to establish my offshore financial trading organisation.

We piled the family into the car and drove from Switzerland across France to Roscoff in Brittany, where we caught the overnight ferry to Cork. Our furniture and belongings were to follow later by van.

As soon as we had rented a house in Limerick and arranged a place for Peggy at the local school, I set off downtown to organise a telephone connection. The government was determined to make the Irish phone service the best in Europe but, although it was not nearly as difficult as getting a telephone in France, the application procedure still took the better part of a day. Finally, the official gave me my completed application form.

'I was worried for a while,' I told him.

'Oh, and why might that be, sir?' he asked.

'I was in the pub last night and somebody said the telephone company was going on strike.'

'The things they say. You shouldn't believe half of what you hear in the pub.' He smiled at me. 'Do I look like I'm on strike?' he asked. 'Is the office closed? Do you see any pickets?'

'No, absolutely not,' I assured him. 'You've been most helpful and efficient.'

He smiled again. 'We do our best, sir. We are only here to serve the public.'

I examined the papers carefully. 'I don't see any dates for the installation of the phone,' I said. 'How long does it usually take after the paperwork is completed?'

'It's usually done within 24 hours,' he replied.

I grinned approvingly. 'I'm very impressed,' I said. 'I've just moved here from Switzerland and even the Swiss aren't that efficient. So I should be up and running some time tomorrow then?'

'Well, maybe not tomorrow, sir,' he hesitated. 'You see, there's a wee problem.'

'A problem?'

'You see, the telephone installers' union is on strike.'

'But you said you weren't on strike.'

He nodded. 'Indeed we're not. It's the installers' union. They're on strike.' He smiled with a sympathetic affability. 'They're part of the Department of Posts and Telegraphs. Nothing to do with us.'

'How long are they on strike for?'

He shrugged. 'Nobody knows.'

'How long have they been on strike?'

'Since lunchtime. Today.'

'Today!' I repeated stupidly.

He nodded and smiled disarmingly. 'Ironic, really. If you had come and ordered your phone yesterday, it would be installed by now.'

Jude and the girls loved Ireland and swiftly made friends. The house was always full of kids and every day Jude had a new amusing story to tell about something that somebody had said to her in the shops or on the way to school. Life in Ireland was perfect, except that I had no phone.

Howard and I had started doing a lot of business in Thailand at this time. One of our colleagues, Phil Sparrowhawk, had recently made a number of influential contacts there and 'Thai sticks' had become the latest fashion among American smokers. It was imperative that I have a phone. For a while, I survived by using the phone in my local pub, Durty Nelly's, or by renting a room for the night in the Shannon Shamrock Hotel, but increasingly I was spending Monday to Friday in London or Zurich solely in order to use the phone to communicate with Bangkok.

Every time I enquired at the phone company, I was reassured with 'Och, sure, it can't be much longer now. They'll probably be back to work next week.' But the weeks followed one upon the other and month followed month without any resolution to the strike. What made matters worse was that there was some sort of parallel transport strike in progress. All our furniture and possessions were in storage in Cork and there was no way to transport them across country to Limerick.

Jude had joined the Limerick tennis club, which was near our house and which had a working telephone, so at least I was able to talk to her when I was away. Peggy, already fluent in Italian, was now learning Gaelic and would proudly teach me new Irish words on my fleeting visits home. But the strain of not seeing Jude and the children was becoming too much for me and finally we decided to return to France. 'At least we'll have a phone,' I said.

We drove across Ireland and spent the night in Rosslare, ready for the morning ferry to Cherbourg. We were all sad to be leaving Ireland but happy to be together as a family again. After we'd had dinner and put the children to bed, Jude and I sat in the hotel's residents' lounge drinking Irish coffee. The lead story on the evening news was, of course, the end of the telephone installers' strike. It began the week we arrived and it ended the day we left, six months later.

So, finally, in late 1979, we returned to Molières and it was as though we had never left. Peggy was back at her old school, speaking French with an Irish/Italian accent, which everyone agreed was *très charmant*, and I once more had a phone. As soon as I had installed a telex machine in the basement – well away from the bedroom – I was back in business.

It was a relief to be back in rural Périgord, where nobody was interested in my business. Nobody cared and nobody was curious. In France, if you cannot eat it, drink it or make love to it, it's not worth talking about. I remember going to Marboutie's bar to use the phone after a long visit to Thailand.

'Ah, Monsieur Patrick,' René Marboutie greeted me as he poured a welcome glass of Ricard, 'I haven't seen you for a long time. Where have you been?'

'Funny you should ask, René,' I replied smugly. 'I was in Thailand buying silk for Jude. I left Hong Kong yesterday morning and changed planes in Honolulu and then flew on to Los Angeles where I spent the night. I flew out of LA this morning to New York and then non-stop to Paris.' I paused, confused. 'No, I guess it was last night I left New York. I've got all my time zones mixed up.' Marboutie watched as I added a little water to the glass. 'Anyway, today at lunchtime, I took an Air Inter from Paris to Bordeaux and then took the first train to Bergerac. I took a cab from there and he just dropped me off outside. Look,' I pointed, 'there are my suitcases. I'm just going to telephone Jude to come and collect me.'

At the mention of Bergerac, Marboutie's face came alive and, for the first time, he showed an interest in my boastful ramblings. 'Ah, you were in Bergerac. How was it? They say that the weather's been really bad this past week. Lots of rain. Bad for the vines.' He shook his head gravely. 'You mark my words: this year's will not be a great vintage.'

[1][1]

MONEY

It was never the money that led me to a life of crime; it was the drugs, the travel and the implicit promise of sex. Indeed, I am embarrassed to say that I've made more money as a regular salary slave in the past 20 years, since I left prison, than I made during my 20 years as an international racketeer. Nevertheless, during those two decades I was certainly exposed to a lot of money. I spent a lot of it and I spent time with people who had far too much of it. One of the very few people I have ever met who was never affected by money and who never expressed any interest in it was Jude.

When I first met Jude, she was working as a waitress at a restaurant called Fagin's Kitchen in Hampstead. During the day, she worked as a wig designer in Savile Row, the fashionable Mayfair street where Michael Durani bought his suits and the Beatles had their office. She designed wigs for all the movies that were being made in London during the '60s and as a result knew many of the actors and actresses of the time. Despite working so close to Carnaby Street and the fashionable centre of 'swinging London', she always had her own sense of style and preferred buying second-hand clothes at Portobello Market, near her Notting Hill flat, and transforming them into something uniquely her own. When long straight hair was the fashion and most of the girls I knew would be bent over the ironing board pressing their tresses before going out in the evening, Jude cut all her hair off and adopted the gamine look years ahead of its time. Although she was always strongly against breaking the law, she was in favour of breaking the rules, an attitude that remains unchanged to this day. She was never a 'bad girl' but she was always a naughty one. With her short-cropped hair, her large dark eyes and her mischievous smile, I was immediately captivated. She was also blessed with a quite extraordinary body.

Fagin's Kitchen was near the top of Haverstock Hill and was the hippest spot in Hampstead at that time. You would see the occasional Beatle there or perhaps a member of the Monty Python team. Peter Cook was a regular and so was Tom Stoppard. Unfortunately, as an articled clerk at Price Waterhouse, I could seldom afford to eat there, unless my father was in town and willing to treat me. But once Jude and I started dating and she introduced me to the owner and the staff, I would go there after the pubs had closed and eat leftover food from the kitchen while waiting for her shift to end. I once invited Alec Singh for dinner after work. We had been conducting an audit in north London and I scandalised him by arriving at Fagin's in jeans and an open-necked shirt. Alec, of course, arrived in his pinstripe and bowler hat. Babs, an old friend and my former landlady in Brighton, and the photograper Miki Slingsby were regulars at Fagin's, and the evenings spent hanging out over a chicken Kiev with such friends were among my happiest. I was still blissfully poor and money had not yet affected me.

Gradually, I started spending more of my evenings at a different kitchen and my life inexorably changed. Howard Marks had introduced me to Graham Plinston and, in addition to collecting suitcases of hashish from various European airports for him, I started handling Graham's accounts. Graham had a Victorian house in Shirland Road, near Maida Vale Tube station. The house was large but extraordinarily untidy and the only place to get comfortable was the kitchen. Graham's girlfriend Mandy, a tall, sweet-natured blonde, was a dedicated shopper and, like many dope dealers' chicks, was devoted to the art of conspicuous consumption. The house was filled with the results of her various expeditions to the West End and every room had piles of unworn dresses and unopened carrier bags from London's more fashionable stores. Mandy made occasional attempts to impose order on the chaos but Graham was equally untidy and every room also contained piles of the carpets he brought back from his trips to the Middle East. As a result, everyone lived around the kitchen table.

The house was often shared with Mandy's parents. After a lifetime in the Colonial Service, her father had retired as governor general of some South Pacific atoll and had bought a home on Alderney, one of the Channel Islands. Whenever they got bored with island life, which was often, they would stay with Graham and Mandy at Shirland Road. They also liked to visit because of Sam, Graham and Mandy's two-year-old son.

If Tony Soprano's kitchen, in the American TV series, epitomises Home Depot chic, Graham's kitchen was Danish Modern. Everything was built from varnished pine by Eddie, our local handyman, and every surface gleamed with the same monotonous golden hues. Mandy's mother would spend all day beside the sink or at the stove, cooking and baking. She chatted incessantly with Mandy, who spent her time hopefully moving piles of junk from one surface to another in a fruitless attempt to tidy up. Her father would sit at the kitchen table with Graham and me, smoking his pipe and reading the *Daily Telegraph*, while Sam spread his toys all over the floor, climbed on our knees or crawled over the table, leaving a trail of sticky fingers and half-digested food across our paperwork.

Mandy's parents came from an entirely different world and were quite oblivious to the nature of our work. The phone rang constantly and Graham would conduct none too subtle conversations with Ernie in California, Howard in Oxford or Big Dave in Afghanistan. Graham's various dealers would join us at the kitchen table to give their reports on market conditions around the country, or sometimes to deliver great wads of cash, which Sam would gleefully attack and scatter among his toys. Meanwhile, I would have pages of accounts, with their neatly ruled columns of debit and credit, spread over the kitchen table as I tried to tally kilos of hash imported with kilos sold. Thick bricks of £20 notes, tightly bound with rubber bands, were stacked among the pots and pans near the sink, and Rizla rolling papers littered the table among the coffee mugs and sticky, half-eaten jars of Gerber macaroni-and-chicken purée for toddlers. Mandy's father would push a pile of banknotes aside to empty his pipe in the ashtray while his wife debated which dress to wear for the Queen's garden party the following week.

'Sam, put that money down!' Mandy yelled. 'Get it out of your mouth!'

'Kent don't look like they've got any decent batsmen this year,' grumbled her father, a cricket fanatic, as he folded the paper. 'If Cowdrey can't pull them round I don't fancy our chances for next season.'

Graham replaced the phone in its cradle and turned to me. 'Big Dave says he's got a load of primo sitting in the warehouse but he thinks there are political problems brewing. Either the Pashtuns will revolt or the Russians will invade.'

'I can't wear the blue one again. I wore it last time we went to the Palace.'

'Come on, Mummy, let's go shopping and get you something spiffy. Something to make Prince Philip want to pinch your bottom!'

'Maybe Big Dave should truck it to Karachi and have Shemsi fly it from there,' I suggested.

'Bloody rain again,' said the dad, staring out the kitchen window. 'There goes my afternoon at Lord's.'

'No,' Graham replied, 'Shemsi will just want to increase his cut. He's already getting too greedy.'

'Oh, Graham,' Mandy wailed, 'Sam's eating the money again. Can't you keep it all somewhere else?'

Mandy was always trying to persuade me to bring Jude to the house. 'I love the way she dresses. She's so clever. We could go shopping together and she could give me all the gossip on the Beatles.'

Jude walked past the Beatles' Apple office in Savile Row on her way to work every morning and one day was astounded to see 'Hey Jude' in large letters scrawled across the pristine white front of the building. For a long time, she was convinced the Fab Four were sending her a message and Mandy continued to believe that Jude had a special relationship with the band.

But Jude seldom joined me at Shirland Road. Although she found Mandy entertaining company and a generous friend, Jude was too independent-minded for Graham's world, where chicks were expected to be ornamental but subservient. She preferred working two jobs and earning her own cash.

'There's too much money there,' she complained, 'and it's all dirty.'

'That's because Sam keeps playing with it,' I joked. 'He sticks it down his nappies.'

Jude disapproved of my deepening involvement with dope smuggling and she left me for someone more stable soon afterwards. I stayed on at Graham's kitchen table and counted the money.

* * *

I also sat at Ernie's kitchen table and helped him count his money after an especially busy season in the summer of 1982. There were a lot of investors and, even without the endless bickering and distrust, the accounting had become extremely complex. My professional training was sorely needed.

At that time, Ernie had a large mansion on the beach at Malibu and we sat at the kitchen table for several weeks just trying to calculate how much money had been made and who should get how much. When I had completed the numbers, my report showed that the enterprise had grossed 40 million dollars, in cash. Even by Ernie's standards, that was considered to be 'a bunch'.

Mark, one of Ernie's distributors in Seattle, had a million dollars of Ernie's money and kept phoning to ask what he should do with it. Ernie was too busy at the time to deal with it and kept telling Mark to sit on it. Ernie had just got hold of a prototype WaveRunner jet-ski and most of his free time was spent riding it off the Malibu shore. In the end, Ernie refused even to take Mark's phone calls and told me, 'Tell him to just stick it in a box and forget about it. We'll deal with it later.'

Mark was understandably uncomfortable having a million dollars of somebody else's money just lying around his house. Eventually, he rented a Learjet and flew to Malibu to deliver it in person. Mark and his friend carried a wooden crate into the house and asked Ernie where he wanted it. Ernie glanced up from the football game he was watching on TV and said, 'Oh, anywhere's fine, man. There. Stick it next to that couch.' He was on the phone to his bookie and had a lot of money riding on the game – less than a million, it must be said, but potential new money is always more exciting than boring old money. Ernie lived for the latest roll of the dice.

Mark was taken down to the beach to inspect the WaveRunner and was given a hair-raising ride through the surf behind Ernie. He got the royal treatment but I could tell that he was upset that Ernie was displaying no interest in the money. He never counted it, never even looked at it. When Mark returned to Seattle the following evening, the box was in the same position and hadn't been moved or opened. It remained there for the rest of the summer; for all I know, it sat there for years afterwards.

Unfortunately, that story was told many years later in a South Florida courtroom and, from that moment onwards, our fate was sealed. The jury had struggled with the prosecution's complicated arguments about predicate acts and the other legal niceties upon which they were building their racketeering and conspiracy charges. It was obvious that the jury had trouble understanding exactly what we were being charged with. However, once Mark told the story about the box with a million dollars, their attitude changed. Everyone can picture a box with a million dollars of cash in it.

Under questioning by the prosecutor, Mark described phoning Ernie to collect the money and how Ernie was always too busy. That was something the jury could easily grasp. These guys had so much money that they couldn't even be bothered to get off their backsides and collect a box with a million dollars in it! They must be guilty!

I don't know all the reasons why Mark became a prosecution witness but I am sure that part of his motivation was no more complex than hurt feelings. It's not every day that you give somebody a million dollars in cash. It is only human to expect some expression of pleasure and gratitude from the recipient. Ernie's offhand 'Oh, stick it over there' eventually cost him a prison sentence of 40 years.

I was aware of Mark's hurt feelings during his visit, which was why I was careful that he didn't see our other box while he stayed in the Malibu house. There was a large antique oak trunk beside the front door. About four feet high and five feet long, it had originally been a New England linen chest. Ernie called it 'the petty-cash box' and it was filled with bundles of money to the tune of several thousand.

Whenever anybody needed money for shopping 'or whatever', they would simply reach in and help themselves before leaving the house. Whenever the level of cash fell, we would simply tip in another suitcase.

Another of Ernie's partners, this one from San Francisco, visited the house while I was there. Jeffrey had been arguing with Ernie for weeks about the accounts. He was convinced that he was owed about $500,000 more than Ernie had paid him and the dispute was becoming increasingly acrimonious, which is always bad for business. Jeffrey controlled the northern West Coast business, including Hawaii. Ernie invited him to visit so that I could go over the numbers with him and, as a gesture of friendship, offered to pick him up at LA airport.

'Let's do it in style and mess with his head,' Ernie said. Val Johnson drove us to a Cadillac dealership and Ernie bought a brand-new 1982 Fleetwood Limousine for about $28,000. At LAX, I parked the limo outside the terminal and sat in the driver's seat while Ernie collected Jeffrey at the gate. The two of them reclined in the back seat smoking joints and drinking Jack Daniel's from a crystal decanter while I drove us up the Pacific Coast Highway to Malibu. The new Fleetwood Mac album, *Mirage*, was playing on the eight-track and, as I watched Jeffrey and Ernie in the rear-view mirror, Stevie Nicks sang about eyes and lies unfurling.

Jeffrey was very impressed and admired the deep black gloss of the car's bodywork when we eventually arrived at the house. 'I love the car, Ernie,' he said. 'That's the most amazing ride I've ever had.'

Ernie turned to me and said, 'Give him the keys.' Putting his arm around Jeffrey, he said, 'She's all yours. All the papers are in the glove compartment. Tomorrow you're going to have the smoothest ride back to San Francisco.'

That was the end of that. Jeffrey dismissed the dispute over the half-million as not worth pursuing. 'We've all made plenty, why sweat it?' he said. He spent the rest of his visit playing with Ernie on the WaveRunner. Ernie, however, was not going to give *that* new toy away.

'See?' he said the next day as we watched Jeffrey head north in his new Fleetwood limo. 'I've just made half a million and it didn't even cost me thirty grand.' Having been born rich, Ernie understood money and how to use it in ways the rest of us would never master. He understood the psychology of wealth.

I visited Jeffrey a few months later at his mansion on San Francisco's Nob Hill. He'd got rid of the car by then but was still touched by Ernie's gesture and was worried that he might appear ungrateful. As he explained, a Cadillac limo is probably the worst car in the world to own in San Francisco. Not only was it too long to fit in the garage of his house and impossible to park in the street but, because of its long wheelbase, he was always getting stuck at the tops of the city's many steep hills. Jeffrey was constantly finding himself in the humiliating position of being unable to move while the front and rear wheels lost traction with the road and the car balanced on its central chassis at the summit. 'The only way I could move was to get a bunch of jeering tourists from a trolley car to push down on the trunk so I could rev the back wheels to shoot me forward. Man, you should have seen the sparks fly as I scraped over the summit! I could have killed somebody.'

Jeffrey was a very refined person, so the idea of being humiliated in front of a group of Midwestern tourists was more than he could bear. 'So I gave it to one of my people in Oakland. There're no hills there and anyway he's black, so he loves it.'

'There's no there there either,' I couldn't stop myself from saying, and Jeffrey gave me one of those looks that Americans reserve for British 'humor'.

Jeffrey had introduced me to his attorney when I first arrived in America. I was an international fugitive at the time and it seemed only prudent to have a lawyer. Don represented several top dope dealers in the Bay Area and soon became a close friend. With his other clients, we would go for meals in fashionable San Francisco restaurants and try to outdo each other in our extravagant displays of wealth. It was easy for the sommelier to anticipate our choice of wine because it would always be the most expensive bottle on the menu. If he had another bottle, not on the menu but more expensive, we would have a few of those instead. Anything less than a 50 per cent tip was regarded as being cheap and everything, of course, was paid for in cash.

This is not a criticism of American flash. Exactly the same desperate display of prosperity was made by English dope dealers when they had unlimited money. Nor, I must confess, was I any different. Throughout the '70s and '80s, in Europe and the USA, I was as guilty as the others of squandering my money in ridiculously expensive restaurants. All I can say in my defence is that I really do enjoy sitting at a good table and eating too much rich food and good wine.

When I look back on those years, it is not the mindless squandering of money in which we all indulged that I regret. The silly money all went back into the economy and permitted waiters to save for their first mortgage deposit or car salesmen to complete their MBAs. What I feel guilty about is all the bottles of Margaux, Lynch Bages and Chateau d'Yquem that were wasted on wasted louts. After all the years those precious bottles of Bordeaux's noble heritage had been carefully tended and guarded, they were knocked back with no more appreciation than if they had been bottles of lager. The $500 in cash per bottle can always be replaced but those are bottles that we will never see again and, more importantly, never drink again. They cannot be replaced.

So, as a racketeer, I did experience the rock-star, dope-dealer, VIP-lounge, money-no-object lifestyle for a short while. Unfortunately, it is very difficult to write about because, quite frankly, it is very boring. The first time you do any crazy extravagant thing, it is very exciting, exactly how you imagined it to be in all your wildest fantasies. Afterwards, once you have experienced that first heady taste, everything else is an anticlimax. What was once unimaginably exotic quickly becomes the norm and rapidly becomes boring unless it can be surpassed. Flying first class instead of coach or staying in large hotel suites instead of regular rooms simply becomes standard and loses its fun – until you can no longer afford it.

In many ways, new money, like drugs, is the opposite of sex. The first time you have a thousand or so dollars in your pocket and realise you can spend it on whatever crazy thing takes your fancy, or the first time you get a cocaine rush, are moments you will never forget and pleasures that you can never repeat, however often you may try. The first few times I had sex, however, were generally messy, awkward and embarrassing. Unlike drugs and sudden money, sex is an acquired pleasure that simply gets better the longer you practise it. The first wad of solid cash and the first heroin buzz, though never to be forgotten, pale when compared with the joys of repeated sex with someone you love.

I hate to sound trite but once you can buy whatever you want, there is no pleasure left, just a hunger that can never be assuaged. I've known many very rich people in my life and few of them have been happy.

I had a rather morose friend at college who came from an extremely wealthy and cultured background. He was consumed with guilt about his incredible fortune and tried to disguise his wealth by being mean and cheap. In the left-wing, liberal environment of Sussex University in the '60s, Dave worried constantly about money.

'What's up with Dave?' somebody might ask. 'He's looking more gloomy than usual today.'

'Didn't you hear? One of his aunts died last week.'

'Oh, were they close?'

'No, he's never met her. She lived in New York.'

'So why the gloom?'

'She left him a million dollars in her will and he doesn't know what to do with it.'

Many wealthy people I've known have been like that, especially those who inherited their wealth. Their fortune is a burden that weighs upon them constantly. In addition to the guilt they feel for having it, they are also tortured by the fear of losing it, and they worry that people only like them for their money. Unlike dope dealers or self-made millionaires, who put all their positive energy into making money and making that money grow, those who inherit money often do the opposite. Their energy goes in other, negative directions and they worry endlessly about their investments and the rising cost of living. They are always looking for deals and can quote the price of everything.

Of course, sudden wealth can be just as destructive as inherited wealth. My sister Natasha has almost always been poor. She leads one of the richest and happiest of lives but she has never been cursed with money, except just once. In the late '70s, she sailed a yacht loaded with pot from Morocco to Scotland and made a large amount of money. Natasha came to visit us at Campione d'Italia to ask for advice about investing her new fortune. When I collected her at Lugano railway station, I could tell she had changed. She still looked scruffy and unkempt but she was dishevelled now in expensive clothes. More to the point, her radiant smile and infectious cheerfulness had gone. Her optimistic recklessness had been replaced with an apprehensive vigilance and I soon learned that she had quarrelled with most of her friends. She did not listen to any of my advice and was suspicious of my motives. She stayed with us for only a few awkward days and after she left we lost all contact for several months.

The next time Natasha and I met was at my best friend Miki's house in Hampstead. We all went down to the pub and Natasha asked if I could lend her a fiver to buy the next round of beer. 'I'm totally broke,' she told me happily.

'What happened to all your money?' I asked.

'Oh, I don't know. I just blew it all,' she smiled. 'In the end, I just wanted to get rid of it. I feel much better now.'

And indeed she did look much better, back to her old carefree self. She has remained happily poor ever since.

Howard, on the other hand, positively thrives on money and the more he made, the more he used. Howard liked money not for its own sake but in order to spend it – not quietly and discreetly but conspicuously and as lavishly as possible. He had an almost mystical approach to money and loved the energy it demanded as well as the energy it created. Howard believed that to keep the rivers of money flowing you must allow it to pour and splash freely and that as soon as you tried to divert some of it or control the current, the stream would dry up and the flow go elsewhere. This is an easy philosophy to hold during the rainy season when the river is in full flood. But during the dry season, it takes an act of faith to hold those sluice gates open and not try to conserve a little. That was the tension that he most enjoyed, spending those last few dollars – taking the giant risk – and then, just at the last moment, generating a new gush and a new flood. Howard had to live up to his image of fabulous and careless wealth, even when he was broke. He believed money was drawn to money and that as long as rich people thought he was also rich, they would be attracted to him.

Howard was never interested in saving or hoarding money, not even for his children. He genuinely thinks that inherited wealth is bad for the recipient and that the accumulation of wealth blunts 'the hunger'. Howard always fought to maintain the vitality and alertness that are part of the hunger and he believes that rich children grow up spoiled and ill-equipped for the battle of life. He even worried that his business partners, if they became rich and successful, would become soft and careless, so he would encourage everybody to gamble their all on the next roll of the dice.

That was why I never made any money as a racketeer. Whenever I managed to accumulate any money, Howard would always encourage me to squander it recklessly – not that I offered much resistance. The end result was that when I was finally arrested, after some 20-odd years as an international money launderer, I had not a penny to my name. The federal agents were incredulous and, I sensed, even embarrassed on my behalf. I had the FBI, the DEA and the IRS all combing through my house, my computer and my bank records looking for hidden wealth, until they were finally forced to concede it didn't exist. The only reason they did not seize my house was that it belonged to the bank. It was extremely humiliating. I was almost tempted to invent secret millions hidden in the Cayman Islands, if only to regain my self-respect and professional stature. My wife suggested, persuasively, that this would not be a good idea.

Nonetheless, after my impressive life of crime, it was most embarrassing to have so little to show for it. It didn't just make me look bad, it made the federal agents look bad also. On the one hand, they described me to the judge as a powerful international financier with bank accounts and shadowy corporations all over the world. On the other hand, they had to concede that I had no assets with which to actually hire an attorney. They raised no objection when the judge appointed the public defender to represent me but they looked embarrassed and I shared their pain. As far as I could tell, the public defender appointed to my case had handled few, if any, racketeering cases before and preferred making plea bargains to going to trial. As with most things in life, you get what you pay for, but at least I didn't have to pay out hundreds of thousands of dollars in legal fees like my co-defendants.

Even worse humiliations lay in store following my release from prison in 1990. A BBC camera crew arranged a visit to my house in order to interview me about my racketeering background and life in an American jail – the usual sort of stuff. When they arrived at the house, they were horrified at what they saw and made no effort to disguise their disappointment. 'This doesn't look like a drug lord's compound,' they grumbled. 'We expected something a little more palatial.'

'I was living undercover,' I offered shamefacedly, but the producer still looked cross and betrayed.

'We'll have to shoot it outdoors, in the garden,' she decided. 'At least we can use the pool.'

'And the palm trees,' said the cameraman. 'Look, there's bloody coconuts on that one. We can use that for the opening shot.'

The producer was somewhat reassured but still unhappy. This was obviously not how the assignment had been described to her back in London. As my wife and awkward teenage daughters watched from the sidelines, the suburban banality of my life became apparent. It was obvious that she was not going to be hobnobbing with any jet-setting celebrities while sipping an exotic rum drink with an umbrella in it.

'Can't you look a little more languid?' she snapped at me. I was confused because she had asked me to change out of my jeans and Guinness T-shirt into something 'more Miami Vice' and I was trying to look sinister.

Eventually, by conducting the interview beneath a palm tree on the far side of the swimming pool and by placing the camera in the neighbour's garden in order to make a longer shot, they were able to create an acceptable facsimile of an exotically degenerate racketeer's retreat. Certainly, I thought, based on my own memories of grey, wet English suburbs, my little tropical garden would look positively sybaritic to the cold British viewers.

Had Howard not persuaded me to throw away my ill-gotten gains on the next roll of the dice, I would have presented a far more credible gangster when I was finally exposed to the gaze of the BBC audience. As it was, in my wardrobe from Sears, I merely looked like a languidly sinister minor hood.

The one time I did manage to accumulate any capital, about $150,000, I gave it to my friend Juan Dejesus to invest. Juan and I had known each other since the early '70s but nevertheless I never again saw my investment. It was not that Juan would steal other people's wealth; he simply believed that he was better qualified to look after it than they were. In my case, he knew I was clueless about money and quite likely to do something foolish if he ever gave it back to me. By holding onto it, he was doing me a favour and protecting my interest.

It was in an effort to get my money back that I first moved to Miami in 1986. Juan had invested my money in a smoked-salmon factory in a questionable neighbourhood populated by hookers and crack dealers. The last time I heard from Juan, he was living on the border of Suriname and Guyana, and he assured me that my investment in a local diamond mine looked extremely promising.

While Howard was a gambler in the philosophical sense, Ernie was a gambler in the real sense. That was the 'other business' that he would leave California to attend to. He loved the casinos of Nevada and whenever we visited we were always treated to luxury suites and given the royal treatment by the management. Ernie was always convinced that he was a serious and successful gambler but I have sat and watched him lose hundreds of thousands of dollars in one sitting at the craps table. But he ignores those evenings and remembers only the successes. The problem was that Ernie always had so much money that it was impossible to tell whether he was winning or losing – and in many ways it was a meaningless question. Nevertheless, the warm reception we always received when we entered the casinos leads me to suspect that Ernie was good for business and his gambling successes were largely in his own head. The only time I have seen a pit boss smile was when Ernie sat down at a table. When he wasn't in the casino, Ernie bet on sports games. His bookie was available on the phone 24 hours a day, every day. He lived in a large house in Bel Air and always drove the latest model Mercedes. He was very fond of Ernie.

I have never been interested in gambling, even though I have spent many hours in casinos. I feel extremely upset when I lose money and think of all the better things I could have spent it on. What's more, I get very little pleasure when I win. Somehow, it doesn't seem like real money. Back in the '70s, Michael Durani was a friend of the management of the Clermont Club in Berkeley Square. This was where Saudi princes and English aristocrats came to squander their fortunes at the card tables. Michael, like me, was not particularly interested in gambling but he had an arrangement whereby the club would front him a couple of thousand pounds so that he could play the tables. At the end of the evening, he would return the initial stake and all his winnings. We would simply have enjoyed an amusing evening, a free meal and some decent champagne at no cost. What was interesting was that we usually won. We were relaxed and had no emotion invested in our play, and somehow that attracted a run of good luck. Had we been worried about our money, we would have played differently. That was why the club fronted us. We generated a nice atmosphere that encouraged other people to sit at the tables and join the play.

As a professional money launderer, I was, of course, obliged to spend a considerable amount of my time in casinos. There was a very large casino in Campione and business would often take me to Monte Carlo. Because I am not a gambler, I could enjoy watching the people and the naked display of their emotions as they moved around the tables. Casinos are wonderful places to observe the human comedy in the raw.

For a while, before the laws were tightened, we were able to use the Nevada casinos for laundering cash. We would simply purchase a few hundred thousand dollars' worth of chips and then trade them back after a couple of hours for a cashier's cheque worth 5 per cent less than our original purchase. Eventually, that loophole was closed, but I continued to visit the casinos, if only to accompany Ernie on his 'other business'.

In the '80s, however, I stayed at the casinos for more mundane reasons. We were living in Santa Cruz and liked to take the children skiing during the winter. Because most people cannot resist a flutter when they are in a casino, the prices of rooms, food and especially drink were extremely low, as an incitement to get visitors inside the casinos. Jude, the children and I would spend a wonderful day on the ski slopes and then return to the casino in the evening for a delicious meal and a large, comfortable room. For non-gamblers, it was the perfect deal!

I was a fugitive at that time and my cover was editing a monthly newsletter called *The Offshore Banking Report*, aimed, obviously, at people with money. The newsletter was published monthly and cost $250 for a 12-month subscription. I had about 700 or so subscribers and published 24 issues before the Internal Revenue Service closed me down. Each month, I would focus on a different tax haven or banking centre around the globe. I gave my readers excellent value for money. I had visited all these places and actually conducted business there. I knew the lawyers and I knew the banking regulations and my subscribers loved it. Initially, I placed small ads in the *Wall Street Journal* and *The Economist*. I drew my own cartoon of three swarthy Mafia types under the heading 'It's not just for the bad guys'. I also advertised in various US legal journals and indeed most of my subscribers were attorneys. However, the big surprise was to discover that the second-biggest class of subscribers was dentists from the Midwest. I very quickly switched my marketing efforts to regional issues of the American Dental Association magazine.

Obviously, the attorneys who subscribed were advising clients, using the information I provided at $20 a month for $200 an hour. The dentists, however, were representing themselves. Certainly in America, dentists do make a lot of money and consequently live in large houses and drive fancy cars. I spoke to several dentists and they explained that, while they made a great deal, they had never received any training on how to handle their cash. Additionally, though this is pure speculation, I would think that spending the best part of your day staring into 'open-oral-orifice situations' (as one Californian dentist described it) leads to a lot of daydreaming: 'Why don't I take the money and move to the Caribbean?'

Tom Sunde told me that he was the son of a dentist. 'That's what my old man did,' he confided to me, when we were sitting in a Scottish castle designing Norwegian firewater labels. 'He took off for the Bahamas with his hygienist when I was 12 years old. It's such a boring job, man, looking into people's fucking mouths all day. That's how dentists stay sane, thinking about money and tits while they're drilling away.'

Tom's other theory about dentists was that, as a profession, they were in the best position for admiring the female cleavage. 'Think about it, man,' he would explain. 'You're staring down their fucking dresses all day long. Just looking at all those tits – it's got to make you horny.' According to Tom, this daily exposure to female charms was why dentists, as a profession, had the highest divorce rate in the country. (They also have a very high suicide rate, although I'm sure this has nothing to do with cleavage exposure.) Rich people contemplating a divorce tend to hide their assets from their spouse in advance, and moving it offshore to a secret tax haven is one of the best methods. That is the major reason, I think, that so many dentists subscribed to my newsletter.

In 1984, I had been happily publishing my newsletter for a couple of years and paying corporate taxes through my company, LaneHouse Publications, when I received a visit from my local IRS agent. He was very nice and he handed me back my tax return. 'We didn't audit you this year,' he said, 'because your tax return seems to match all your financial records.' He paused, gave me that look that only federal officials and casino pit bosses can give and then he said, 'We will audit you next year and the first thing we will request is your subscriber list.'

He didn't know I was just a little guy with zero legal backing. Had he known I was an illegal immigrant and a fugitive, he could have crushed me on the spot. However, I suspect that he didn't want to get into a First and Fourth Amendment legal argument about invasion of privacy, so he was giving me a warning. I'm a big believer in warnings. Warnings are good and I took this particular one to heart.

I sent the following letter to all my subscribers:

> This is the final issue of *The Offshore Banking Report*. After mailing this issue, I will destroy the subscriber list on my computer. I will have no further way of contacting you, unless you contact me first. If you still have a prepaid subscription, I apologise. You have my address if you wish to ask for a refund.

None of them ever asked for their money back.

It was 1984 when I retired from the offshore banking business and I assumed until recently that the world had changed and my knowledge of Swiss banks and Liechtenstein trusts had become long out of date in the subsequent years. I was therefore pleasantly surprised to discover a US Senate report dated 17 July 2008 and entitled *Tax Haven Banks and US Tax Compliance* that could have been lifted from the pages of *The Offshore Banking Report*. In my newsletter, I had described how to incorporate in Liechtenstein and how to use the corporation's bearer shares to control numbered accounts at Swiss banks like the Union Bank of Switzerland (UBS) or the Swiss Bank Corporation (SBC), to manipulate assets, own property or conduct business anywhere in the world. Twenty-four years later, according to the Senate report, nothing had changed and all my old practices and suggestions were still valid in the twenty-first century.

Ironically, the report (as well as a recent Florida grand jury indictment) described how Swiss banks target wealthy clients by courting them at prestigious cultural events such as Art Basel Miami Beach. UBS actually sponsors Art Basel and in 2006, when I was director of a local wine appreciation programme, I solicited UBS to donate free Swiss, French and German wine for an event I organised called The Wines of Basel. Finally, two of my greatest lifelong interests were brought together – fine wine and international finance.

I do not believe that money is the root of all evil, rather the contrary; lack of money is far more pernicious. However, I have certainly learned that illegal money has a corrosive effect on everything it touches.

Our 1960s dope-smuggling enterprises began with the 'love and peace' premise that the more people smoked dope the more relaxed and gentle the world would become. As we started making money from smuggling, however, the nature of the business changed. Today, in the twenty-first century, the drug business causes almost as much suffering and death as religion.

Just as Natasha discovered, sudden wealth changes your perception of the world and your relationships to other people. Its effects are corrupting. You quickly lose contact with the everyday concerns and values of people outside the business. You get used to solving problems by buying your way out. 'Everybody has their price' becomes a deep-seated mantra. There is also an arrogance that comes with easy money, an arrogance that spills over into your personal life, making friendships hard to maintain. There came a point in my life when I could have afforded to eat my meals at Fagin's Kitchen every night of the week if I had so wished, but all my old friends were no longer in touch and I would have had to eat alone.

Not only is easy money corrupting, it is also addictive. After you have made a few thousand pounds for a few hours of easy work, it is very hard to return to a regular job, whether you earn five, ten or twenty-five quid an hour. Most people never manage the transition and remain hopelessly addicted to the promise of easy money. Even as their probation officer forces them to return to normal life, they remain always alert to the possibilities of a quick, easy deal. That's the real reason why so few dope dealers are ever able to rejoin the regular workforce. I was lucky – I had a wife who promised to kill me if I even thought about returning to a life of crime – but most people are not blessed with such good fortune.

And that's a pity, because, as I can testify, crime is not necessarily worth the trouble. As embarrassing as it is, I have to accept the fact that I've made much more money as an ordinary employee than in all my years as a racketeer.

But still, I do miss travelling first class!

1|2

DRUGS AND POLITICS

As previously noted, it was not the money that attracted me to this life of crime, it was the drugs.

English people can be divided into two groups, Francophiles and Francophobes. For whatever reason, I have always been one of the former. From a young age, I have loved French literature, French food and French wine. French music, of course, has always been bad and, since the arrival of Johnny Hallyday in the early '60s, has become truly insufferable.

My parents sent me on school exchange visits to France from the age of about 13 and I quickly developed a fascination with and love for all things French. It may have been no more complex than the fact that Hervé, my exchange pal, had two beautiful sisters, Chantal and Simone, with both of whom I was in love. Possibly, it was because I once saw his equally beautiful aunt stepping out of her shower, naked. Whatever the reason, I fell in love with France.

When I was around 16, my girlfriend Sue introduced me to Baudelaire's *Les Fleurs du Mal* and Rimbaud's *Une Saison en Enfer*, both of which celebrated the pleasures of hashish. I soon discovered Théophile Gautier and his Hashish Eaters' Club and quickly became obsessed with French nineteenth-century literature, a passion that has continued to this day. I have even published a book on Marcel Proust, who consumed a wider variety and quantity of drugs than any other major literary figure. Along with a curiosity about hashish, I developed a fascination with absinthe, which was the subject of so many French poems and paintings. I also loved Coleridge's 'Kubla Khan', which he reportedly wrote under the influence of opium.

It was in Paris that I had my first taste of hashish. Hervé's elder brother, Henri, would take the two of us by train from Versailles, where they lived, to the narrow, cobbled streets of the Left Bank. The kebab sellers had not yet taken over St-Michel in the early '60s and the Rue de la Huchette was still romantic and mysterious. Henri, who was a student at the Sorbonne, would huddle in a dark corner to make his purchase and then the three of us would descend the stone steps of the quays and sit beside the Seine, watching the dark river flow past while we passed the pipe back and forth. With a well-thumbed copy of Camus protruding from the pocket of his black leather jacket, his five-o'clock shadow and his nonchalant sophistication, Henri remained my hero for many years.

Opium, absinthe, hashish – I wanted to taste it all and to escape the narrow, middle-class confines of my miserable, boring, suburban, bourgeois existence. I was a horrible teenager and I shudder when I think what my poor parents had to suffer. During the day, I was forced to wear the brightly coloured school uniform of Queen Elizabeth's Grammar School – a dark-blue blazer with yellow piping and the Queen's coat of arms in gold, a peaked cap and grey flannel trousers. But as soon as I was home again, I would change into my other uniform of black sunglasses, black polo-neck sweater, black plastic jacket (I could not afford the leather one I dreamed of), black jeans and cowboy boots. I thought I looked pretty cool and that all the people who made fun of me, starting with my family, were simply demonstrating their pathetic bourgeois prejudices.

I would ride my bicycle through the gloomy streets of Finchley all the way to Hampstead and, having hidden it around the corner, I'd casually saunter into one of the many coffee bars where the existentialists hung out. The guys all had real leather jackets and the girls had long silken hair, short skirts and long legs in black stockings. They arrived in MG convertibles with the hoods down and they smoked Gauloises cigarettes. I dreamed hopelessly of having one of those girls lean her head on my shoulder while I explained the theories of Jean-Paul Sartre between puffs of my Gauloise.

After indulging my fantasies for about an hour, I would glance at my watch, as though remembering a gallery opening I was expected to attend, and saunter out into the night. 'Who is that tall, dark-haired man who sits all alone?' I imagined the girls asking each other with a hint of a French accent. 'He seems to conceal some secret sorrow. There is a romantic mystery about him that I would like to explore.' Back around the corner, I would climb onto my bicycle and pedal furiously back to Barnet in a desperate effort to meet my parents' midnight curfew.

I knew that somewhere in the coffee bars of Hampstead it was possible to get hold of hashish and opium, if not absinthe, but I was never able to find a source. It is hard to project a cool hipster image on a bicycle. I therefore took advantage of a school adventure holiday to Morocco in 1962 in order to develop my own source of hash. With a couple of masters and some old boys down from university, about ten of us drove across France and Spain in an old Bedford van to take the ferry to Tangier. We spent three weeks touring Morocco, driving as far south as Casablanca, then through Marrakesh, over the Atlas Mountains and out into the desert. We returned to Tangier via Rabat.

I became friends with one of the old boys whom I'd known slightly when he was a year ahead of me in the sixth form and who was already studying philosophy at university. Each evening, we would leave the others at the camp and hitch-hike or walk to the nearest town, where we would spend the night wandering around the medina, drinking beer and smoking dope. Looking back, I cannot believe that no harm came to us. One morning, we were so wasted we woke up on the lawn of Barbara Hutton's house in Tangier. Other nights were spent in a café with William Burroughs and his friends. Burroughs' taste for good-looking young boys was well known but we emerged unscathed and even remained in contact with him for several years.

The exotic sounds, smells and sights that I discovered on that first trip to Morocco were so different from anything that I had dreamed of in England that I became a passionate orientalist. I hitch-hiked to the Middle East whenever I had the chance. For many years, I flirted with Islam and I read everything by and about Richard Burton, the

Victorian explorer who visited Mecca in disguise. I would sit in my bedroom at home in Barnet smoking hashish and reading Sufi poems while listening to Arab music on my mono LP player. My mother had a housecleaner once or twice a week, who also cleaned other houses in the neighbourhood. Through the local kids' grapevine, I heard her reports of my strange behaviour. 'He's a right weird one, that eldest son,' she would tell people. 'Always wears those sunglasses, even at night, and he sits in his room with the door locked and funny music playing.' She'd give a knowing sniff. 'Smoking those foreign cigarettes and doing God knows what strange things.'

By the time I started university in 1965, I had various contacts for buying hashish in Hampstead and I immediately located and became friends with all the other first-year dope smokers at Sussex. Between us, we always had a source of hash and would pool our money for a trip to London to maintain our supplies. That's how most people first got involved in dope dealing: purchasing extra from their supplier so that they could sell to their friends and keep some for themselves. However, my main interest during my first year was turning on the world to LSD.

Before attending university, I had spent several months hitch-hiking around North America with my school friend Charles. Armed with a well-thumbed copy of Jack Kerouac's *On the Road*, we headed for San Francisco, the home of the Beats.

William Burroughs had given me a note of introduction to the poet Lawrence Ferlinghetti, who owned City Lights bookstore on North Beach. For a young, rebellious, drug-obsessed English schoolboy, City Lights in the mid-'60s was as close to heaven as it's possible to get. Ferlinghetti was extremely generous and not only introduced us to everybody but also took an interest in our education, advised us on books to read and gave us the run of his shop. It was Ferlinghetti who encouraged us to enrol in a summer psychology course at the University of California, Berkeley.

With our Beatle haircuts and English accents, Charles and I quickly acquired two girlfriends, both from New York and both attending the psychology course. In addition to being attractive girls with healthy and unselfconscious appetites for sex and drugs, Cindy and Barbara also owned a car, a '58 Chevy, which they allowed us to drive. Charles and I could not believe our good fortune. It was as though we had woken up and found ourselves in the middle of a Beach Boys song. Our English school friends would never recognise us now!

Unable to grow a beard like Charles, I used Cindy's mascara to extend and enhance my sideburns. My friends were too solicitous of my feelings to explain that, when we went dancing in San Francisco's many jazz clubs, my sweat made the mascara streak until it dripped off my chin. Happily unaware of this, I revelled in my cool hipster image.

On the first morning of class, the professor gave us all some blotting-paper tabs containing LSD. He was an old friend of Timothy Leary and had recently returned from visiting him in Millbrook, NY. Leary had suggested turning on the class as a way to prepare them for the rigours of the course. At lunchtime, Cindy, Barbara, Charles and I all jumped into the Chevy and headed for Muir Beach to sample the acid. It was my first visit to a nudist beach, the sun was shining, the views were beautiful and the sight of so many naked women made my head spin. My first LSD experience was something I will never forget. I've had lots of acid trips since then but nothing ever compared to the beauty of that day. I believed I was in total harmony with the universe and I finally felt at peace with God. With hindsight, of course, I realise that – with a '58 Chevy in the car park and a beautiful girlfriend lying naked beside me in the Californian sunshine – I hardly needed drugs or anything else to be at peace with God. But such is the ignorance of youth.

We didn't leave the beach until after midnight and none of us was ever the same again. We looked at each other as we returned slowly to the car and we knew that we were different.

'I know what,' said Cindy. 'Let's drive to Mexico.' Cindy came from a wealthy New York Jewish family and her brother was shooting a film in Acapulco. 'He'd love to see us. They always need extras,' she assured us. So we loaded up the Chevy that same night and headed south for the Mexican border as the sun rose. We never did return to class.

In 1966, Leary gave a speech in which he told his listeners why they should take LSD: 'Like every great religion of the past, we seek to find the divinity within and to express this revelation in a life of glorification and the worship of God. These ancient goals we define in the metaphor of the present: turn on, tune in, drop out.' I had anticipated him by almost three years and dropped out of Berkeley after less than a day.

Unlike in England at that time, pot was extremely easy to find in California and even easier to get hold of in Mexico. We floated down to Acapulco in a haze of pot smoke and descended into the town with the Rolling Stones' latest release, 'Satisfaction', blaring on the radio. Cindy's brother was delighted to see his sister but not to meet a couple of penniless, long-haired, stoned-out English proto-hippies. He had no need for extras and soon banned us from the set.

In order to survive, I got a job singing in a nightclub on the beach. The only song I knew the words to was Ray Charles's 'What'd I Say' and, being stoned and knowing no better, I just sang it over and over every night for a couple of weeks. To say that I knew the words is something of an exaggeration. I knew there was something about a red dress and possibly shaking that thing but, for the most part, I just kept yelling, 'Tell me what'd I say,' with the occasional 'yeah' thrown in until the musicians stopped playing.

Obviously, I had not been hired for my singing ability but because I was English, had long hair and the American tourists from the Midwest thought I was exotic. They all wanted their photographs taken with me. But being exotic will only take you so far. Eventually, the management could no longer stand listening to 'What'd I Say', the Mexican band all threatened to resign and my singing career came to an ignominious end.

In the meantime, Cindy had been badly stung by a jellyfish and we put her on a plane back to New York. Charles and Barbara were on the verge of breaking up and we had no money, so Charles and I decided to hitch-hike back to the US border.

We rode part of the way with a young couple from the US Embassy and they put us up for a few weeks at their apartment in Mexico City. At one of the parties they invited us to, I became friends with a then unknown South American writer and told him about our LSD experience. He was fascinated by our stories and invited us to join him on a visit to the jungles of Yucatán to taste the magic mushrooms at a Native American religious festival. Yucatán was completely isolated in those days and Cancún was not even on the government's drawing boards. My new friend had organised a whole group of us to drive through the jungle in Land Rovers towards the southern border with Guatemala and British Honduras.

We arrived at a bare hillside just as the sun was setting and joined thousands of indigenous people who had travelled on foot from all over Central America. There was a lot of singing and dancing and chanting, and the trip leader tried to explain the significance as best he was able. Eventually, we were all given a handful of various herbs and dried mushrooms, which we washed down with a bowl of vile-tasting tea. Then we lay back on the ground while the drugs took effect. I remember very little of that particular night; in my memory, it has merged with various other psychedelic experiences that I've had since. Vivid colours, sounds and smells all overlapped, my senses merged and I became one with the universe.

What I have never forgotten is the final effects of the drug, just before the sun rose. I was lying on my back on the bare earth feeling an irresistible urge to kill. I was surrounded by thousands of other people, also lying on their backs, and all I wanted was to stab them all with a large knife and rip their hearts out. I wanted to crack their ribs and tear the flesh from their bones. I wanted to sink my teeth into their throats and drink their blood. I felt an insatiable thirst for blood. But I could not move. As the sun rose swiftly above the jungle, I lay paralysed, unable to satisfy my lust to kill and destroy. But with the first touch of sun on my skin, the effects of the drug vanished, movement returned and all over the hillside people began to sit up and move around stiffly.

Driving back to Mexico City, feeling embarrassed and ashamed, I hesitantly told the others of my experience. Everyone had felt the same bloodlust and we had all shared the same murderous rage. My friend explained that thousands of people on the hillside would have had an identical experience. Had we not all been paralysed, there would have been a massacre. That was when I first learned that illicit drugs had a dark side.

It took several more months to hitch-hike back to New York for the plane home to England. It took more than a month just to get through the cruel and desolate deserts of Durango and Chihuahua to the border towns of Juárez and El Paso, where, you may recall, we spent a couple of months smuggling rum across the Rio Grande until we'd saved enough cash to move on. But the journey from Texas through the Deep South took even longer and was much worse than crossing the deserts of Mexico.

In 1965, the good folks of Louisiana and Alabama did not look kindly on long-haired troublemakers with funny accents. We were tossed into county jails several times and were lucky not to be lynched. We heard of several lynchings on our journey through Mississippi. Just the previous year, Klansmen had tied Charles Moore and Henry Dee to a tree and beaten them with sticks before throwing them into the Mississippi, where they drowned. A month after that, James Earl Chaney was murdered along with two other civil rights activists by a mob of Klansmen. Charles and I, as obvious 'outsiders' and 'pre-verts', were the constant subject of suspicious disapproval as we moved from one little Southern town to another. Unfriendly mobs would gather whenever we stopped beside the road to hitch-hike; little kids would throw stones at us and teenage boys, drinking beer in their pick-up trucks, would drive slowly past shouting insults. Even today, I still feel uncomfortable whenever I see a crowd forming. 'No Niggers' signs were everywhere in the South, and even in El Paso the Grand Wizard of the Ku Klux Klan was given an official welcome by the mayor during our stay. It is hard to accept but sobering to realise that I witnessed all this little more than 40 years ago.

In New York, I made contact again with a fully recovered Cindy and she drove me upstate to Millbrook, where she introduced me to Timothy Leary. It was at Millbrook that I had my first controlled and guided acid trip. With readings from the Tibetan Book of the Dead, Bach concertos playing in the background, vases filled with flowers and wall hangings stirring lightly in the breeze from the open windows, it was a truly mystical experience. Leary explained to all of us that this was the only way to experience LSD and that it should always be consumed in a controlled environment such as this. One of the other visitors at Millbrook was a fellow Englishman called Desmond O'Brien. We quickly became friends and agreed that the Millbrook experience needed to be exported to England. We had become disciples of a new religion.

Back in Britain, I wasted no time in contacting friends at Berkeley to send over supplies of LSD. In 1965, acid was still (just) legal in California as well as in England, so we had no problems shipping it from the psychology department of UC Berkeley to the Sussex University Psychedelic Association. I'd made the Psychedelic Association a sub-branch of Desmond's World Psychedelic Centre in London. Even my South American writer friend sent some packets of psilocybin mushrooms and peyote, which were also perfectly legal at that time.

Desmond was a rather dissolute aristocrat with a small house in Pont Street Mews, just behind Harrods, and he seemed to know everyone in London. All the creative spirits and intellectuals of the new London drifted through his house. Desmond managed to mix rock stars, painters, poets and academics with the bright young things of the British aristocracy. All of us had been liberated by LSD and pot and were determined to liberate the rest of society. Britain's rigid class system was breaking down, along with the old ways of doing things and looking at the world. The Establishment was the enemy and LSD our weapon of choice. It was an exciting time to be alive.

The first time Desmond invited me to visit him at his country house, I asked him for directions. 'Just take a train to Crewe,' he said, 'and ask for me at the taxi rank.' Crewe is a fairly large and important English town and the idea of just giving a random taxi driver a name with no address sounded crazy. But, sure enough, when my girlfriend Sue and I arrived at the railway station, the first taxi driver we asked said, 'Mr O'Brien? Sure, jump in.'

We drove out of Crewe into the bucolic countryside and, after passing through several picturesque Shropshire villages, we arrived at the grounds of a small castle. 'Been in the family for generations,' Desmond said, ushering us into the main hall, where a vast Jacobean table was laden with slabs of Pakistani hash. 'Care for a smoke?'

Not only was the castle filled with ancient furnishings but the extensive grounds were filled with eighteenth-century follies – ruined abbeys and mock Greek temples. When taking an acid trip at the castle, it was very hard to tell fantasy from reality; everything was already so unreal.

The LSD that we imported and distributed through the World Psychedelic Centre was never sold. We just gave it away. We genuinely believed we could change the world and make it a better place if we could only get everyone to take a trip. I'm embarrassed now to realise how naive we were, and how dangerous. In this age of jihadist terrorism, I blush to remember seriously discussing how we could introduce LSD into the London water supply.

But, like today's jihadists, I was a man with a mission. The nuclear threat and the Vietnam War were at their height and the world seemed to be hurtling towards self-destruction. If only everyone would drop acid and find their inner harmony, perhaps peace would have a chance. I took it all very seriously and organised structured psychedelic sessions on the Sussex campus, complete with incense, classical music and readings from the Tibetan Book of the Dead. The student newspaper called me 'LSD Lane'. Soon after I'd organised a large on-campus event at which Desmond O'Brien was to address the students and hand out sugar cubes impregnated with LSD, all our grand schemes were dashed to pieces by a magazine called *London Life*. An advertisement for their forthcoming exposé appeared in the *Evening Standard*:

LSD – THE DRUG THAT COULD THREATEN LONDON

Just for kicks, some famous artists, pop stars and debs are 'taking a trip' on LSD – one of the most powerful and dangerous drugs known to man. It produces hallucinations. It can cause temporary insanity. Kicks like this may be bought at the appalling cost of psychotic illness or even suicide. It is banned in America and elsewhere – but is still available in London, quite legally. Still more appalling – just half an ounce of LSD could knock out London. Socially, the stuff is dynamite. *London Life* magazine has investigated LSD fully and has uncovered a social peril of a magnitude which it believes demands immediate legislation . . . to stop the spread of a cult which could bring mental lethargy and chaos. *London Life* reporters have also traced the man who calls himself Mr LSD. He has given them an astonishing series of interviews. Read all about him, and about LSD, in this week's *London Life*.

Then *The People* followed suit, printing another piece on the Psychedelic Centre:

THE MEN BEHIND LSD – THE DRUG THAT IS MENACING YOUNG LIVES

The drug is LSD-25 – lysergic acid diethylamide. It is by far the most dangerous drug ever to become easily obtainable on the black market. LSD, which is said to give 'visions of heaven and hell', is used legitimately by psychiatrists to produce carefully controlled hallucinations. In the wrong hands, the hallucinations it produces can lead to utter irresponsibility, disregard for personal safety and suicidal tendencies. IT IS, IN FACT, A KILLER DRUG. We have obtained evidence of 'LSD parties' being held in London.

'Mr LSD' was, of course, my friend Desmond O'Brien and the *London Life* story was picked up across the British press, with lurid stories of drugs, sex and rock 'n' roll. (Ironically, it was *London Life* that, the following year, voted me and my girlfriend 'London's Coolest Couple' and sent us on a luxury holiday to Hawaii.) The university authorities were not impressed. Desmond's visit was cancelled and the Sussex University Psychedelic Association was promptly shut down. Within weeks, the Government passed new laws that made possession of LSD illegal and it was placed at the top of the dangerous drugs list. Had I not been so obviously serious and academic about my involvement with LSD, I would probably have been expelled from Sussex but, after some stern warnings, I was allowed to continue my studies.

Despite these admonitions, talking about drugs, reading about drugs, thinking about drugs and taking drugs became the centre of my universe. Studying literature and philosophy, I managed to relate everything I read to some aspect of the drug experience. Originally, the literary aspect was an important part of my obsession and I would gather friends to read the Tibetan Book of the Dead or a Sufi poem while altering our consciousnesses. But my friends were growing increasingly bored with my rather bossy insistence on mystical mumbo-jumbo and preferred to mix their drugs and to listen to Jimi Hendrix rather than the Brandenburg concertos.

I had always taken a very serious and rather prudish attitude to drug taking and did not approve of the increasingly casual, recreational approach of my fellow students. However, as dope smoking suddenly became more widespread, all my old elitist and snobbish reservations were swept away. In 1966, Dylan released 'Rainy Day Women #12 & 35', with its rallying cry of 'Everybody must get stoned!' The genie was out of the bottle and the psychedelic revolution had begun.

My downward spiral was no different from and no more interesting than anybody else's. I discovered speed and started dropping 'black bombers', this rapidly led to Methedrine and cocaine, and very soon I was injecting anything I could lay my hands on, from LSD to heroin. In a very short space of time, I changed from a pompous, elitist mystic into a sensation-fixated junkie.

I became officially registered as a drug addict and received prescriptions from my doctor for government-issue heroin and cocaine, which I collected from an all-night pharmacy in Kilburn, aptly named Bliss. To this day, when I hear the Stones' 'You Can't Always Get What You Want', with its talk of drugstores and prescriptions and its fine distinction between what you want and what you need, I think of that place. My favourite drug was liquid Methedrine, which came in small glass ampoules manufactured by Burroughs Wellcome. It was one of the first products I had ever seen with a bar code on the packaging, and my friends and I were convinced these were Chinese I Ching characters. We would spend hours arguing about whether the symbol on the boxes represented K'un (the receptive, earth) or Chen (the arousing, thunder). For many years after this, I continued to associate Burroughs Wellcome with Chinese mysticism.

By the time I was in my early 20s, I had a wide circle of very creative and sometimes famous friends in London and Paris as well as New York, San Francisco and Mexico City. It would be nice to be able to say that this is still the case. Unfortunately, as my focus on drugs increased, my ability to make or keep friends declined. If I did not quarrel with them, insult them, steal from them or throw up on their furniture, then I committed the worst sin of all: I bored them. There is nothing more boring than a drug addict. Even Sue, my childhood sweetheart, finally abandoned me because I had become so boring in my obsession. She also objected to me calling her 'man' all the time. I called everybody 'man', partly because I thought it was hip and partly because my brain was so wasted that I could no longer remember names.

My serious-drug-addict phase lasted two or three years. The life of every drug addict is universally the same and always tedious to describe. The addict becomes entirely self-absorbed, cunning, manipulative, dishonest and interested only in the next score. Any concept of morality or even human decency is swallowed by the need for another fix.

I visited my close friend Paul one day at his basement flat in Ventnor Villas in Hove. I found him on the floor, dead, with a syringe still protruding from his arm. Instead of giving him mouth-to-mouth resuscitation or calling an ambulance, I rifled through his pockets to find his stash of drugs, which I immediately took possession of. I also stole his LP of Bach's *Musical Offering* and his copy of *The Hero with a Thousand Faces* by Joseph Campbell. That such wondrous examples of human creativity should be coveted by a lost degenerate provides yet another example of life's rich contradictions. 'Well, he doesn't bloody need them any more,' I would have said if asked.

I'm pleased to report that Paul was not in fact dead, just unconscious, and these days he holds the Chair of Mathematics at a very prestigious university. I eventually replaced the drugs and returned the book and LP, though we argued for a long time about how much heroin was in his pocket when I emptied it. But Paul was very forgiving of my behaviour and completely understood. 'Of course, man. I would have done exactly the same.'

Despite my self-destructive tendencies, I have always been blessed with a strong sense of self-preservation. Somehow, I continued my studies at university, while all my friends dropped out or died. Eventually, I managed to graduate with a second-class honours degree in literature.

After I graduated in June 1968, I continued to live in Brighton, dealing enough drugs to feed my habit and generally pursuing a sordid and aimless existence. Deep down, I was unhappy, and I knew that I needed to change my life – but only after the next fix. By late summer, I'd been arrested on a minor possession charge and that was enough to give me the impetus to change.

After attending the funeral of yet another friend, a beautiful young lady called Maggie, I hitch-hiked north to my parents' new home in the Staffordshire village of Acton Trussell. They had always maintained a bedroom for me, even though I had long ago left home, and I locked myself in my room for three or four months while I fought my demons. The family never asked questions and a tray of food was always left outside my door in case I was able to eat. After about three months, my brother George gave me an avocado stone that he had positioned with toothpicks in a glass of water so that the root was beginning to grow. Within a matter of weeks, a stalk grew from the top of the stone and then some leaves. I watched the new life sprout and I changed the water every day.

> I remember, I remember
> The roses red and white,
> The violets and the lily cups –
> Those flowers made of light!
> The lilacs where the robin built,
> And where my brother set
> The laburnum on his birthday, –
> The tree is living yet!

One day, I carried my new avocado plant down into the family kitchen and placed it on the windowsill. My long journey was over and I was cured.

In many ways, I was lucky to have had my drug experience at such an early age, before drugs became such a social scourge. There was no social acceptance of junkies, as opposed to potheads, during the '60s. We were a despised minority and it was therefore much easier to quit drugs – if you really were determined to do so. In the '70s and '80s, however, when coke and smack became more easily available, fashionable and widely accepted, quitting drugs became a much more difficult challenge. I have seen far too many families destroyed since then. Even cannabis is no longer the mild hallucinogenic that it was in the '60s. Today's pot, industrially produced in hydroponic labs, is far more powerful than the stuff that we used to smoke and I've seen too many of my children's generation ruin their lives through pot alone, without even touching harder drugs.

Howard and I never had any professional dealings with hard drugs and nor did our friends. We dealt only with cannabis, nothing else. I never even met any cocaine dealers until I went to prison in Miami. The Federal Metropolitan Correctional Center of Miami is an exclusive finishing school in the cocaine world, a place where the elite of the South American drug trade gathers. It is filled not just with cocaine smugglers and money launderers but also with Colombian cartel kingpins, deposed dictators and Bolivian army generals, not to mention corrupt US drug agents and Mexican contract killers. All these men had just one thing in common: cocaine and the vast sums of money it generates. They would sit around the inmates' chow hall discussing the benefits and drawbacks of different brands of money-counting machine like other people compare brands of coffee maker.

'The Braun is good, I agree, and it's fast. But it overheats after five million and you have to let it cool off for a half-hour.'

'That's why I like the De La Rue Brandt. It only does 1,200 notes per minute but you can run it all day long and it never gets hot.'

Listening to these men, I quickly understood that Ernie and Howard, even with all their millions, were small fry indeed. The amount of money generated by the South American cocaine trade is beyond imagining. I was always impressed when Ernie rented a Learjet but these guys owned their own fleets of Gulfstreams and Boeings. They had their own armies.

For as long as that sort of vast and unimaginable wealth can be generated, the cocaine trade will continue to flourish. For every cartel leader extradited to Miami, there will be two more to take his place. For as long as drugs remain illegal and the 'War on Drugs' continues to be fought, the demand for the latest model of money-counting machine will keep growing.

After decades enjoying my role as a smuggler, I am now both embarrassed and ashamed to have ever been part of the drug trade. The innocent world of '60s pot smuggling, in which young gentlemen had fun-filled adventures in exotic lands, no longer exists. Messing around on the North-West Frontier, we naively felt we were participating in a modern Great Game, taking part in some Kiplingesque romance. There was no violence then and very little dishonesty. It all worked on trust and a common desire to have fun. Pieter's friend with the axe in Wales was the exception not the rule. Today, we live in a sadly different world in which the violence and corruption of drug trafficking have undermined our social fabric and threaten many of our freedoms. The drug trade has truly become a force for evil, but it is the War on Drugs that fuels it and gives it its power for evil.

Unfortunately, there is no politician with the courage to declare the War on Drugs to be a failure or to campaign for legalisation. If drugs were legal, the profit motive, the syndicates and the violence would vanish overnight and the government could move its resources away from enforcement and into education. But that will not happen in today's political climate.

I, however, have absolutely no right to criticise the politicians; I am completely unqualified to do so. Not only have I never fought for a political cause or been active in a political party, I have never even voted. I'm afraid I have been apathetically apolitical all my adult life.

My parents were both lifelong members of the Conservative Party. My father's heroes were people like Reginald Maudling and Edward Heath, while my mother preferred Sir Winston Churchill and Harold Macmillan. They both loathed Harold Wilson and the Labour Party and referred to socialist politicians as 'horrid little men'. My mother never forgave the socialists for defeating Churchill at the end of the war and was convinced that the Labour Party had no other goal than to deliver England to the Russian Communists. When Russian tanks rolled into Hungary in 1956, she explained that the same thing would happen to England if we ever voted Labour. The fact that we were betrayed by the Americans in that same year, when they abandoned us in Suez, simply reinforced her determination to keep Britain as a world power by voting Conservative.

My mother was raised in a grim Irish working-class street, where her widowed mother worked her fingers to the bone washing laundry while she and her eight siblings slept four to a bed. Nevertheless, she always maintained the manners and the attitudes of an English duchess and instilled in her children the belief that we were natural aristocrats and born to rule. Never being terribly interested in politics, I accepted my mother's beliefs unquestioningly until I was in my mid-teens, when two things occurred to change my attitudes.

My parents were always trying to make me join the Young Conservatives. The YCs would often have a hop at the weekends and my mother was convinced I would enjoy the dancing and meet 'a nice girl'. I grudgingly attended a few of these dances but soon discovered that all the girls had thick ankles, dressed in long tweed skirts and had names like Samantha and Annabel.

'All right then,' my mother finally capitulated, 'go to the Young Socialists dance if you want to but you won't have nearly as much fun. You'll see. It'll just be a group of horrid little men whining and complaining about the monarchy. You never listen to anything I tell you anyway. The Conservative Party was good enough for Churchill, but if you think you're better than him . . .'

In fact, my mother was completely wrong. I had much more fun at the Young Socialists dance. All the girls wore tight jeans or short skirts with high boots and they had names like Lindsay and Paula. They strummed guitars and sang Joan Baez songs with soft, sad voices and wore tons of black mascara. I was enthralled. I was also able to wear my dark glasses and black plastic jacket instead of the Harris tweed with leather elbow patches that my mother insisted I wear to the YC hop. At the Young Conservatives, we had danced to Cliff Richard or the Everly Brothers; at the Young Socialists, we danced to the Rolling Stones. I immediately decided to become a socialist.

Soon after this, it was revealed that Kim Philby, an aristocratic member of the Establishment and a senior member of British intelligence, was also a Russian spy. We quickly learned that a whole group of Establishment figures who had studied at Cambridge at the same time as my father were traitors and Soviet agents. My mother was forced to concede that they were all members of the ruling

Conservative Party – not socialists at all. I would not be surprised if the revelation about Kim Philby's betrayal was responsible for the political cynicism of many people of my generation. I certainly never trusted any public figure after that and even my mother became less strident in her support of the Tories.

For a brief period after the Philby revelations, I did join the London Federation of Anarchists but only so that I could attend the Anarchist Ball in 1963. The girls wore extremely tight jeans that looked as though they'd been painted onto their long legs, or the very shortest of short leather skirts with fishnet stockings. The main appeal of the anarchists, of course, was all the talk about free love, a political position of which I was strongly in favour.

And that pretty much sums up my lifetime's experience of politics.

Natasha, on the other hand, became an active socialist at a very young age and moved progressively to the left throughout her teens. By the time she graduated from Essex University in the early '70s, she was hanging out with members of the Angry Brigade. This was a minor, home-grown English version of the Continental terrorist groups like the Baader–Meinhof Group and the Red Brigades. They did bomb a few banks but only one person was ever injured. Natasha's radicalism mellowed over the years and these days she sounds more and more like my mother as she fulminates against all these lazy louts living off the welfare state.

There was a lot of political activity at university during the '60s, including endless protests against the Vietnam War and the nuclear bomb. My experiences with politically inclined fellow students only served to confirm my cynicism. Without exception, the ones who preached peace, liberty and freedom were mean to their girlfriends. That was the first time I was able to observe a correlation between love for mankind in general and contempt for actual individuals such as girlfriends and classmates. Most of the lefties attracted moneyed, beautiful girlfriends and would then proceed to mock and criticise their wealth while busily squandering it on expensive hi-fi systems and eating in fancy restaurants where they could sneer at their bourgeois dining companions.

I don't believe any political goal justifies violence. Even though I strongly opposed the Vietnam War, I felt embarrassed and ashamed when one of my friends threw a bucket of red paint at the US ambassador when he visited Sussex. I hated the angry self-righteousness of the left-wing activists.

However, I must admit to one occasion of revolutionary activism, when I joined the students of the Sorbonne in their revolt against the government of Charles de Gaulle.

During the months of April and May 1968, there were very few classes at Sussex as we were all supposed to be revising for our final exams in late May and early June. Although I did very little actual studying, I did attempt to cut back on my drug use and some of my more destructive social habits so that I would be in good shape for the exams. I moved out of the shooting gallery in Ventnor Villas where I'd been living and took a room in the university dorm in order to avoid my fellow junkies.

My mother, who, unknown to us, had learned that she had cancer, had somehow organised an audience with the Pope and planned for the whole family to drive to Rome for the occasion. She persuaded me to accompany them by offering to employ me as the chauffeur and, seeing this as a way to clean up my act, I graciously consented.

The engineering company of which my father was chairman at that time maintained a splendid Daimler stretch limousine, reserved for formal occasions, when it was driven by the company chauffeur. When the chauffeur was not driving the directors to Royal Ascot or other important meetings, he spent his days polishing the paintwork and making sure the engine was maintained in perfect condition. He had never married and had worked for the company for 30 years; the car was his life. When he discovered that the company chairman was planning to fill it with children, take it out of England and drive through foreign countries on the wrong side of the road, he nearly died. He raised every sort of objection but eventually had to accept that he was just an employee, while my father was chairman of the board. He watched forlornly as I drove the family out of the factory gates onto the main road and headed for Dover.

'Don't worry, Faversham,' my father called out the window as we drove slowly past. 'We'll look after her. We'll have her back in a couple of weeks.' I will never forget Faversham's eyes as I drove away. He ignored everybody else and just stared at me. He knew I was bad news. It wasn't just the long hair and hippy clothes; he had looked into my eyes and seen the soul of a Daimler destroyer. He knew.

It really was a lovely car. Everything was polished walnut and stitched cowhide, and, with three rows of luxurious leather seats, it accommodated the whole family comfortably. We glided across France effortlessly and then reached the autostradas of Italy, where the aristocratic but repressed English automobile was finally able to fulfil her destiny.

Because the car was so well built and so solid, there were no vibrations and no distracting noise from the outside world, however fast one drove. The passengers were isolated from reality in a luxurious cocoon and only the chauffeur (and his father) was aware that we were travelling at speeds of up to 160 mph as we traversed the Italian peninsula towards Rome. My father and I never discussed it but, sitting next to me on the front seat, he was just as aware as I was of the needle slowly inching higher and higher; just like me, he enjoyed the private thrill of this display of raw power and blistering speed. If my mother had had any idea that we were doing even 80 mph, she would have been furious. Some things fathers and sons just need to share.

We arrived in Rome and met Pope Paul VI at St Peter's Basilica. Despite being an atheist, I remember being quite overwhelmed, not just by the pomp and ceremony but also by the presence of the Pope himself and the powerful intelligence that seemed to emanate from him. I was holding my baby brother Marcus in my arms at the time and the Pope made a beeline for us both. Gesturing to one of his cardinals, he took a large gold medallion on a ribbon and placed it around Marcus's neck. He then looked deep into my eyes, as though he could see my troubled junkie soul, and smiled at me. I received a great sense of peace that stayed with me for a long time.

After a few days in Rome, we all drove happily back north towards the Swiss border, planning to return to England via the German Rhine Valley. My mother felt much better after meeting the Pope,

I still had my beatific inner glow from the papal smile and Marcus had the Pope's heavy gold medallion, which he swung by its ribbon, cracking everybody over the head until finally it was taken away from him. Unfortunately, by the time we reached Milan, the car had started making funny noises. Initially, these were audible only at speeds in excess of 140 mph but eventually they became noticeable at any speed.

'There is an authorised Daimler agent in Milan,' my father announced after consulting one of his guides. 'We'll spend a couple of days exploring the city while they repair the car.' But the problem could not be solved in two days. New parts were needed that might take weeks to arrive. So the whole family flew back to England carrying just the necessities on the plane and leaving everything else in the car, including the medal from the Pope.

I left my father to explain to Faversham that there might be a delay before the car could be shipped back from Italy ('nothing to worry about') and returned to my studies at Sussex. On my first evening back in the dorm, I saw a television news report about the student takeover of the Sorbonne in Paris. It looked like one big party celebrating free love and there were even shots of bare-breasted girls smoking reefers on the banks of the Seine. One of the poems I was studying for an exam was *The Prelude* by Wordsworth, part of which describes the pleasurable excitement of a previous French Revolution:

> Bliss was it in that dawn to be alive,
> But to be young was very Heaven!

I decided that, in the cause of academic research, I needed to visit Paris and so within 24 hours of returning to England I was once more crossing the Channel, hitch-hiking through the night to Paris.

I had no idea what the students were protesting about or why everyone was so angry with President de Gaulle. I didn't really care. There were lots of intoxicatingly pretty French and German girls, lots of wine, lots of pot and everyone was very friendly. During the days, we pulled up cobblestones around the Boulevard St-Michel and shouted rude slogans at the CRS riot police. At night, we sat around bonfires, discussed the meaning of life in several languages, ate and drank, smoked endless joints and, if we were lucky, got laid. I decided that I liked being a revolutionary. I started wearing a beret and a beautiful French girl with long legs and a short skirt told me I looked like Che Guevara. Wordsworth was spot on: to be young was very Heaven!

Unfortunately, as May drew to a close, my time was up and the final exams were calling. While assuring all my new friends that I was off to England to spread the revolution among the students there, I actually returned to sit my exams, earn my bourgeois degree and eventually begin a career as a chartered accountant.

One other incident worth recounting occurred before I abandoned my role as a left-wing revolutionary and left Paris behind me.

Nobody could possibly have foreseen, except of course poor Faversham, that when the finally restored Daimler was carried back to England on a special transporter, it would pass through Paris during a revolution.

I did not see the incident myself but heard various accounts from all sides. Planning to drive straight through Paris, travelling up the Boulevard St-Michel, over the Seine and north via the Boulevard de Sébastopol towards the Normandy coast, the transporter driver was surprised to find his road blocked by hastily erected barricades and gangs of long-haired students. The gleaming paint and the deep polish of the luxury limousine was too symbolic a capitalist target for them to resist and the students attacked it with a fury. All the windows were smashed with hurled cobblestones, the leather upholstery was ripped with knives and the lovingly polished paintwork was dented with rocks and the Cuban heels of angry boots. The Pope's medallion was never seen again.

By the time the car was delivered to England, the insurance company had already decided that it was beyond repair. My father's company, having no further need of a full-time chauffeur, gave Faversham two weeks' notice. I don't think he really cared; his heart had already been broken.

Sadly, the Paris revolution of 1968 was just a light-hearted harbinger of the political violence to follow. Living in Europe during the '70s, with Baader–Meinhof in Germany, the Red Brigades in Italy, the IRA in London, Fattah and Hezbollah in Paris, there was bloodshed and intolerance everywhere we went.

Jude and I were living on the Italian border when the Prime Minister, Aldo Moro, was kidnapped and executed by the Red Brigades. Our car and even Bridie's baby seat were searched by armed police each time we went to Como for the weekly grocery shopping. We spent a lot of time in England during the '70s, when the IRA were bombing pubs and restaurants from Guildford to Birmingham and even exploded a bomb in the House of Commons car park, killing an MP. In 1974, I was staying in Paris when Carlos bombed Le Drugstore, a café on the Left Bank, and in 1977, just weeks after Bridie was born, Fauchon, our favourite food shop in Paris, was destroyed by a bomb. During this whole period, the world seemed to fall apart; planes were hijacked on a regular basis and the threat of violence was everywhere. It seemed as though Yeats's apocalyptic poem 'The Second Coming' had been specifically written for the '70s.

And now, of course, 30 years later, things have degenerated even further; the blood-dimmed tide has indeed been loosed and the worst are all too filled with a self-righteous and passionate intensity. In the '70s, blood was shed in the name of politics; today, it is shed in the name of religion.

To return to the politics of the drug trade, I make no apologies for my involvement with pot smuggling over the years. I still believe it is a benign recreational drug that should be legalised. The only effect pot has ever had on me is to make me drive more carefully, be more gentle and thoughtful in what I say, laugh at silly things and make love more often and more slowly.

I do feel remorse for breaking the law, however, because of the corrosive effect that lawbreaking has on your personal life and because, in the end, it was my innocent wife and children who had to pay the price. With hindsight, instead of breaking the law, I should have become politically active and worked to change it. If we had succeeded in changing the law, the War on Drugs might never have been launched and hundreds of thousands of prisoners, prison guards, DEA agents, racketeers, judges, smugglers, politicians and cartel bosses might all be living completely different and more productive lives today.

The only one of my friends to become seriously involved in politics is Howard Marks. Since his release from prison, he has run several political campaigns on a 'Legalise Cannabis' platform. He was defeated when he ran for Parliament and was rejected by the Government when he applied for the post of drug tsar. Howard based his official application on his extensive personal experience. Nevertheless, I am sure he will continue his lone campaign and that is the one and only political cause that I find myself able and willing to support.

[1|3]

VIOLENCE

José and his men knew I was planning something. Tension and unspoken hostility had been building for weeks, ever since I'd started asking questions about the large deliveries of fresh lemons to the warehouse. I had fired Garry and Anna a week earlier but that had been relatively simple. I had taken possession of their keys to the factory and told them I would also confiscate the company van if they ever returned. Beneath their bravado and Anna's not so veiled threats, I think they were both pleased to be out of the business. The future of European Smoked Fish Inc. was starting to look very bleak.

But José and his men were a different kettle of fish. There were at least a dozen of them; they were all lean and mean with the sort of tattoos you only get in prison and most of them carried fish-gutting knives in their belts. Unlike Anna and Garry, they had no intention of leaving; they had a very nice little business, which they would fight to maintain. Juan was not much help. 'Just get rid of them, Patrick,' he pleaded. 'Otherwise we'll all end up in prison.'

I often worried about going to prison, but only for handling international funds without completing all the required paperwork. 'An unintentional oversight, Your Honour,' I would explain. 'I'm very sorry and I promise I won't do it again.' This time it was different. This time I could go to prison for murdering half the population of Miami, or at least those who had had the misfortune to eat in a seafood restaurant serviced by our company.

It was Garry who had brought José into the business, long before I became involved. 'We had all this space we weren't using,' he'd explained to me when I'd confronted him about it, sweeping his arm around to indicate the vast warehouse. 'José pays us $1,000 a week in cash for the use of our cold rooms. He minds his own business and keeps out of our way. What's the problem?'

I wasn't ready to tell Garry about the lemons and so I ignored his question about 'the problem'. 'So where's the weekly cash he's been paying?' I asked.

Garry looked shifty and Anna looked angry. In fact, Anna always looked angry. From the time she was born in Hungary, life had treated her badly and she lusted for revenge. She raised her eyes from the workbench, where she was slicing fresh gravadlax with a very large and sharp-looking knife. 'What for you always prying and asking?' she shouted in her thick Slavic accent, waving the knife in my direction. 'There's operating expenses, always the bills, always the money going. And what from Juan do we get for all our hard work? Where is the money he promise? Without José's rent we have nothing.' She snorted and returned to attacking the fish with her knife. 'All we get from Juan is some nosy parker poking around what he don't understand. Better be careful he don't cut hisself,' she added darkly.

Once I had hidden the knives, Anna and Garry were quickly dealt with, but getting rid of José would require more muscle than one stout middle-aged Englishman could muster. Luckily, I was friends with one of the local hookers. There were lots of hookers near the factory; in fact, one could say there was a plethora of prostitutes in that particular part of Miami, but Hortense, being Haitian, was the only one who spoke French. The inside of the warehouse was bitterly cold, mainly because of all the giant freezers blasting away while José and his men left the doors open as they worked. Our electricity bill alone was more than a thousand dollars per week and I was always cold. The low temperature reactivated the venom in the spider bites I had acquired in Guam and little red spots would appear on my arms and legs. It had baffled a succession of doctors until I'd been sent to the School of Hygiene and Tropical Medicine in London.

'It's spider venom,' they told me.

'What can be done about it?' I asked.

'Nothing that we know of.'

'But why does it always flare up in the cold?' I asked.

They shrugged. 'We don't really know.'

'So what should I do?'

'Try to keep out of the cold,' they advised.

Yet another reason to live in Miami.

Just to warm up, I would often sit outside on North-West 10th Avenue and smoke a cigarette in the sunshine, which was how I became friends with Hortense. The strip in front of our warehouse was her working territory and she would patrol it in bright-red vinyl hot pants, thigh-length white vinyl boots, a long feather boa and very little else. I would practise my French on her as we puffed Marlboros in the hot Florida sun during our work breaks.

Hortense told me she had a brother, Pierre, who ran a building crew in north Miami, in an area known as Little Haiti. Pierre and his men were always looking for work and she would be happy to introduce us. For a hundred dollars, I bought two hours of her professional time and she changed into a simple black dress and shoes in my office before joining me in the car. The transformation was amazing; she was actually attractive.

We met Pierre in Churchill's Pub. This was an incongruous bar in the heart of Little Haiti, popular with British expats and Jamaicans, who all came for the English beer and loud reggae music. Pierre was very large and very black, almost blue. He was probably 6 ft across the shoulders, and tall. Just what I was looking for. We quickly settled on a price for him to provide a cleaning crew of a dozen men to work in the warehouse for a week.

'The main thing to clean out are some Cubans,' I told him, and his eyes gleamed.

'*Sont des salops,*' he told me. '*Sont de la merde.*'

Relations between the Cuban and Haitian communities in Miami are never very good and in the mid-'80s, following a new influx of Haitian boat people, they were extremely bad.

Pierre and his men reported for work at 8.30 on Monday morning, as arranged. They reminded me somewhat of the platoon of marines that Howard and I had hired in Scotland. None of them had tattoos but they were all large and muscular and most of them carried baseball bats. I ushered them into the smoking room, where we prepared the salmon, and waited for José to arrive.

José and his men rolled in around 10 a.m. and I could hear them loading crates from a van into one of the freezers. They were easy to hear because they always talked at the tops of their voices. I suspected they spent their weekends at Key West, shouting insults at Fidel Castro across the Florida Straits.

Leaving the other men in the smoking room, Pierre and I wandered past the loading docks to the main freezer. José looked up suspiciously and when he saw Pierre he muttered something like '*swarzer maricon*' and spat on the floor.

'I'm afraid I'm going to have to ask you to leave, José,' I said, waving some papers at him. 'We had a visit from the Dade County health inspectors over the weekend,' I lied, 'and they're closing us down – something about contaminated fish. I want you and your men to pack all your stuff and leave before the inspectors come back.'

'Fuck you,' José replied. 'I knew you was trouble when I saw you. This is my place. This is my business. I work hard for this. Fuck you, cocksucker. You go fuck yourself. I'm not leaving.'

Previously, José had always pretended that he did not speak English, forcing me to address him in my broken Spanish. I was impressed by his sudden command of the language. 'I'm sorry you feel like that, José,' I said, 'but I really am going to have to insist.'

The other men had stopped working and were gathered in a sullen group behind their leader. I don't know how much they understood but they knew it was trouble and appeared prepared, even anxious, to deal with it.

I held up a photocopy of José's Social Security card, which I'd found among Garry's papers in the office. 'This is your Social Security card, I think. Would you like me to give this to the health inspector when he comes?'

José pulled an evil-looking gutting knife from his belt and moved towards me. 'Give me that, you cocksucker,' he said, 'or I cut your cojones.'

As he thrust the knife towards me, Pierre grabbed his wrist with one hand and his bicep with the other. He lifted José off the ground and, with all his strength, smashed his arm against the door jamb of the freezer. There was a sickening sound of breaking bone and the knife clattered to the floor.

While José's men watched in disbelief, Pierre threw their leader to the floor, where he writhed in agony, screaming what I could only surmise were Spanish obscenities. Shaking off their surprise and pulling out their knives, the Cubans moved towards us.

I don't think I'd been in a fight since I was a small boy in the school playground. I could not believe this was happening. I was beyond fear. I could not even wet myself. The whole thing erupted so unexpectedly, I was stunned. I had thought that threatening José with the health inspector would be sufficient and had never imagined that I was going to be confronted by a dozen bloodthirsty Marielitos armed with sharp knives.

As the Cubans moved towards me, I was rooted to the floor, paralysed with fear. Suddenly, my attackers stopped and, from the look of shock on their faces, I realised that Pierre's men had emerged from the smoking room. The sight of a bunch of angry Cubans with knives is certainly frightening, but the sight of a dozen six-foot-tall Haitians wielding baseball bats is even more so.

It was scarcely even a fight. It was over as soon as it started. Before the first baseball bat landed, the Cubans turned and ran. Pierre and his men carried José out to his pick-up truck and dumped him in the back. We changed the locks on all the doors and Pierre's men remained on guard, night and day, for a couple of weeks. But José never returned and I've not seen him since.

I had to pay Hortense, of course, for all the business she lost while her brother was guarding the warehouse (she claimed he was unaware of her profession) but I suspect she just moved around the corner and swapped territory with one of her colleagues.

* * *

The strange journey that had brought me to instigate an interracial conflict in the back streets of Miami had begun 13 years earlier in an office on Wall Street. Like many good stories, it started off with money.

While a good Hartmann case was always my first choice for moving large sums of money around the world, certain situations required something more commodious, if less elegant. For a taxi ride from the Plaza Hotel on Central Park to Wall Street, I favoured army-surplus kitbags made from heavy-duty canvas. In addition to holding far more cash than any case on the market, they were cheap and could be tossed aside when the cash had been delivered.

Hotel porters would struggle with the heavy bags when loading them into a taxi and the driver would summon help from the doorman when wrestling the bags from the taxi into the bank. I was willing and able to carry half a million in a Hartmann case but I refused to put my back out while carrying a couple of million in cash. However, I always tipped generously.

At his Wall Street office, Juan's people would rush to help with the kitbags as soon as the doorman announced my arrival. Juan and I would wander off for a leisurely lunch while his staff counted the cash.

From the '70s through the go-go, greed-is-good decade of the '80s, Wall Street had an insatiable hunger for cash. The world of gargantuan stock deals, mammoth mergers, insider trading, takeovers and BSDs (big swinging dicks) described in *Liar's Poker* and *The Bonfire of the Vanities* was fuelled by bribes, kickbacks and under-the-table arrangements. All of this activity required hard physical cash, so whenever I arrived on Wall Street with a Hartmann case or a kitbag full of it, I was welcomed as a BSD. The rivers of cash that were so difficult to dispose of elsewhere in the world evaporated on Wall Street like morning dew on desert sands.

My friend Juan Dejesus was chairman of the board of a holding company that, among other things, handled foreign-exchange activities for the international bank Deak-Perera. Under his command, trading rooms full of brokers yelled into telephones and exchanged millions of dollars in foreign currency every day. Juan knew all the players on Wall Street and was aware not only of their foreign currency requirements but also of their need for US currency – in cash.

If anyone else was joining us (Nicolas Deak, for example), we would usually walk to the World Trade Center and have lunch at Windows on the World. But if it was just Juan and me, we would take a cab uptown to one of his favourite Italian restaurants and spend the next few hours discussing the menu and what to eat next. In the cab back downtown, we would discuss possible choices for dinner later that evening. Juan was a man whose passion was for food and, wherever we ate in New York, the chef would always hurry out from the kitchen and offer to make him something special.

One particular restaurant, Romano's, in the basement of a skyscraper near Little Italy, always served us a Dejesus salad as soon as we arrived, even before our first glass of wine. It was a nice enough salad – tomatoes and basil with olive oil and garlic – but it had no special ingredients that I could recognise. Eventually, I asked Romano for the story behind the name. He looked at Juan and Juan grinned and nodded his consent while the owner explained. Juan had been a regular patron for several years when he learned that the restaurant was closing down. The lease had come to an end and the landlords were preparing to sell the whole 32-storey building. Juan made a few enquiries and within weeks had become the new owner. Romano was given a new 20-year lease and then Juan sold the whole skyscraper again at a profit. Before finalising the sale, however, he made one other arrangement. He built a greenhouse on the roof of the building, next to the air-conditioning units, and included access to the greenhouse in the restaurant's lease. Whenever Juan phoned to reserve a table, Romano would send a waiter by elevator to the roof to pick fresh tomatoes and basil for the Dejesus salad. That was why it was special; it was freshly picked.

This was just one example of Juan's ability to turn any situation to his advantage. Many years later, in 1983, living in Santa Cruz, I was on the phone to Juan when the Coalinga earthquake struck us. One minute I was having a quiet phone conversation and the next the whole house was shaking, the concrete floor was buckling and my new Apple II computer was sliding off the desk to crash on the floor. Against a background noise of breaking glass, I shouted, 'Juan, I have to go! We're having an earthquake!'

As I dropped the phone, I heard Juan shouting, 'Grab hold!'

Grab hold of what? The phone? Anyone who has survived an earthquake, especially a 6.4 monster like this one, knows there is little to grab onto. That is what is so frightening: nothing is stable; everything is shaking and collapsing. Even the ground is no longer solid and a concrete floor becomes like sand. I crawled under my desk and grabbed hold of my head between my knees.

I later learned that I had completely misheard what Juan was shouting. He was actually calling orders to his traders and telling them to 'Buy gold!' In that instant, he had realised that he had maybe a 30-second lead on the rest of the world, and he knew exactly what to do. As soon as the news of a major Californian earthquake hit the wire, the price of gold would shoot skyward. This is a natural reaction of the market when faced with any catastrophe. By the end of the day, the price of gold would have returned to normal. But Juan was 30 seconds ahead of the market and thus was able to buy gold at pre-panic prices and sell it again a couple of minutes later just when news of the earthquake reached Wall Street. He made hundreds of thousands of dollars from that phone conversation and bought me a new IBM computer to replace my Apple – as well as many good Italian meals.

Juan's network stretched from Hong Kong and Tokyo to Bahrain and Zurich, and he had close friends in every major city around the globe. All his friends had a need for disposable funds to use on Wall Street and Juan always had a market for cash. By the time we returned to his office from lunch, my bulky kitbags would be emptied, the money counted and the funds transferred to a bank in whatever country I had chosen. If one of Ernie's couriers had delivered a bag of cash to my New York hotel in the morning, I could have it sitting in a Hong Kong bank before Juan and I had even finished digesting our dinner later that evening.

* * *

I first met Juan through a contact at the Foreign Commerce Bank in Zurich, which was part of the Deak-Perera group. Initially, I was unwilling to switch my accounts from my bank in Geneva because I was more comfortable speaking French than German. 'Oh, nothing to worry about,' my Swiss banker friend assured me brusquely. 'They're a very nice group of fellows. It's American owned, so they all speak English.' Eventually, I did open an account in Zurich and another with the sister bank, Bankhaus Deak, in Vienna. Eventually, after I'd proved myself a worthy and active customer in Europe, I was introduced to the founder of the group, Nicholas Deak.

Deak had been a founding member of the Office of Strategic Services – predecessor of the CIA – in the Second World War and there were many stories of his exploits behind German and Japanese lines. After the war, he became one of the world's most important gold traders, with the largest foreign-exchange empire in the western hemisphere. He had 57 offices in the US and many others all over the world, including the banks in Zurich and Vienna.

Deak and I had dinner a couple of times in Zurich and he insisted that I visit him the next time I was in New York. I would love to say that I became a close friend of Nicholas Deak. He was probably the most fascinating person I have ever met. Unfortunately, the few times I did meet with him I was so in awe of his legend and his conversation that I could only mumble platitudes and stare at him like some star-struck teeny-bopper.

The morning that Ernie's hooker abandoned me in my hotel room with $100,000 in grubby notes, I took a cab to visit Deak's office at 29 Broadway, on the corner of Wall Street. The office was a large and impressive oak-panelled room on the 21st floor, with commanding views uptown towards the Empire State Building. Deak seemed delighted to see me and invited me to join him for lunch. Awkwardly, I pointed to my suitcase.

'I wonder if you can help me. I seem to have acquired rather a lot of cash and I don't really want to lug this into a restaurant.'

'No problem at all,' he assured me. 'You can leave it here. I'll lock my office when we leave.'

'Actually,' I continued, nervously recalling my first transaction at Latimer's, 'I wondered if it might be possible to transfer it to my account at Foreign Commerce.' And then I added, rather unnecessarily, 'In Zurich.'

'Ah,' said Deak. 'How much cash are we actually talking about?'

'One hundred thousand,' I mumbled, wishing I were somewhere else.

'Hmm.' Deak raised an eyebrow and looked thoughtful. 'The problem is there are all these tiresome government regulations, you know. I'm afraid we just can't handle that amount of cash.' My heart sank. 'However,' he said brightly, after a pause, 'I do know somebody who might be able to help you. Come with me and I'll introduce you to Juan.' From the 21st floor, I followed Deak, with my suitcase, down in the elevator to the basement of the building.

Both Deak and Dejesus were conservatively dressed in dark suits and both had thick hair brushed straight back, with distinguished silver 'wings' above their ears. But where Deak was tall, elegant and leonine, Juan was dark, short and stocky, more bull-like. Nicholas Deak could speak five languages without a trace of an accent while Juan's English could not disguise his Cuban origins – not that he ever tried. He rose when we entered his office and, as he approached, his rolling walk reminded me of a boxer or a wrestler.

'Juan, I'd like you to meet Patrick Lane, one of our good clients in Zurich.'

Juan held out his hand. His grip was powerful. When he smiled the saturnine darkness lifted from his face and his eyes twinkled with humour. 'Welcome to the basement,' he said in his thick accent.

'Think you can have this transferred to the Foreign Commerce Bank?' Deak asked casually, indicating my suitcase.

Juan took the case from me and weighed it expertly in his hand. He raised his bushy eyebrows. 'Five hundred?' he asked.

'No,' I said, 'only one hundred. I'm afraid there's a lot of small denomination bills.'

'No problem,' Juan replied. 'Three per cent to have it there tomorrow. Two per cent if you give me a couple of days.' I nodded and Juan called an assistant. 'Have this counted and then prepare a transfer for FCB.' He turned to us both and looked at his watch. 'Señors, is it time for lunch?'

As I've mentioned elsewhere, I had lunch in Windows on the World with two of the best-connected bankers on Wall Street and all I could think about was Angie, the hooker who had delivered the cash. I barely listened as Deak and Juan described a whole new world of financial possibilities. Nevertheless, even though he was 15 years older than me, Juan and I became immediate friends, with a shared passion for red wine, garlic and anchovies. That first meeting, in 1973, was some 35 years ago and yet we have remained friends ever since. He attended my 50th birthday party in France and, although he lives a reclusive life on the jungle border between Suriname and Guyana, he occasionally calls on his satellite phone and we discuss favourite recipes and menus.

Juan's life changed dramatically in 1984 when his eldest son, Carlos, was diagnosed with leukaemia. Carlos was 21 years old and had just returned from his honeymoon when he received the diagnosis. Juan immediately dropped all his complex business affairs and flew to Seattle to install his son in the Swedish Hospital. For the next nine months, he did not leave Carlos's bedside and every day he was hooked up to a machine that took his blood, removed the platelets and added them to Carlos's blood. I visited him there and it was heartbreaking to watch Juan trying to conduct business over the phone, lapsing in and out of consciousness as his blood drained away. Despite the best efforts of everybody, nothing worked and Carlos died within the year.

Juan returned home to find his company in collapse. The glory days of his Wall Street empire were over. Most of what he had created over the years was destroyed. A few weeks later, Nicholas Deak was murdered.

Juan needed to rebuild his business and he offered me a job as his assistant with the grand title of vice president. The IRS had recently closed down my *Offshore Banking Report* in California, so I was ready for a new adventure. Also, I discovered that my own $150,000 that I had entrusted to Juan was now tied up in a smoked-salmon plant in Miami. In addition to my other title, I therefore became president of European Smoked Fish Inc. and moved my family, despite the vocal objections of my children, from Santa Cruz to Miami.

The fish factory was located on North-West 10th Avenue in Miami's warehouse district. It has become a little more artsy and bohemian in recent years but in the mid-'80s the area was populated entirely by crack dealers and hookers. I would arrive at the factory in my suit, carrying my briefcase and Compaq portable computer, and make a mad dash for the door, terrified that I would be killed in the short distance from the car.

Conditions inside the factory were not much better. Garry was managing the plant when I arrived and it was he who had had the bright idea of leasing the warehouse, spending all my money to import fish-smoking equipment from Germany and producing tons of high-quality smoked salmon. The smoker itself was the size of a small house and in addition there were two freezers, each the size of a basketball court. There was no business plan and no accounts, just shoeboxes full of invoices and bills to show what had happened to my life savings. There was also a remarkable lack of smoked salmon.

My plan was to get a handle on the paperwork, gain an understanding of the operation and then sell the business as quickly as possible. Forget making a profit; I just wanted to salvage what I could. This was easier said than done. The first problem to deal with was the Cubans. Garry had rented out space to a group of Cubans who were paid to collect crates of spoiled fish from various Miami fishmongers for incineration. Instead of disposing of the fish, they were bringing it to our warehouse to be repackaged and sold to seafood restaurants in the name of our company. That I discovered this was thanks to my training as an auditor. Going through Garry's abysmal paperwork, I tried to understand why we were purchasing so many crates of fresh lemons.

The reason turned out to be that José's men would tip the crates of spoiled fish onto the floor, straighten them out and soak them in fresh lemon juice, and then repackage and freeze them as snapper or grouper. They had been doing this for months before I stopped them and it was a miracle that the population of Miami wasn't wiped out by some horrible version of ciguatera or diphyllobothriasis.

With Garry and Anna gone and José and his gang disposed of, I found myself in possession of a vast fish-smoking plant and no idea what to do with it. Juan and I quickly learned that the only way to sell it was as a 'going concern'. In other words, it needed to be an operating business before anybody would consider buying it. Or, to put it another way, it was off with the pinstripe suit and on with the wellies. In addition to accountant, pot smuggler, snail rancher, ladies' underwear rep, money launderer and editor, I now added fish smoker to my CV.

We hired the manager of a smoked-salmon factory in Vancouver to fly down and spend a month teaching me the rudiments of the business. We had booked her into a Holiday Inn but in the end we were both working so hard that she would crawl home with me and sleep on our sofa. A few hours later, the two of us would be back at the factory. The smoking machine was certainly top of the line, state of the art and, as I have mentioned, the size of a house. Carol Fisher (that really was her name) not only taught me how to smoke fish in the machine but also how to dismantle, clean and repair it. She taught me how to buy salmon from Norway and how to gut it, fillet, cold smoke and slice it. She taught me about knives and how to use and sharpen them. She taught me about fishmongers and restaurants, about marketing and packaging. In one month, she offered me her twenty years of experience, and I soaked it all up.

Thanks to Carol's expert tuition, I became a damned fine smoker, though I say so myself, and, for the next year, we produced some of the best smoked salmon on the Eastern Seaboard. Jude worked full time selling it to the most exclusive restaurants in Miami and we also sold to the cruise lines that sailed from Miami and Fort Lauderdale. We even sold to some of the airlines. Juan promoted our salmon to the private dining clubs on Wall Street and each week I would ship a small container to New York.

But it was back-breaking work and I was sometimes working 20-hour shifts in the freezing cold with nobody to assist me and only my old spider bites to keep me company. Twenty years later, the pains in my back serve as a constant reminder of those days wearing the rubber boots. The salmon, which I flew in from Norway, averaged 9 or 10 lb each and I needed to smoke a minimum of 40 at one time. They all had to be filleted before smoking and soaked in brine for 20 hours. The smoking cycle itself could last anywhere between 13 and 20 hours and required constant monitoring. North-West 10th Avenue became my home and I was soon on first-name terms with all the hookers and crack dealers.

On my occasional visits home, Jude would make me strip naked and hose me down to remove the smell of fish before I entered the house. Of all the terrible things I have done to my poor children through the years, the worst was making them come to the fish factory after school and wait while Jude and I worked.

'But, Daddy, it's so smelly and yucky.'

'Be quiet and do your homework.'

Despite Jude's success at selling the fish, the overheads left very little money for living. For 12 months, we lived on salmon. Sam the poodle turned pink and to this day my daughters refuse to look at salmon. Oddly enough, I still love smoked salmon and retain a very discerning palate for it.

There's not much I'm proud of in my life. I've been a lucky husband and father, an innumerate accountant, an accidental racketeer, a mediocre money launderer – but I really was a good smoker! Juan and I managed to sell the business in 1988 and I invested my proceeds in a desktop publishing business called Mr Write. A few months after selling European Smoked Fish, I was arrested. But at least it wasn't for poisoning Miami's gourmets.

* * *

Just before my move to Miami, on 18 November 1985, while Juan and I were having one of our long lunches at Romano's, Nicholas Deak was murdered by a deranged woman with a .38-calibre revolver. After a lifetime of adventure, parachuting into the Balkans behind German lines and tracking down Japanese gold in the jungles of the Philippines, it was ironic that he should have suffered such a meaningless fate.

When Juan and I returned to the office with a postprandial glow, it was crawling with armed police and I feared the worst. But it wasn't an FBI raid, just a random act of New York violence. A seriously deranged schizophrenic with a long history of mental problems had wandered off the street into the Deak-Perera offices and shot the bank's receptionist. Hearing the gunfire, Deak emerged from his office and was shot through the heart. He died immediately.

Had Juan and I taken a shorter lunch break and not indulged in a second bottle of wine and the cheeseboard, we would have returned to the office earlier. It could have been us lying in a pool of blood instead of Mr Deak. There was a lesson to be learned there and I have never, to this day, resisted a second bottle of wine or cut short a good lunch to hurry back to the office.

In all my years as a racketeer, with the exception of the meeting between José and Pierre in the Miami warehouse, that is as close as I ever came to violence or murder.

14

KEEPING A LOW PROFILE

None of my circle was ever very good at keeping a low profile. Howard delighted in seeing himself on the front pages of the newspapers even when he was on the run, which was most of the time. Graham wore gaudy silk suits to Christie's wine auctions and would purchase expensive cases of rare Bordeaux vintages while journalists took photographs. We drove expensive cars, spent most of the days in pubs, most of the evenings in restaurants and simply assumed that nobody would notice.

In 1971, Graham and I decided we needed an official business as a front for our various illegal activities. I established Zeitgeist, meaning 'spirit of the times', which seemed appropriate for our venture but was not exactly a low-profile name. We rented a four-storey building in Little Venice from the Church Commissioners and registered it as the official London offices of Zeitgeist. Warwick Place is a very small, beautiful street of white-painted Regency buildings adjoining the Regent's Canal and round the corner from Richard Branson's houseboat. Our building was number three. Four was a bookshop, five was Didier's restaurant and six was the Warwick Castle pub. Except for the occasional visit to California or Afghanistan on business, we had no need ever to leave Warwick Place. It had everything a man could want.

The plan was to use the ground floor as the office for Zeitgeist and the first floor as the centre for all our smuggling and racketeering strategy sessions. I moved into the flat on the top floor. Graham's place in Shirland Road was nearby.

The Church Commissioners managed the property portfolio for the Church of England, one of the largest landowners in the country. Many of its holdings were slum tenements and at one point the Church of England owned most of the brothels in London. The Georgian terraces of Little Venice were one of their more respectable investments. Unfortunately, the Church Commissioners would not allow us to use the ground floor for office space. The lease stipulated that it had to be a retail store open to the public.

'Let's hang our carpets on the wall and call it a carpet shop,' I suggested.

'Brilliant!' Graham said. 'We can put outrageous prices on them and people will leave us alone.'

What had started as a cover for our trips to Iran and Afghanistan had quickly turned into a passion. Graham, who had been collecting oriental carpets for years, enjoyed teaching me all he knew and I soon acquired my own collection of antique tribal rugs. Every trip to the Middle East added new rugs to our collections. Graham's house was filled with piles of folded carpets, so Mandy was delighted when we moved them all into our new shop, which we called Hamdullah, meaning 'Thanks be to God'.

Hanging the rugs on the walls of the shop permitted us to enjoy our collections and we rotated them on a regular basis. We even hired a beautiful Swedish girl, Kristina, to sit in the shop all day and frighten away customers with our ridiculous prices. Unfortunately, Saudi oil money was pouring into London in the early '70s and Arab princes had started buying up oriental carpets. The more we asked, the more they paid and the shop quickly became successful, which was never the idea. What had been merely a front for laundering money ended up making cash.

Because the official address of Zeitgeist Ltd was 3 Warwick Place, we were legally obliged to display the name outside the building. However, this was forbidden by the terms of the lease. We were caught between the Church Commissioners and the Department of Trade and Industry.

'Why not write it in Arabic?' I suggested. 'That way everyone will assume it says Hamdullah even though it actually says Zeitgeist.'

'Brilliant!' Graham said. 'Michael Durani can translate it for us.'

The deviousness of the project appealed to Michael and within a few days he found us a Pakistani signwriter who painted the large gold Arabic letters above the shop.

Michael assured us that the sign said 'Spirit of the Times', but for all I know it could have said 'Allah Smiles on Those Who Canoe'. In any event, we felt that we had done our best to fulfil our legal obligations and so Zeitgeist opened for business.

Warwick Place was a busy place in the early '70s. In addition to our bustling carpet shop, we also operated a property company. We would buy derelict buildings in various parts of London and then employ a crew to gut and renovate them. Because of all the Arab oil wealth pouring into the city, property prices were going through the roof and we were selling at a handsome profit.

On Fridays, after lunch, I would drive around London in my BMW with a boot full of cash and deliver the weekly payroll to our various building sites. George, who was now 20 years old, had moved to London and, without telling anyone he was my brother, was working as a labourer for one of the building crews.

Jude, disapproving of my new flashy lifestyle, had completely abandoned me by the time I moved to Warwick Place and I was exploiting my freedom with a new girlfriend, or two, every week. At the time, I tended to wear white linen suits and when I delivered the payroll to the building sites in my left-hand-drive BMW, I was conscious of what a dashing man-about-town figure I must appear. The men were, naturally, always pleased to see me and were suitably grateful when I paid for several rounds of beer in the nearest pub after work. With a hip apartment in one of London's more fashionable districts, a smart German sports car, money in my pocket and trendy suits, I was highly aware of my good fortune and anxious not to lord it over others less privileged than myself. I made a point of being 'one of the chaps' and insisted that all the workers 'just call me Patrick'.

Years later, my brother George finally told me how I was regarded by the workforce. When they saw my car drive up to the building site, one of them would shout, "Ere comes that ponce with the money. Let's see what nancy-boy gear he's wearing this week.'

'Look, he's wearing a white suit. What a prat!'

Blissfully unaware of my reputation as a stuck-up git, I would return to Warwick Place, satisfied with my paternal role as a generous boss and popular man of the people. One of the sobering effects of writing a memoir is realising what an insufferable jerk one must have been at various stages in life. I have already described what a pretentious and self-centred teenager I was but now I see that I had grown into an even more selfish and ostentatiously arrogant young man. The only consolation is that I now feel less bad about my current incarnation as an elderly curmudgeon and grumpy old man.

In addition to the shop, the offices and my top-floor flat, 3 Warwick Place also had a genuine old brick wine cellar, which extended under the road. Howard was to become a serious wine connoisseur in later years but in those days, as part of his rough, Welsh, salt-of-the-earth persona, he was strictly a beer drinker. Graham and I, however, quickly filled the cellar with a collection of good Bordeaux, which we purchased at Christie's and Sotheby's auctions by the case. Had we kept the collection, I suspect that it would be worth several million pounds at today's prices but, unfortunately, when we eventually left Warwick Place with only a few hours' advance notice, we had time to collect nothing but our passports. The wine was seized by our building-site workers in lieu of their final pay packets, which I had failed to deliver due to my sudden and unannounced departure from the country. It still hurts me when I think of the fate of all those cases of Pomerol and Margaux: 'What a fucking wanker! Look at all this frog's piss – no bloody lager!'

The second time I built a wine collection was when we lived in France. This was a much more modest affair but nevertheless represented several years' worth of collecting from the local vineyards. Again, I had to leave the country at somewhat short notice but at least this time the seized wine was better appreciated. Several senior police officers from Paris and London came to inspect my house after our departure and they stayed in a local hotel owned by a friend of mine. I have the consolation of knowing that they fully appreciated my collection and let my friend know what excellent taste I had as they diligently worked their way through my racks of dusty bottles.

By the time I had to flee London, I also owned a small house in Kentish Town, which the authorities knew nothing about. That house contained a small wine collection and I looked forward to drinking it some time in the future. Meanwhile, I had made friends with a local dignitary in Périgord – a good person to have as a friend and a bad person to have as an enemy. He had a magnificent wine cellar and I spent several enjoyable evenings exploring some of his vintages. His son was a student, a pot-smoking friend of mine, and during the Christmas vacation I gave him the key to my London house. Apparently, he and his girlfriend ran out of money while they were in London. Being a resourceful young man, and his father's son, rather than spend his last few pounds in the pub, he drank his way through my wine collection instead. 'You don't have a corkscrew in your house,' he grumbled later. 'We had to push the corks into the bottles with a knife.' He promised to replace my wine collection with bottles from his father's cellar. Unfortunately, he also discovered LSD at about the same time and spent the next two years in a sort of otherworldly trance. He is a respectable lawyer these days and eventually inherited his father's cellar, so possibly the next time I see him I'll remind him of his promise.

The trouble is, I no longer collect wine. I have a wine rack in which I keep a few bottles of everyday plonk but, after losing three magnificent wine collections, I now drink good wine as soon as I get my hands on it. I currently teach a wine appreciation course at the local university and often have access to good collectable wine. I don't drink it straight from the bottle, of course – I will always wait long enough to get a glass and a corkscrew – but I don't wait much longer than that. I celebrated my 60th birthday quite recently and was given several decent bottles of wine. They were all gone within the week. Wine collecting is for wankers!

Beyond the carpet shop and the property development, the main business at Warwick Place was moving large quantities of cannabis around the globe, by plane, by boat or packed inside VW camper vans. Most of our working day was spent in the Warwick Castle and in fact we had the pub's phone number on our Zeitgeist business cards. Howard lived in Oxford but spent as much time in the Warwick

Castle as anyone else. In the evenings, we tended to eat in Didier's, which we treated like the corporate dining room. We had far too much money, we travelled the world and we lived in London, which was still the most exciting and creative place on earth. The Beatles had recently disbanded but the Stones were still rocking and Paris Hilton had not even been conceived. We changed our girlfriends daily and even though, with hindsight, I can see what a bunch of arrogant, self-satisfied and self-centred little fops we were, life was wonderful and we loved every moment of it. Being low key was never an option.

* * *

In 1977, Christopher Boyce (the subject of the book *The Falcon and the Snowman*, played by Timothy Hutton in the subsequent movie) was sentenced to 40 years in prison for a combination of spying for the Russians and cocaine dealing. About the time we arrived in America in 1980, he escaped from the top-security federal prison at Lompoc and vanished into the inhospitable deserts of central California. He also moved immediately to the top of the FBI's Most Wanted List. He was eventually captured a couple of years later in Washington State on his way, via Alaska, to join Kim Philby in Moscow. During his time on the run, when most people in his situation would have kept a low profile, Boyce became a professional bank robber in Idaho.

I identified strongly with Boyce, not because I was a Russian agent or even a bank robber but quite simply because he and I became fugitives at the same time, in 1980. A sort of karma united us and I was anxious for his continued freedom. When the story of his life on the run became public, I felt even closer to him. Our interpretation of keeping a low profile while on the run was similar. He became a bank robber, while I started publishing a newsletter for money launderers.

The Offshore Banking Report was published from my new home in Santa Cruz and, in between delivering the kids to school or attending PTA meetings, I would sit at my computer and write articles about Swiss numbered bank accounts or anonymous corporations in the Cayman Islands. My company was called LaneHouse Publications and I was a member of the Santa Cruz Chamber of Commerce. Jude and I attended all the Chamber's meetings and all our friends were from the Chamber or the PTA. I would give free copies of my newsletter to my new friends, who loved it. My racketeering friends, however, were appalled. 'That's so uncool, man. You'll get us all busted.'

There are two schools of thought on living undercover and I will call them the English and the American schools. The American school is based on a transient society (especially in California), where everybody is from somewhere else and on their way to somewhere else, you don't know your neighbours and so you simply keep to yourself and mind your own business. The English school's approach is the opposite. Get to know your neighbours, participate in all the local activities and let people see you for who and what you are. Obviously, you do not tell people you are an illegal immigrant or an international fugitive (American tolerance stretches only so far). But let them see you being yourself, just doing regular things, whether it's volunteering at the PTA or getting drunk and loudly defending the British monarchy.

We had a wonderful five years in Santa Cruz and made lifelong friends. They all accepted that I published this interesting newsletter and that I had various wealthy clients whom I needed to visit from time to time. The rest of the time, it was early-morning tennis with Bob, barbecues at our house and pool parties at Nancy's. We all had kids the same age and shared the same lifestyle. We went to the beach or skiing at Lake Tahoe with the kids. We drove to the wine country and hosted drunken pool parties without the kids and we all supported the local school.

It was the local elementary school that first taught me how non-judgemental our Californian neighbours could be. The principal was a stout middle-aged lady who would have looked quite at home at one of the Queen's Buckingham Palace garden parties. She was the epitome of respectability and we were all happy to submit our children to her benign maternal care.

We were therefore surprised to hear that the school principal had been arrested for stealing. The PTA raised funds by organising bingo evenings on the first Wednesday of every month and the parents dutifully attended and purchased their $20 entrance tickets. Apparently, while we were all chanting 'sixty-six, clickety-click', a new security camera in a school office captured the unwitting lady with her dress raised and her girdle lowered as she stuffed bundles of PTA bingo money into her voluminous knickers. The police discovered she had been doing this for months and had accumulated several hundred dollars, which she spent on her much admired collection of Amish needlework samplers, all of which featured an inspiring religious theme.

Somebody from the PTA organised a fundraising tea party one Saturday afternoon to raise money for the principal's defence. We all stood around making polite small talk with the woman, trying not to think what she might have sequestered in her knickers (we knew she didn't wear a thong, but then nobody did in those days). As a fugitive racketeer, I felt quite smugly virtuous for once.

Publishing *The Offshore Banking Report* was an odd occupation, it is true, but so were many of the things my Californian neighbours did. My neighbour Steve Wozniak, for example, had developed this combination of TV and a typewriter that he called an Apple. That was much more weird than publishing a newsletter. Anyway, people were supposed to be doing unusual and creative things in California. That was why we were all there. The newsletter was so successful that it came to the attention of the IRS and they gently suggested that I close it down. By that time, I was hooked on computers and in 1983 I switched from international finance to software – a much more low-profile occupation.

* * *

My sister Natasha is somebody who shares my inability to maintain a low profile. After we finally managed to bribe a judge to release her from prison in Mexico, she crossed the United States border illegally with her fiancé, Stuart, and their son, Albi. They lived for a few years in San Diego on a yacht owned by a senior executive at California's Bank of America. Natasha's job was simply to sail the yacht to whichever West Coast destination the executive planned to visit. It was a forty-six-foot two-masted schooner with several luxury cabins and everything built in polished mahogany or teak. For maybe four or five weeks out of the year, they lived on the boat as servants. For the other forty-seven weeks, the yacht was their private luxury home.

After the birth of their second son (my godson Thomas), Natasha and Stuart, now married, decided to return to the UK to give their sons a proper English education. With the money they had saved, they purchased their own yacht, *Sundancer*, a 30-ft trimaran, and, leaving San Diego in late 1986, sailed south to the Panama Canal. At this time, Panama was experiencing some turmoil, which resulted in the US invasion three years later, and the overthrow of President Manuel Noriega. Noriega was later to join me in the Federal prison in Miami in 1989. But that's another story.

Following various student protests and demonstrations, control of the canal was disrupted and, as a result, Natasha's yacht was slightly crushed by a Japanese oil tanker and, we later discovered, suffered serious structural damage.

Her plan was to visit me in Miami on her way back to Europe. As a convicted pot smuggler with a Mexican prison record, she would obviously not be welcomed by the US authorities. Nevertheless, she planned to sail up from Panama, slip quietly into a friend's berth in Coconut Grove harbour and then spend a few days with me. After that, her plan was to sail to the Bahamas and thence across the Atlantic. A quick, quiet, low-profile, beneath-the-radar visit, in other words.

In the event, Natasha arrived just south of Key West in October 1987, slightly ahead of Hurricane Floyd, which had followed her from Nicaragua. Because Floyd did not do much damage when it passed over Miami, it is always referred to as a minor hurricane. However, when you are on a small boat, the word 'minor' seems remarkably inappropriate. As Stuart struggled to lower the sails, he called to Natasha that the pontoon had broken off. 'Put out a Mayday!' he called.

The US Coast Guard in Key West responded instantly, asking if they were in immediate danger, and Natasha, shouting to be heard over the howling wind, replied, 'Yes, we are in immediate danger and I have two young children on board.' In the days before easily available GPS units, Natasha could calculate her position only using a sextant. In the predawn light, drifting with no sails, out of sight of land and being pounded by giant waves, it was impossible for her to provide the Coast Guard with a precise location. Although they put out an immediate search team, they might never have found the yacht had it not been for a nearby motor vessel, *Monkey Business*, which had been listening to the transmission and was able to confirm Natasha's exact position.

After two terrifying hours, and thanks to *Monkey Business*'s constant radio monitoring, US Navy and Coast Guard helicopters appeared overhead and lowered the rescue harness to lift the family off the yacht. But, tossed around in the 15-ft waves, the corkscrewing *Sundancer* was an impossible target and eventually the pilot admitted defeat. 'Don't worry,' he said. 'If your boat sinks, we'll be able to fish you out of the water.' *Sundancer* held together and eventually a 41-ft Coast Guard launch arrived and somehow, bouncing around in the giant waves, Natasha, Albi, baby Thomas and finally Stuart were all transferred to the safety of the larger vessel.

A Coast Guard boarding party climbed onto *Sundancer* with a pump and some flotation devices but decided that the structural damage was so bad that the yacht was doomed. Natasha listened to their exchanges on the radio: 'She's breaking up. We can't save her.'

'What do you want us to salvage?' they asked as Albi and Thomas looked overboard and watched the only home they had known settling sideways in the pounding seas. Natasha was heartbroken. 'My photo albums,' was all she could say.

Looking around the doomed yacht, the Coast Guard captain, realising that *Sundancer* was more than a boat, it was a home, decided to save it. Getting on the radio, he made contact with the US *Shearwater*, which was a 110-ft cutter with a crew of 17 and a top speed of over 30 knots. The *Shearwater* was part of a unique Coast Guard division tasked, as a public affairs pamphlet noted, with 'maritime law enforcement, targeting [their] efforts towards the interdiction of narcotics and controlled substances smuggled into the United States by sea'. From the time it was first commissioned in 1982 until it was decommissioned in 1992, *Shearwater* seized pot-laden yachts and motorboats, cargo ships and freighters on a sometimes daily basis. It intercepted so many drug shipments into the United States from the Caribbean and South America that the ship and crew received an endless number of Commendation Medals from the government. *Shearwater* was every pot smuggler's worst nightmare.

It was also my sister's salvation, and the skipper, Lieutenant Russell, and his crew could not have been kinder. The family was transferred from the launch to the cutter, where a doctor was able to take care of them while crewmen from the various boats salvaged *Sundancer* with large inflatable flotation devices.

Despite the worsening weather conditions, Lieutenant Russell was determined not to lose Natasha's home and so, towed by the large Coast Guard cutter and escorted by the Coast Guard launch and a US Navy hydrofoil, with a red-and-white Coast Guard helicopter and grey Navy helicopters hovering overhead, Natasha finally made her discreet, below-the-radar entrance into Key West. When the family stepped onto dry land, they were officially welcomed by the mayor of Key West, the chief of police and reporters from the *Key West Citizen* and NBC *Keys News*.

Monkey Business was also in the news not long after Natasha's dramatic arrival. In May 1988, front-running candidate for the Democratic presidential nomination Gary Hart decided to take a private cruise to Bimini as a break from the pressures of political campaigning. The *Miami Herald* and the *National Enquirer* subsequently published photographs of the candidate on board the *Monkey Business* with an attractive and scantily clad young lady who was not his wife. He dropped out of the race a few days later.

Natasha's low-profile visit to the USA was front-page news for weeks and featured on TV almost daily. Wherever they went in Key West, people would stop them with offers of food, jobs and money. The only federal agency that did not get involved was the INS, the immigration service. Natasha and her boys fell in love with Key West and its people and they continued to live there, as illegal aliens, for years while they slowly rebuilt their boat. Twelve years after their spectacular arrival, they finally sailed across the Atlantic and returned to England.

Oddly enough, after almost sinking Natasha's boat in 1987, Hurricane Floyd continued across the Atlantic to Europe where it became known as the Great Storm of 1987, the most severe storm Britain had experienced since the Great Storm of 1703. It caused the deaths of approximately 23 people, some embarrassment to a top

BBC meteorologist and the windows of my father's seafront home in Brighton to be smashed.

* * *

In addition to sharing an unusual attitude to keeping a low profile, Christopher Boyce and I had another connection.

When my family and I lived in Santa Cruz, we had two cars. I owned an extremely large Fleetwood Cadillac, which all Europeans buy when they move to the US, and we also had a VW camper. This was a classic Santa Cruz hippy van with a peace symbol on the front and a pink 'Nuke the Gay Whales' bumper sticker on the back.

In the summer of 1981, we decided to drive up the Pacific coast to visit some old friends, Dick and Joanne, in Seattle, Washington. I had met Dick in Europe during the Vietnam War, when he had been stationed with military intelligence in Germany as a Russian-language specialist. He would go into East Germany from time to time on official business but the rest of the time he monitored Russian transmissions along the border. Needless to say, he was an expert on all the regional variations and subtle nuances of the Russian language.

One Saturday, we decided to drive from Seattle to Port Townsend at the northern end of the Olympic Peninsula. I had recently read a rave review in the *Wall Street Journal* of a local restaurant that roasted a whole cow, completely covered in garlic and rock salt, every couple of months. We drove to the restaurant in the VW bus and arrived in plenty of time for the 7 p.m. start. The meal was delicious. The beef was filled with flavour and melted like butter on the tongue, while the smell of garlic filled the grounds of the outdoor restaurant. Dick and I had far too much wine to drink and so Joanne drove us along the shore of Puget Sound, heading back to Seattle.

After leaving the restaurant, we drove through Port Townsend and could not help noticing a number of solitary men in suits sitting in parked cars and on park benches. 'They look like goddamn government spooks,' Dick said. Spotting my CB radio, he added, 'Let's have some fun.'

Puget Sound is a deep-water port for America's Pacific Fleet. There are hidden submarine bases there and all sorts of stuff you don't want to think about. It's a high-security area at the best of times.

'Let's pretend we're Russian spies in a rubber raft with a leak and we're looking for our submarine,' Dick suggested.

'What a splendid idea!' we all agreed.

For the next hour, until the booze started to wear off and he got bored, Dick carried on several conversations in fluent, idiomatic Russian between a Soviet submarine captain and some Russian spies in a rubber dinghy who were returning from a mission. It was all jolly good fun and we had a good laugh before we eventually returned to Dick and Joanne's home and collapsed into our beds.

The newspaper headlines the following morning focused on the arrest, the previous evening, of Christopher Boyce as he was preparing to board a fishing vessel to Alaska. He was arrested as he left a restaurant in nearby Port Angeles. His plan had been to cross the Bering Strait and reach Siberia. The FBI had been closing in on him for weeks and that evening, while we were playing games on the CB radio, we probably had most of the FBI and CIA agents in the country within 20 miles of us actively looking for Russian agents. No wonder they've still not caught Bin Laden! He is somebody who definitely knows how to keep a low profile.

15

MY DAD

WEDNESDAY, 13 SEPTEMBER 2006

Father died today. Or maybe it was yesterday. We had not spoken for 30 years, so a day here or there makes little difference. My sister called me from England to give me the news but I already knew, as soon as I heard her voice on the phone. I could have spared her the grief and said, 'I know,' but I was playing for time and I made her spell it out.

'Who's this?'

'It's me. Natasha.'

'Oh, hi, Tasha. I thought it sounded like you but you don't usually call this early – or during the week.'

'Well, it's about Dad.'

'Oh, yes? How's he doing?'

'He's dead. He died this morning at three.'

That's the same time that my first child, Peggy, was born, exactly one year after my mother died. She was also called Peggy. But I didn't bother saying any of that to Natasha. She had her own sorrows.

I don't know why my father cut me out of his life and refused to talk to me. It could have been because I was a racketeer, of course. It was not a profession of which he approved. But, unfortunately, I think it was more than that. In many ways, I wish that had been the reason; it would have made things simpler. Once I'd stopped being a racketeer, there would have been the possibility of reconciliation. But, with no specific reason for the estrangement, I was left to assume that he simply did not like me or anything about me. In his view, I was a disappointment to the core. And now, of course, it is too late to do anything about it.

Natasha said, 'At least he gave us a most wonderful childhood. He looked after us until we were able to look after ourselves.' This is true. My childhood memories are filled with family outings, trips in the car and my father's endless lists as he tried vainly to organise us.

I remember when I left home for university, my father very seriously said, 'I hope you know there's always a home here for you.' I didn't really understand what he meant at the time. Of course there was a home there for me. With the selfishness and ignorance of youth, I never questioned that this was my home and that I had a right to it. It was only later, when my own children left home, that I understood what he had said – and by then it was too late to thank him. True to his word, several years later, when I was fighting my heroin addiction, I returned to the family. They had preserved my room and I found salvation and recovery in my father's home.

> I remember, I remember
> The house where I was born,
> The little window where the sun
> Came peeping in at morn;
> He never came a wink too soon
> Nor brought too long a day;
> But now, I often wish the night
> Had borne my breath away.

My father was a very dignified man and always wore a jacket and tie, even when we went on camping trips. These days, campsites have bathrooms and flush toilets, electrical outlets and even Internet connections. When I was a child, a campsite was just a muddy field where you could pitch your tent while you looked for some strategically placed bushes in lieu of a bathroom.

I remember once my father had telephoned ahead to reserve us a place in a campsite near Hamble, on the Solent. It was in the grounds of a country estate owned by a retired brigadier. We were all told to be on our best behaviour, as this was not a site where children were normally permitted to stay. Usually, the guests were other retired people on sailing holidays. When we drove up to the main house, a military-looking man with a clipped moustache strode across the gravel driveway to meet us. My father got out of the car and my mother hissed at us to 'sit still and be good'.

Both men wore identical dark corduroy trousers and Harris tweed jackets and, as they neared each other, they both held out their hands to shake.

'Mr Lane?'

'Brigadier Jones?'

'How d'you do?'

'How d'you do?'

No sooner had their hands met than my father threw back his head and a vast green and yellow stream of vomit erupted from his mouth and hit the brigadier full in the face. The poor man was covered in it but he barely flinched.

'Oh, I'm most terribly sorry,' my father said. 'I've had this stomach flu all day and getting out of the car must have exacerbated it.'

My mother rushed from the car with a handkerchief to mop up the damage but her gesture was entirely futile. The man needed hosing down with a water cannon.

'My dear lady, please don't bother yourself,' the brigadier said. 'I'll wash it off later. Worse things happen at sea, don't you know?' He turned and looked at us children in the back seat. 'Better get these youngsters in their tent while it's still light.'

After a shocked silence during which we recovered from the sight of my father behaving in such an unlikely and undignified manner, we all started hooting with laughter and imitating what we had just seen.

'Mr. Jones? . . . Braaaghfff!'

'How d'you do? . . . Graaacht!!'

'Daddy, why did you throw up on that man? I thought we were s'posed to be on our best behaviour.'

My poor father was forced to relive that incident for many years and whenever we were told to be on our best behaviour there would always be sniggering until one of us made some disgusting vomit noises.

Although we must have severely tried his patience at times, he never hit us. I don't believe I was ever hit or beaten by my father. My mother, on the other hand, beat us regularly. Her anger was like a summer storm. It was sudden, violent and swiftly finished, although not before she'd grabbed the nearest stick and smacked us with it. I remember her chasing me out of the house once and following me around the garden with a stick while I ran just ahead of her, dodging around trees and bushes until she finally caught me. We were both out of breath. 'I can't even remember why I wanted to hit you,' she gasped, and we both started laughing. But my father never, ever raised his hand in anger. He just looked endlessly disappointed and as I grew older his disappointment only increased.

My father died today, or yesterday, or whenever, during an operation to implant a pacemaker. My wife and daughter think the operation failed because they could not find a heart but my sister Natasha thinks it was because we, my siblings and I, broke it long ago. Certainly we put a lot of strain on his heart. My own history of drunken arrests and criminal misdemeanours has been well documented already. Natasha herself could add her involvement with the Angry Brigade and subsequent years in a Mexican prison to the list.

My brother George deserves his own book, possibly entitled *The Three Horsemen of the Apocalypse*, as war, revolution and falling property prices did seem to pursue him wherever he went. After abandoning Europe for places east at an early age, he truly became one of Buchan's lean brown men. The family lost all contact with him except for the occasional sighting on the shores of the Oxus or in Afghanistan, Mongolia or the more remote regions of Anatolia. If my father had ever dreamed that George would follow his footsteps as a corporate executive, such hopes must soon have been abandoned.

My other siblings brought my father no greater comfort. Judy, after becoming a teenage mother while still at school, eventually married Howard Marks, Britain's most notorious and headline-hogging drug smuggler. My youngest and sweetest sister, Masha, is the only member of the family who never gave him grey hairs but by then he was too weary to properly show her much love or recognition. And my youngest brother, Marcus, made the most dramatic exit of all from the family circle.

Marcus is 19 years younger than me and by the time he was in his teens, Judy, Howard and I were already fugitives living in various parts of Europe. George was doing mysterious things in Lebanon, and Masha and Natasha were both living on yachts in the Caribbean. Marcus was an angelic-faced young boy in a Brighton boarding school. My father had remarried and Marcus did not feel comfortable in the house; he spent most of his school holidays with Jude and me in France.

I'm so pleased that I had daughters and not sons. Just as I've spent my life fruitlessly yearning for approval from my father, my two brothers have sought love and approval from me, which I have been unable to give them. I don't know why. I love them both and am proud of them both but I just cannot share or demonstrate my love. I have young male assistants at work to whom I provide strong and warm mentoring; I have loving relationships with my sons-in-law; but I have antagonistic relationships with both of my brothers.

Marcus left his boarding school to join Jude, Peggy, Bridie and me in Molières for Christmas in 1979. He was 15 years old and this was his opportunity to bond with his elder brother and make plans for his future. He felt rejected by his father and stepmother and must have hoped that his big brother could provide the guidance he needed. A couple of days after Marcus arrived at our house in France, I received a call that the mysterious *Karob*, the salvage ship that had vanished into Antarctica, had made contact and that my presence was required in Scotland. Marcus stayed with Jude and the girls and I am sure had a wonderful time, but he never made the connection with his big brother that he so desperately needed and deserved.

He returned to school in January 1980 but by April Howard had been arrested and I had become a fugitive. Desperate for love and contact with his family, Marcus used his saved pocket money to buy a really cheap ticket on Bulgarian Airlines to join George in Beirut. The flight to Lebanon went via Sofia, the capital of Bulgaria, and Marcus had a few hours to wait between flights. The Cold War was in full swing in 1980 and the Soviet KGB tended to use the Bulgarian secret service for its more brutal 'wet jobs', such as assassinating the Pope or killing émigré dissidents with umbrellas.

Bored in the airport at Sofia, Marcus purchased a postcard and a local stamp and sent the card to my father in Brighton. My father had already been alerted by the school that Marcus had gone missing and was phoning around the family to see if any of us knew where he was. Marcus's postcard arrived two days later with its Bulgarian postmark: 'Dear Dad, have decided to enrol in the KGB like your friend Philby. Love Marcus.' Marcus eventually achieved a certain notoriety as a gun-toting chauffeur for one of the warlords in the Bekaa Valley.

To be fair to my siblings, whom I love immensely, I should put the above observations in perspective. Natasha has been happily married for almost 30 years and is the proud mother of two fine young men. George, equally happily married and with two charming children, earned his doctorate at the University of London and, with four or five books already published, is a leading authority on the early Mongol Empire. Judy and Howard have three delightful children, the eldest of whom is a successful barrister, journalist and published author. Masha is an international driving instructor and the mother of two beautiful daughters, and Marcus, after many adventures, became a skilled cabinetmaker, with a very successful atelier in Majorca and wealthy clients all over Europe. None of which seemed to prevent my father from being disappointed.

Judy and I were not invited by our father's wife to attend his funeral but we received reports from our siblings. The surprising thing was how many people attended – hundreds of them. We had no idea that he knew so many people. George was appalled to discover how many of my father's friends didn't even know he had any children. Natasha told me that she must have been approached by at least 15 or 20 people who told her they regularly had lunch with my father, at least once a month. They all described him as a fascinating conversationalist and a great lover of good food and drink. Indeed, that is how I remember him, even when I was a child. My parents were forever giving and attending parties and my father was always surrounded by acquaintances. But I can never remember him having a friend. Nobody was ever able to get close to him, even his family. He was an extremely private man and, I suspect, profoundly lonely.

MY DAD

Being very well read and intelligent, he could talk effortlessly and entertainingly on any subject as long as no emotions were involved. I remember when I was about 11 or 12 years old, my mother had obviously persuaded him to give me 'the talk'. She made a big point of going out for the evening with Natasha after the younger children had been put to bed. My father and I were left alone to have dinner together undisturbed. I knew that it was to be a significant evening because of the many meaningful looks my mother gave my father before she left, but I wasn't sure what to expect. I had a few glimmerings about sex at that age and some vague understanding of the plumbing and mechanics involved. But I could never have related the concept to anyone I knew and certainly not to my parents.

As my father spoke, I had no idea that he was talking about sex and spent a rather bewildering evening listening to him describing the pollination of flowers by bees and making some rather mysterious observations about the plumage of male birds. The only part of 'the talk' that related to humans was the rather cryptic observation that 'some chaps like other chaps' and I should always be careful. He was obviously relieved when my mother returned home and once again the two of them exchanged meaningful glances. My mother, presumably embarrassed by what she imagined to be my newfound knowledge, told me to clean my teeth and go to bed. 'And don't forget to say your prayers.' I lay awake for hours but instead of saying my prayers I puzzled over the significance of 'some chaps like other chaps'. It was not until many years later, when we were standing together in the kitchen and I told my father that I was gay, that I finally realised what he had been referring to.

During the last few years of his life, my brothers and sisters would be invited to his house for the occasional dinner party and everything was fine as long as nobody discussed anything personal. George would talk about the situation in the Middle East and Natasha would discuss sailing or the latest advances in GPS technologies. As long as no emotional or personal matters were raised, my father's conversation was brilliant and he was endlessly knowledgeable and entertaining. I remember once sitting in the restaurant of the railway station at Le Buisson, having dinner before we put my father on the night train to Paris. He had been staying with us a few weeks in Molières. The dinner conversation ranged from the Arian heresies of south-west France to the Aryan theories of the Nazis. Jude asked him where the Aryans came from and my father proceeded to draw a map of Eurasia on the white paper tablecloth. If I had had an atlas in front of me, I could never have copied the map that he drew in freehand and from memory. Every bay, every inlet and every headland from the Aran Islands to the Aral Sea and from Sicily to Scandinavia was swiftly drawn onto the tablecloth while he explained the prehistoric movements of the Celts and the Proto-Indo-Europeans around the two continents. The breadth of his knowledge came as no surprise; he had been the ultimate authority on everything since I was a small child. What surprised me was the effortless way he drew the map and the extraordinary accuracy of the details. After we put him on the train, I retrieved the map from the restaurant table and when we returned to Le Moulin I compared it with an atlas; the details were perfect.

Through my job at the university, I spent a large amount of time with young people, who told me about their problems with boyfriends and girlfriends – and their parents. Just a week or so before my father died, one young man said to me, 'You must think I'm pathetic, already in my mid-20s and still having unresolved issues with my father.'

'Not at all,' I told him. 'I'm in my 60s and I still have unresolved issues. My father and I have not even spoken for 30 years.' And now, of course, we never will.

My father, Kenneth Alexander Lane, was the son of a submarine captain in the Royal Navy who spent many years away at sea. When he was home, he was a reserved and very demanding disciplinarian and my father always addressed him as 'sir'. My father left home at an early age to study nuclear physics at Cambridge. He worked with C.P. Snow during the Second World War on some obscure part of the Manhattan Project. Predictably and stupidly, I would refer to him as Dr Strangelove during my rebellious teenage years and he would look pained and disappointed.

My parents met during those years, in the middle of the war. He was a Cambridge physicist and she was a young Irish girl who had left her home in Belfast to seek her fortune in London. She was employed by the Government to show Pathé newsreels to people sheltering in the

Underground during air raids. The experience of living and working in London during the Blitz had a profound effect upon the rest of her life. Her admiration for the British monarchy was formed when she saw the King and Queen visiting the devastated families in the East End night after night and symbolically refusing to leave Buckingham Palace. I must confess I have inherited her monarchist loyalties, despite the apparent family dysfunctions of recent years. And, of course, Winston Churchill's defiance during those awful years became her definition of manhood, statesmanship and courage – again, an article of faith that I have inherited from her.

But the greatest lasting impression that her war work had on her was of the death camps. Towards the end of the war, several times in one night, she would show films of the liberation of the concentration camps. She could never forget the horror of those images. From a young age, I learned about the sufferings at Treblinka and Auschwitz and it was many years before I was able to overcome the deep hatred for the Germans that my mother had instilled in me.

Anti-Semitism was still quite common among the middle classes when I was growing up in England. Jews were not allowed to join many golf clubs and anti-Jewish jokes were still socially acceptable. My mother was incensed by any form of anti-Semitism, not because of any kind of liberalism (God forbid) but because of the awful images of human cruelty she had been obliged to show and watch during the war. Thanks to my mother, I have inherited an enormous admiration for the history and the culture of the Jews and I remain, like her, a blind supporter of Israel.

I don't know what my father felt about the Jews or even the monarchy. But whatever his beliefs, unlike my mother's and my own, they would have been based on reasoned logic and rational research, not emotions and passion. My father was always the Cambridge rationalist.

We would often visit Cambridge on family outings in the car and my father would show us around Christ's College, his alma mater, and take us for punting expeditions on the River Cam. We would rent a punt at Silver Street and then go for a pub lunch in the garden of the Anchor pub, overlooking the river. My mother would point to all the young students in their college scarves and black gowns and say, 'You can be one of those one day if you study hard and do your homework. Your father would be so proud.' I would watch the young men enviously. They seemed more like young gods with their pints of beer and their pretty girlfriends and I yearned to join their group. I pictured myself having intellectual conversations and making them laugh with my witty remarks about Wittgenstein as I brought over another round of beer. 'You remind me of a young Bertrand Russell,' I imagined one of the girls whispering in my ear.

'Daydreaming will never get you to Cambridge,' my father told me. 'Hard work and determination is what counts. You need to improve your maths.' I knew he was right and I resigned myself to a future in which the young gods of the Anchor pub, and the pretty girls who shared their golden glow, remained for ever out of reach.

In the event, many years later, I somehow managed to get good enough A level results to be accepted by Cambridge and finally had the chance to make my father proud. But I let him down again. Cambridge in those days, like Oxford, had a male to female student ratio of about 95:5. A new university had opened the year before with a male to female ratio of 50:50. Sussex University was located in Brighton on the south coast and quickly developed a reputation for sin, sun and sex. The newspapers were filled with articles about girls in small bikinis reading Kafka on the beach. The Jay twins, the beautiful daughters of a senior cabinet minister, were both students there and when they were not reading Kafka on the beach, according to the popular press, they were hanging out at parties with the Beatles and the Rolling Stones. I never even hesitated. I applied for Sussex and got accepted.

My father was not pleased and told me that, once again, I had chosen the easy and superficial option and that my values were entirely shallow. He was absolutely correct but the thought of a 50 per cent female student body and Kafka and bikinis overwhelmed all memories of Wittgenstein and the Anchor pub.

Many, many years later, I was employed as international business director for a software company based in Philadelphia. We purchased a UK distribution company in Cambridge and consequently, when I was in my late 40s and early 50s, I spent a lot of time in Cambridge.

I became and remain a close friend of the managing director, Paul Ward, and we spent many hours exploring the pubs and restaurants of Cambridge, including the Anchor.

I had forgotten all about the place until Paul took me there one early July evening after work. As we crossed the bridge and entered the garden of the pub, all the memories of family visits came flooding back. I remembered my mother's words of hopeful encouragement and my father's resigned glance as he passed out the glasses of lemonade for the children. I remembered my own yearnings and my fantasies of clever repartee about Russell and Wittgenstein. Where were the young gods? I looked around for the golden boys and girls of my youth but all I saw were awkward and pimply-faced young men in T-shirts shouting obscenities at the football match on the television above the bar. My father would have been disappointed and, for once, it was not my fault.

Paul and I visited Christ's College and I asked Paul to take some photographs of me standing in the quad, outside my father's old room. I suddenly remembered, and told Paul about, the faded scars on my father's wrists. I'd forgotten all about them until that visit to his college. I proudly showed Paul the high brick wall around the grounds, still surmounted with broken bottles embedded in concrete. My father had badly cut himself when climbing over the wall back into the grounds after a late night in the pub beyond the curfew hour. My mother had told me that story several times, proud that my father too had once displayed a wild streak. 'There's no need to keep reminding him of that,' my father would object. 'Patrick already has more than enough bad habits as it is.'

George was in regular contact with my father by then and I sent him the photographs of me, the 51-year-old son, standing proudly outside his college room. My father said he did not need to look at the photographs, he remembered what his college looked like. 'That's the nice thing about Cambridge,' he said. 'It never changes.'

I never told Paul why I wanted him to take the photographs. If a 24-year-old student could feel pathetic about having unresolved issues with his father, as a 51-year-old father of two, I felt doubly shamed.

Sending photographs via my brother was just one of the ways I tried to communicate with my father over the years. I don't know how many letters I wrote, many of which were posted and many of which were not. Some were short, factual reports about my daughters as they grew up and some were long, impassioned pleas for forgiveness. I don't know if he read any of them.

Then there were the phone calls, especially when I lived in California as a fugitive. California is eight hours behind Greenwich Mean Time, so when it was midnight at my home in Santa Cruz, it was eight in the morning in Brighton where my father lived. By midnight, especially if I had decided to phone my father, I would be roaring drunk; at eight in the morning, he would always be sober. This is not the best way to revive a delicate relationship and I cringe when I recall some of the brief phone calls during that period. Luckily, I remember very little about them.

I was actually in Brighton the last time I spoke to my father. With my youngest daughter Bridie, who was about nineteen or twenty, I was visiting Masha and her two daughters. Bridie asked if I could possibly arrange a meeting for her with my father. Bridie is very family oriented and the only close relative she had never met was her grandfather. Rather than surprise him with an unexpected visit, I decided to wait till breakfast and telephone in the morning.

'Hello.'

'Dad, this is Patrick calling from Masha's. I'm just leaving Brighton for London but wondered if you would like to meet my daughter Bridie before we leave. I can wait in the car.'

'Oh. Thank you for calling. Goodbye.'

I went upstairs to tell Bridie, who was still asleep. She woke immediately and listened intently as I repeated the conversation. Unlike her elder sister Peggy, Bridie is very reserved and demure. I had never heard her use a swear word in her life. She looked at me thoughtfully and then put her hand on mine. 'It could have been worse, Dad. At least he didn't tell you to fuck off!'

And it's true, it could have been worse. At least my father got to say goodbye. Unfortunately, he put the phone down before I was able to say goodbye myself.

1|6

MOBS, SPOOKS AND YETI BALLS

OR HOW THE WEST WAS SAVED FOR DEMOCRACY AND MY ROLE IN IT

Anyone who has travelled by public transport in London on the day of a major football match can attest to the frightening potential for violence of a British mob. Alcohol-soaked gangs of young men roaming the streets in search of kicks quickly destroy any lingering images of English reserve. American mobs are equally frightening, as Charles and I discovered as we hitch-hiked through the South in 1964. We would be standing by the side of the road at the edge of some little town when a few curious and bored children would gather to watch us. Soon, they would be joined by their elder brothers and sisters, slightly intimidated by our long hair and strange proto-hippy clothes.

On the outskirts of town, where the tumbledown shacks gave way to cotton fields, as the bullfrogs croaked in some distant pond and the cicadas chirped endlessly all around us, they would stand in ominous silence, watching. The heat was oppressive; sweat ran down the insides of our tie-dyed T-shirts and thunderheads gathered on the horizon, preparing for a late-afternoon downpour. Eventually, a group of young men would arrive in a pick-up truck and join the others, maintaining their distance but growing in confidence with each furtive slug from the bottle.

The muttered jokes and nervous laughter would become increasingly threatening and the sense of menace palpable. Soon, the insults grew more open, accompanied by sticks and small stones. We were never sure whether it was better to walk further away from town and risk a private beating or to return to the centre and hope that some adult would take pity and give us a ride away from the developing mob. Cops would often drive us out of town and dump us a few miles away. 'These are decent law-abiding folk here,' they'd explain. 'We don't want no trouble.'

My usual ploy was to walk across the street, seemingly unconcerned, and address whoever I decided was the ringleader of the mob. 'Know how to read?' I'd ask in an exaggerated English accent. 'Then read this,' I'd say, pulling out my British passport, which in those days was a very impressive hard-cover affair with gilt writing and the royal coat of arms. 'Read it out loud for your friends,' I'd insist.

'Her Britannic Majesty's Secretary of State,' some acne-scarred youth would carefully read, stumbling over the curlicued script as though back in the schoolroom, 'requests and requires in the Name of Her Majesty all those whom it may concern to allow the bearer to pass freely without let or hindrance and to afford the bearer such assistance and protection as may be necessary.'

'Very good,' I'd say. 'Do you understand all those words?' There would be a series of awkward nods. 'Now turn the page and look at the photograph.'

By now the mob was mine, hostility replaced by curiosity.

'Why, that's you. Look, you guys, that's him, Patrick Lane.'

'Do y'all know the Beatles?'

I don't know how many times a British passport has saved my neck and got me out of serious trouble. But those Dixie mobs of good old boys, so easily awed by an official document from the Queen, were no less dangerous for all their youth and simplicity. A drop more liquor and things could have been different, and if Charles and I had been black, they could have casually killed us and nobody would have cared.

An Asian mob is a whole different kettle of fish. For a start, the size of an Asian mob defies all imagining and its seeming unity of purpose would be impossible to organise in the individualistic West. Even a mob of striking French bureaucrats could never match anything to be found east of Suez. We have all seen frightening images on television of vast angry mobs in the Middle East, in Pakistan, Indonesia and Japan, chanting in unison and waving their fists in an endless sea of common hatred. But to confront such a mob in the flesh is to know real fear. The eyes of an English football mob are dim and dulled by alcohol; the eyes of a Southern mob are shifty with inbreeding and guilt; but the eyes of an Asian mob blaze with a fierce and passionate intensity that devours everything in sight.

As Big Dave and I stared at the angry multitudes surrounding the Everest Hotel in Kathmandu, I knew that waving my British passport was not a good idea. Although they were shouting anti-American slogans, the general mood was anti-imperialist. To make matters worse, a taxi had just brought us from the US Embassy and the driver could easily share that information with his compatriots. I gave him all the remaining cash in my pocket as we got out of the cab, and told him we'd need his services later if he could just wait half an hour.

There must have been thousands of protestors surrounding the hotel on all four sides. The Everest was a five-star hotel, one of the best in Nepal at the time, set in a large square that was at this particular moment entirely filled with an angry, chanting mob, thrusting their fists rhythmically in the air and shouting unmistakably unfriendly slogans. In the distance, above the sea of waving fists, I could see the hotel entrance guarded by a small platoon of Gurkhas, armed with assault weapons and their traditional curved and lethal kukri knives. The entrance was perhaps three hundred feet away, a three-minute walk at most. Unfortunately, our route was blocked by a seething mass of inflamed fanatics, wedged shoulder to shoulder and howling for blood.

'Maybe come back later?' I suggested. 'We could go grab a couple of beers while things calm down.'

'Can't,' Big Dave replied. 'They're threatening to burn down the hotel.'

'Ah,' I said, 'I see your point.'

Dave's point was that if they burned down the hotel before we collected our bags, we would lose the million dollars of cash inside the bags, hidden in our room. Half the cash belonged to Ernie Combs and his contact in Florida's Cosa Nostra, while the other half, apparently, belonged to the CIA. I suspected that Dave had a further point, which was that neither of these groups would regard grabbing a couple of beers as an acceptable excuse for abandoning their money. Being physically torn apart and killed by a thousand irate Nepalis might not be the worst fate that we could face. I could not help feeling a certain degree of resentment towards Big Dave; it was ultimately his fault that we were in this predicament.

A month earlier, in April 1980, Howard and I had been in our Soho office on Carlisle Street when Dave telephoned from Nepal. After a typically cryptic Big Dave conversation, Howard put down the phone and said, 'Sounds like he's got a supply of primo Nepalese Temple Balls. If we can get him the cash, it's all ours – the whole harvest.'

The last thing we needed at that time was more hash. We still had well over half the 20 tons of Colombian pot that we'd landed in Scotland on New Year's Eve. England and Europe were awash with dope; the market was flooded. Nevertheless, Nepalese Temple Balls were the holy grail of dope smugglers. Grown high in the Himalayas near the border with Tibet, harvested and rolled into balls by monks, the hashish was as pure and as powerful as anything on earth. It would be criminal to ignore this opportunity. 'Maybe Ernie can take it,' Howard suggested. 'Californians like exotic shit.'

Ernie was delighted. He loved the idea of having exclusive control of something so sought after. He was living in Beverly Hills at the time and decided to market this as a high-end product. 'We'll keep the retail price high and restrict it to the Hollywood crowd,' he told us. 'And the Brits,' he added, referring to the colony of English rock stars who lived there in self-imposed tax exile. 'We'll have to change the brand name, though,' he said.

'Why?' I asked. 'Even Californians have heard of Temple Balls.'

'Yeah, but don't you remember that load of Afghani we moved last year? We branded that as Himalayan Temple Wheels. I don't want any confusion with this new stuff.'

'Just call it Yeti Balls,' Howard suggested.

'What?'

'You know, the Abominable Snowman, up in Nepal. The Yeti.'

'Yeti Balls,' said Ernie. 'I like it.'

The major problem was paying for the product. Most of the suppliers we dealt with in Asia were financially sophisticated. Money could be transferred to their bank accounts in Hong Kong, Singapore or Dubai. In Afghanistan, we could use the Kabul money market. Nepal, however, had no financial infrastructure and Big Dave's contacts would accept nothing but cash, in dollar bills, in Kathmandu. We could not even persuade them to travel to Hong Kong for payment. 'They don't have passports,' Dave explained.

Alec Singh at Latimer's was unable to help. 'We can deliver in Delhi but not in Nepal,' he told me. 'Very primitive people,' he added disdainfully, 'all farmers and herdsmen.' Eventually, Alec transferred $500,000 to my Deak-Perera account in Hong Kong. Juan Dejesus assured me he could arrange a transfer to Nepal.

On 25 April, after an overnight flight, Ethan, my contact in Hong Kong, collected me at the airport, and drove me to my hotel. 'We're having lunch at the US Officers' Club,' he told me, 'so be on your best behaviour.'

'What do you mean?' I protested.

'None of your usual love-and-peace hippy shit,' he said. 'This guy we're meeting is a serious spook. He eats peaceniks for breakfast.'

'So why are we meeting him?'

'He's going to deliver the funds to Nepal for us.'

'How?'

'You don't care and you don't want to know.'

Thomas Lang met us at the door to the club and signed us in. He was a tall man with a deep suntan, a blond buzz cut and civilian clothes that said 'military' all over them. His teeth were strikingly even and white, and he used them to smile a lot. Behind the dark aviator glasses, which he never removed, it was impossible to see if his eyes smiled also.

'How old do you think I am?' he asked when we sat down at the table.

I mumbled something about late forties.

'Fifty-nine,' he said. 'I'm a grandfather.'

He pulled out his wallet and showed us a photograph of a baby.

'Very nice,' I said. I pointed to a second photo of a baby. 'Is that him also?'

'Her,' he corrected me. 'That's my new daughter.' He flipped the page to a photo of an attractive young blonde woman in a bikini. 'That's her mother.'

'She doesn't look like a grandmother,' I said, trying to be tactful.

He put away his photographs, smiling proudly. 'That's my new wife. Married just last year.'

Having established his point – that he was vigorous and virile – he pulled out a transistor radio and placed it on the tablecloth with a conspiratorial wink. Snapping his fingers, he ordered a bottle of Pouilly-Fuissé for Ethan and me ('I know you Europeans like your wine') and a can of Tab for himself.

'You boys are going to get an unexpected treat,' he told us. 'You will be taking part in history today. You'll tell people about this lunch in years to come.' While Tom fiddled with the tuner and adjusted the aerial, I noticed that many of our fellow diners had similar radios. There was an air of barely suppressed excitement in the room. Some of the other diners were in uniform and even those who weren't projected a military air. There was not a woman in the room. Even the uniformed waiters were all male. I felt as though I had infiltrated the Pentagon.

'What's going on?' I asked.

Tom briefly raised his sunglasses and gave me a wink. 'Can't tell you. Have to kill you if I did.' He smiled. 'Gonna pull the Ayatollah's beard. That's all I can say.'

The news started trickling out over the static at the various tables and, true enough, it was a lunch that I shall never forget. President Carter's attempt to free the American hostages from the embassy in Tehran had gone horribly wrong. The US military's bumbling at the Desert One base defined the word 'debacle'. The mission was an absolute disaster. Reports were sporadic and confusing but by the time dessert was served the general picture was clear. The Americans had lost eight men, seven helicopters and a Lockheed C-130 Hercules transport plane and had not even made contact with the Ayatollah's forces. The mood in the room moved quickly from smug anticipation to stunned disbelief and anger.

The waiter had brought only two wine glasses with the Pouilly-Fuissé, so when Tom grabbed the bottle he had no glass to pour it into. Briefly, he considered his glass of iced water and then put the bottle to his lips and simply poured the contents down his throat. I was impressed. It was three-quarters full and he didn't spill a drop.

'Goddamn sand niggers!' he said. 'Fucking Commie stooges!'

'Will this affect our arrangement?' Ethan asked nervously.

'No way, José,' Tom said. 'Makes the success of our mission all the more vital. Teach those goddamn Commie bastards a lesson.'

Anxiously, I wondered what 'our mission' was and what role I was expected to play.

I was too embarrassed to look any of the Americans in the eye, and Ethan and I slunk out of the Officers' Club as soon as we could, leaving Tom to commiserate with his fellow warriors. Back at Ethan's office I used my private telex key to transfer the $500,000 to Tom's numbered account. Ethan explained that 'Tom's people' would deliver the funds to me, in cash, at my hotel in Nepal. The following morning, I left for Bangkok and then on to Kathmandu.

The city was crawling with armed soldiers and despite my cover story, backed up with documentation, that I was a consultant for Compass Travel, Hong Kong, I was treated with open suspicion by immigration control. They examined all my papers and confirmed that I really did have reservations at a nature reserve called Tiger Tops, where I was to research the possibility of canoeing holidays on the upper tributaries of the Ganges.

Big Dave met me at the airport and explained the political background as we took a cab to my hotel. 'Well, it's all the Greens and Blues, see?'

'What are they?'

'The Greens are on the King's side, King Birendra, right? They want to keep things as they are. Keep the old *panchayat* system of government.'

'So what are the Blues?' I asked, having no idea what we were talking about but trying to sound interested. It was like arriving in a strange city and pretending to take an interest in the local team's chances in next Saturday's football match.

'Well, the Blues are the opposition, aren't they? They want to overthrow the old system, get rid of the King and have parliamentary elections, right?'

'Right. So what side are we on?'

'We're Greens. We're on the King's side. The Neps' side.'

'Who's on the Blue side?'

'The Indians. All the shopkeepers in Nepal and most of the businessmen are Indians. Most of the Neps are farmers and herders. The Neps want to keep things as they are but the Indians want change. They want closer ties with India. In effect, they want Nepal to become another Indian state.'

Ethan had already explained to me, before I left Hong Kong, that King Birendra had called for a national referendum to be held in the next few days. I still didn't see how this affected us, though.

'If it's just the Indian shopkeepers who are opposed to the King and he has most of the population behind him, I don't see the problem,' I said.

'You see, the referendum's being held in Kathmandu,' Big Dave explained.

'So?'

'So all the Indians live in Kathmandu. Most of the native Nepali population are out in the country, deep in the jungle or up in the mountains.'

'So they can drive down to vote.'

'No cars, hardly any buses, hardly any roads.'

I was still having trouble trying to show any interest. Some inconsequential referendum in an obscure mountain kingdom was not top of my concerns.

'So we've got to truck them in,' Dave finally explained.

Except when we flew out east to visit him, Big Dave spent most of the year alone with nobody to speak to other than Himalayan pot farmers or yak herders. Consequently, a lot of what he said when he did have an opportunity to speak was unintelligible. At such moments, I didn't even pretend to understand what he was talking about.

'Oh, that's nice,' I said.

Two large, cheap plastic suitcases filled with dollar bills were delivered to my room at the Everest Hotel the following day. These were definitely not Hartmann cases. The man who delivered them had a large hooked nose like a bird of prey and elongated earlobes that reached almost to his shoulders. His business card identified him as the local managing director of an American company. 'My name is Nawang Topkay,' he told us, 'but you can call me Mr Top.'

Big Dave had been quickly counting the bundles of notes. 'I think you've brought us too much money, Mr Top,' he said. 'Looks like a million here.'

'Yes. One million dollars, US,' said Top. 'Half for you, half for Mr Tom.'

'Mr Tom?'

'Yes, Mr Tom at the US Embassy. He wants it for the buses.'

'Ah,' said Big Dave, as though understanding something, 'for the buses.'

This was my first visit to Nepal and I decided it must be something about the altitude – because I could understand nothing. Nothing made any sense.

'We'd better visit your friend at the embassy,' Dave said after Mr Top had left.

'What about the money?' I said. 'We can't just leave it in the hotel room.'

'It'll be fine. The manager's an old friend of mine and anyway the Neps are all honest: very religious people, not into nicking stuff.'

I was uncomfortable about leaving the cash in the room, even if it was hidden under the bed. But it was Big Dave's show.

Tom Lang met us in a small, windowless conference room in an anonymous house near the US Embassy. I assumed it was wired for sound. He explained the international geopolitical ramifications of the buses. 'Nepal is a neutral buffer between China and India,' he told us. 'If the King loses this referendum and Nepal eventually gets taken over by India, that will be a threat to China. The Soviets are in bed with the Indians and they would like to see India pressing on the Chinese borders. The US wants to keep Nepal neutral. We don't want Nepal to become part of the Soviet sphere. Nor do the Brits. And the Pakis certainly don't want the Indians digging deeper into the Himalayas.'

I turned to Big Dave: 'So that's why we're supporting the Greens?'

'You got it,' said Tom. 'The bad guys – the Soviets and the Indians – are the Blues. They want to vote King Birendra out. The good guys, my government, your government, want to support the King.'

'And the Chinese,' said Dave.

'Yeah, them too.'

'But they're Communist as well,' I objected.

'But they're our Commies,' Tom explained.

'So where do the buses come in?'

'Trucks and buses,' Tom said. 'We use this money to buy buses and trucks to ship the farmers and the yak fuckers and anyone who can vote down here to Kathmandu.'

'That way they outnumber the Indians,' Dave joined in.

Apparently, Dave already knew that this was what our money was going to be used for. That was another reason the suppliers wanted it in cash, in country. This was why they (whoever 'they' might be) had made the harvest of primo Temple Balls available to us. They were obviously Greens, or Green sympathisers, and needed cash to further their political ends. Exactly how Tom and 'his people' discovered what was being planned was never explained and was not something that I cared to explore. In any event, Tom's people approved and decided to double the funds available to the Greens.

'You'll need more trucks,' Tom explained. 'And you'll need more money for the Maoists.'

'Why?'

'They control all the roads.'

'Are they our Commies too?'

'Classified,' Tom said. 'I'd have to kill you.' He was still wearing his dark glasses, so it was impossible to see if he was joking.

So that was that. With no signatures, no paperwork and barely a handshake, we had just acquired another half-million dollars to give away to some nameless peasant farmer.

Dave had already inspected the Yeti Balls and arranged ground transport south to India. 'As soon as we hand over the cash, they'll take it across the border by elephant.'

Tom did not want the money anywhere near the embassy, so Dave had arranged to make the transfer at his hotel, the Yak and Yeti. We just needed to collect the bags from my hotel and deliver them to Dave's. That was when we came across the furious mob of chanting protestors surrounding my hotel.

'Oh, shit! Now what do we do?'

'Follow me,' said Dave. Stepping into the violent throng, he gently placed his hand on a shouting man's shoulder. 'Excuse me, please,' he said. 'We need to get through.'

I am about 6 ft 1 in. and Dave is a good few inches taller. The average Nepali is about 5 ft. We towered above the mob and, body by body, with polite but firm 'excuse me, pleases' we inched our way through the heaving mass. Halfway to the hotel entrance, we were easily visible to the armed Gurkhas guarding the door, like two giants slowly advancing towards them. The cries of the mob were deafening and the press of sweaty bodies overwhelming. After about 20 terrifying minutes, we reached the entrance. The suspicious and nervous soldiers kept their HK33 assault rifles pointed at our heads. 'Out of the frying pan, into the fire,' I muttered.

Stepping out from the mob, Big Dave climbed the steps and approached the officer in charge. Barely slowing his stride, he gave a brusque salute and stepped towards the door. 'At ease, Corporal,' he said crisply. 'Tell your chaps they're doing a splendid job.' He opened the hotel door and ushered me through. 'If anyone wants us, we'll be about ten minutes,' he called over his shoulder. 'Keep the door closed and don't let anyone in.'

I was a nervous wreck by this time, barely functioning, but Dave remained cool and collected. Grabbing one of the hotel's ornate luggage carts, he led the way to my room and we loaded the two heavy bags onto the cart.

'These are too heavy to carry,' I panted.

'Exactly,' Dave replied.

Back in the lobby some of the hotel staff emerged from their dark corners, terrified of the mob outside but curious to see what we were doing.

'You two,' Dave commanded, 'help us with this cart.'

While I held the front door open, Dave guided the two porters with the luggage cart onto the hotel steps. After another crisp salute to the Gurkhas and a clipped 'Carry on, Corporal', we descended the steps and re-entered the mob.

The crowd had gone strangely silent while we were with the soldiers, as curious as anyone else about the nature of our activities, but after we descended the steps the chanted slogans began anew and fists were once more punched defiantly in the air. Dave led the way, calming successive protesters with, 'Sorry to trouble you. Excuse me, please. Thank you, sir.' The two porters with the laden luggage cart followed close behind and I took up the rear. Once again, we found ourselves surrounded by a pulsating sea of human fury, only this time we were approaching the mob face to face and not from behind. Desperately, I tried not to catch anyone's eye and made a show of smiling benignly and nodding paternally. 'Thank you so much. Sorry to be a bother.'

Our taxi driver was waiting where we had left him. We heaved one bag into the boot and the second onto the back seat. 'Bung the porters a tip,' Dave said. 'They deserve a good one for that.'

'I haven't any cash,' I said. 'I spent it on the taxi. Give me $20.'

'I can't. All my money's in my hotel room.' For the first time, Dave looked worried. 'We can't stiff them. There'll be a riot.' He pointed to the heaving mob. 'They'll lynch us.'

'Ironic, when you think about it,' I said. 'We're standing here with more than the combined annual income of every single person in the country and we haven't got enough for a tip.'

Dave glared at me. 'When you've finished being fucking ironic, stick your hand in the suitcase and pull out a bill.'

While Dave distracted the driver and porters by gesticulating and mumbling nonsense in Nepalese, I opened the zip wide enough to withdraw a $100 bill from the suitcase and slipped it to him.

There was a reasonably Western-style café on the edge of the square facing the hotel and Dave persuaded the taxi driver to park the cab directly in front, where we could keep an eye on it. We then took the driver and the two porters inside and ordered a round of raksi (like sake but significantly stronger) and beers, with several bowls of the local speciality gundrook-dheedo. The taxi driver insisted on a round of fermented yak's milk. Several rounds later, we decided we had spent enough money to be able to break the $100 bill without upsetting the café owner and we left the happily drunken porters with a fistful of rupees from our change.

Dave sat in the front beside the driver and we finally lurched off for his hotel, the driver swerving from side to side and leaning on the horn with a drunken grin. 'Nice blokes, the Neps,' Dave slurred as we staggered into the Yak and Yeti Hotel. 'You just need to be firm.'

Dave's local contact inspected the bags of money in Dave's room and gave me a small amulet, a silver monkey on a chain. 'Give this to Dr Han when you meet him,' he said. 'It will assure him that all the doings have been correctly done.'

Big Dave stayed in Kathmandu to help organise the buses and trucks while I took a small private plane over the jungle-clad slopes of the Himalayan foothills. I flew to Chitwan National Park, where I was supposed to be doing my canoeing research (as well as inspecting the consignment of Yeti Balls). I was greeted by a large, florid gentleman wearing a three-piece suit and with an infectious smile. 'I am Dr Hanumant Ganapathiraman,' he told me, thrusting a business card into my hand. 'Dr Hanumant Ganapathiraman. BA Oxford (failed)', it read. 'Please call me Dr Han.'

Leading me into a hangar close to the landing strip, he showed me a pile of large white muslin bags, which emanated a powerful and unfortunately unmistakable odour.

'This is for you, I believe,' I said, handing over the little silver monkey god.

'My namesake,' Dr Han said, kissing it and smiling broadly. (Hanumant is the name of the Hindu monkey god.) 'So the doings have most satisfactorily been accomplished,' he said. 'Now let me show you your transport.'

I became aware of two large elephants in a dark corner of the hangar; tethered to stakes, they were drinking water and using their trunks to slap bundles of straw against their backs. 'These two fellows will deliver your goods to you in New Delhi next week,' Dr Han told me. 'They've already been fed and are ready to be on their way.' He clapped his hands and some assistants emerged from the shadows and started carrying the bags of Yeti Balls over to the elephants.

I spent the next few days at Tiger Tops, riding elephants through the jungles and canoes down the river with a group of American travel agents from the Midwest, photographing wild tigers and rhinos to support my cover story.

When I returned to Kathmandu, Dave told me the Greens had won the referendum with 55 per cent of the vote. 'It was a close-run thing,' he said. 'Next time we'll need the Maoist vote as well.'

In the end, all our political efforts proved futile. In June 2001, King Birendra and most of the royal family were brutally murdered at the dinner table by the Crown Prince, who became king for four days before he died of his self-inflicted wounds. National elections were held in April 2008 and the Maoists won a landslide victory. The following month, the monarchy was abolished and a republic declared. Unfortunately, I never did find out from Tom Lang whether the Maoists were our Commies or theirs.

Dr Han was waiting for me the following week in New Delhi. He gave me a list of air waybill numbers for the consignment and detailed delivery instructions to pass on to Ernie Combs in California. Afterwards, we shared a drink in the hotel bar and I asked him how he had brought the hash over the border.

'On the elephants, of course, like I told you.'

'Through the jungle?'

'Oh, goodness me, no! On the main highway to Segauli.'

'But didn't the customs people smell it?'

'Of course. They are not stupid people. They even weighed it.'

'Why?'

'Because they are being paid by the kilo to let it through.'

'So if you were bribing them, why didn't you just use a truck?'

'Ah, but you see, my good fellow, trucks are not my business.

Elephants are my business. For me, your product is just a sideline. The big money is in pachyderms.' I must have looked blank. 'Those two fine fellows are rare Nepalese wild elephants. Very protected. Not allowed out of the country. Not even for bribes.' I still looked puzzled. 'As these chaps at the customs post were so busy counting your Temple Balls and weighing them, they never noticed the elephants.' He smiled delightedly. 'This time next week, they will be in a zoo far away from here.'

I had no further active involvement in the defence of democracy and the free world for another eight years. In 1988, I was called on to help Saddam Hussein in his war with the Islamic Republic of Iran. At the time, I was running my desktop publishing company, Mr Write, in Coral Gables, Florida.

I had invested in the latest computer technology and was successfully producing marketing materials, proposals and brochures for various local businesses. One of my most important clients was a real-estate developer called Bush Klein Realty, part-owned by Jeb Bush, whose father, George H.W. Bush, was to become President the following year. Bush Klein was developing large office blocks along Biscayne Boulevard in downtown Miami and I produced some of their glossy proposals, which were sent to rich and well-connected investors.

These days, even small companies have their own in-house desktop publishing departments but in the '80s the services I provided were unique. As a one-man show, I was faster, more flexible and much cheaper than the normal advertising agencies and the quality of my work was good. We had so much business that Jude joined me full time to work on the printing and binding. Mr Write's reputation spread rapidly and soon the people at Bush Klein introduced me to another development company, Swissco. Swissco was based in Miami Lakes on land owned by the Graham family. Bob Graham, the head of the family, had been governor of Florida from 1979 until 1987, when he was elected senator. He remained Florida's leading senator till 2005 and even ran for the Democratic presidential nomination. Anthony Mijares, the president of Swissco, loved the work I had done for Jeb Bush's company and asked me to work on a large multi-use project he was developing in Orlando. When I first met him, Tony had just hosted a fundraiser that had contributed $50,000 to Bob Graham's senate campaign.

The purpose of my boastful name-dropping is simply to show why I believed that everything I was doing with Swissco was legitimate and had the blessing of the US government. Jeb Bush was later to become Governor of Florida and his brother Governor of Texas and, later still, President. Their father was already Vice President of the USA and had previously been head of the CIA. Senator Bob Graham later became chairman of the Senate Select Committee on Intelligence. These were sophisticated and well-informed business and political leaders. Given Swissco's connections, I never doubted that the company's business was entirely legitimate and above board.

The investment proposals I created for Swissco's Orlando Corporate Center were the best work I had ever done. Tony Mijares told me to spare no expense and I produced a 60-page book, filled with detailed maps, tables, glossy photographs, drawings and environmental-impact studies, all handsomely bound in blue leather. The book was a great success and Tony ordered an initial run of 200. He also introduced me to his partner Carlos Cardoen, chairman of the board and majority shareholder in Swissco.

Cardoen was a Chilean citizen with offices in Santiago, Geneva and Miami Lakes. His company, Industrias Cardoen Ltda, manufactured mining equipment, explosives and military armaments. Although his office in Miami Lakes was on the seventh floor of an ultra-modern glass building, the interior was like an English manor house. The walls were all oak-panelled and suits of armour stood amidst dark leather club chairs, heavy Jacobean furniture and oriental carpets. The walls were covered with Carlos's collection of antique maps of South America and the Caribbean. I love maps and recognised this as an extremely rare and valuable collection.

About the same age, with a common interest in maps and history, Carlos and I got on well. He was an educated man, extremely well read and knowledgeable on many subjects. I took an immediate liking to him and I think it was mutual. Like the narrator of the Stones' 'Sympathy for the Devil', he was a man of wealth and taste.

After a couple of glasses of Scotch, over which we discussed maps and Carlos complimented me on the work I had done for Swissco, he asked if I could produce a similar leather-bound report for his other company.

'What sort of product will we be marketing?' I asked.

'Long-range attack helicopters,' he said.

'Do you have a customer in mind?'

'The government of Iraq. Saddam Hussein is a close friend of mine.'

Unlike the bearded and robed ayatollahs in Iran or the wild and unshaven PLO leaders with their chequered headscarves, Saddam Hussein was generally portrayed as a civilised statesman. When not in crisp military uniform, he wore Western business suits and sported a neat moustache rather than a long beard. He looked like the sort of chap one could do business with. Certainly, he was not perceived as the monster that he came to be seen as in later years.

Iraq had invaded Iran in 1980 and the war had raged back and forth for the rest of the decade. The US had no diplomatic relations with Iran and had not forgiven the Islamic government for the hostage crisis and the humiliation of the Desert One fiasco, which I'd heard about in the Hong Kong Officers' Club. US support for Iraq was no secret and was frequently discussed in Congress. In 1992, Ted Koppel reported on ABC's *Nightline*: 'It is becoming increasingly clear that George Bush Sr, operating largely behind the scenes throughout the 1980s, initiated and supported much of the financing, intelligence and military help that built Saddam's Iraq into an aggressive power . . . Reagan/Bush administrations permitted – and frequently encouraged – the flow of money, agricultural credits, dual-use technology, chemicals and weapons to Iraq.'

With Cardoen's connections to the Bush administration, it was my understanding that he was acting on behalf of the US government in supplying arms to Iraq. So I was delighted to have landed such a large and wealthy customer for Mr Write, and one so well connected to the US administration. That I should also be striking a blow against the bearded mullahs who had humiliated the West and thrown my brother George out of the country was just a bonus.

The first project was a proposal to provide Iraq with the Cardoen Attack Helicopter 206L-III, which was based on the Bell civilian model. My proposal, bound in black leather with the Cardoen logo embossed in silver, was filled with detailed reports about 'hover ceilings', 'fuel flow v. airspeed' and 'dual armament systems'. It was a 50-page book with photographs and tables, and the frontispiece was a letter from Carlos to His Excellency Minister General Hussein Kamel in Baghdad.

Carlos was delighted and flew to Baghdad with several copies of my book to make his presentation. While visiting Hussein Kamel and his ministers, Carlos learned of a new threat that the country was facing. In addition to sending 'human waves' of suicide soldiers, mostly young boys, to cross the mine-filled deserts of eastern Iraq, Iran was also sending frogmen up Iraqi waterways to destroy their oil facilities. Iraq needed to quickly develop an underwater defence strategy.

'Excellencies,' Carlos later told me he'd said, 'I can have a detailed proposal for you within the month.'

'This is very specialised work,' Hussein Kamel objected. 'You have access to such expertise?'

'Mr Write Inc., Excellency, a small Florida company. It is the best at this sort of work. The best.'

Long before Carlos returned to the US, Mr Write was already being prepared to produce this wonderful report. Our first visitor was Tom Lang. He insisted he was not Tom Lang and that he had never heard of Tom Lang, but he had the same dark glasses, deep tan and perfect white teeth.

'So what is your name?'

'Larry.'

'Is that your real name?'

'It's a need-to-know situation,' he smiled.

Larry brought me a fancy-looking camera and a camera stand for photographing documents. He gave the impression that they had come from the darkest corners of CIA headquarters at Langley but I saw a similar model on sale at Target and I also found a small label on the base that said 'Made in Taiwan'. 'Disinformation department,' said Larry when I mentioned this.

Larry reminded me of Tom Sunde, Ernie's sidekick, who also implied at times that he was employed by the CIA. I still don't know if either of them really were spies. If true, I suppose it would explain some of America's intelligence failures.

Over the next couple of weeks, Larry was followed by a succession of mysterious specialists, mainly American, although some were English, some French and others central European. They would arrive at our house, unannounced, usually at mealtimes, and remain till the wee hours, showing me classified documents and explaining the more arcane aspects of underwater ingress, propulsion and demolition.

Mr Write's office started to accumulate a collection of limpet mines and waterproof fuses, which Jude would desperately hide before the arrival of our regular clients for whom we were also publishing brochures. One morning, we had a 9-ft OT 3000M DPV (diver propulsion vehicle) bobbing in our swimming pool when the PTA Entertainment Committee arrived. Black and sinister, it looked like a small nuclear submarine.

'It's for the girls,' I explained. 'We're going to paint it yellow. You know, a yellow submarine.'

'Oh, what fun! Maybe we can use it in the Thanksgiving Harvest Festival.'

When the specialists departed, I would try to digest my notes and write a technical report on the weaponry and techniques they had described. *The Cardoen Underwater Defense Package* was a thick leatherbound report containing detailed proposals on, among other subjects, mine clearance, underwater defence and detection, aggressive defence and the Cardoen Swimmer Delivery Vehicle Fleet.

The book was prefaced with a letter to Hussein Khamel:

Excellency,
Further to our recent discussion during which you communicated Iraq's desire to acquire the most modern and effective equipment for the conduct of underwater military defense, I am pleased to submit this proposal for your consideration.

As an organization owned fifty percent by Iraq, *Industrias Cardoen, Ltda.* has approached the world's leading manufacturers and suppliers in search of the most sophisticated and effective equipment. We have assembled a comprehensive package of weapons and military materials which will cover a maximum of hostile eventualities at a minimum of cost . . .

. . . As you have explained to me, the highest authorities are determined that Iraq quickly become self-sufficient in the production of military equipment. The emphasis on eventual local manufacture and the training of Iraqi personnel have therefore always been of utmost importance to us when selecting our material.

Cardoen was never secretive about the work he was doing for the Iraqi government. About 60 or 70 people were employed at the Swissco/Cardoen offices in Miami Lakes and I became a well-known visitor, using the photocopier, sitting in the public conference room with my papers spread all over the main table. Sometimes they were detailed maps of the Orlando development site; sometimes they were large-scale diagrams of long-range attack helicopters. It was all out in the open.

Several years later, however, after Bush Sr had become President and Saddam had invaded Kuwait, threatening American oil interests, Carlos Cardoen was accused of supplying arms to the enemy. In 1993, Cardoen, Swissco and employees from both companies were indicted on criminal charges. Carlos was publicly disgraced and had to flee the country. All his assets were seized and his companies were closed down. Despite all the claims made in court and in subsequent government reports, I am quite sure that, at least when I was working with him, Cardoen believed that he was acting with the knowledge and support of the US government. The openness with which he conducted his business would make no sense otherwise.

Carlos flew from Santiago to Miami to inspect the report on Sunday, 24 July 1988 and spent the day at my house carefully reviewing it. He was delighted and asked me to prepare ten copies, dated Tuesday, 26 July, to be delivered to his office. He planned to fly to Baghdad that day to present my report.

Unfortunately, on the morning of 25 July, the police forces in Thailand,

Australia, Pakistan, Singapore, Switzerland, Spain, England, Ireland, Canada, California, New York and Florida executed simultaneous raids on a number of private residencies. Among many others, Ernie Combs, Howard and Judy, Phil Sparrowhawk and I were all taken into custody on charges relating to a worldwide racketeering conspiracy centred on Miami.

Obviously, I had been under surveillance for quite some time and yet somehow, the day before the raids, Carlos Cardoen was able to fly non-stop from Chile in his own private Gulfstream jet, collect his white Rolls-Royce at the airport and park it outside my house all day long without anybody noticing or asking questions.

Displaying extraordinary grace under pressure, Jude was able to print, bind and deliver all ten copies to Carlos's office in Miami Lakes on the day I was arrested and he was able to successfully deliver his presentation in Baghdad later in the week. Unfortunately, I was not available to receive his eventual praise, nor the recognition of a grateful nation. I was otherwise detained, in the Federal Metropolitan Correctional Center, MCC Miami. I had finally been busted.

[1][7]

BUSTED

My first time, in 1968, was quite gentle. They rang the doorbell and said, 'Brighton CID. May we come in?' Caught not only by surprise but also lacking any Plan B, I gestured them into the front hall and they removed their hats. Three of the policemen were in uniform and wore helmets but the officer in charge was in plain clothes and wore a homburg.

He looked at the rather vibrant art deco-style painting in the front hallway and said, 'This is rather striking, sir. Reminds me of Klimt. Do you mind if we look around?' I was pretty stoned and could think of no alternative to nodding my consent. It was a five-storey house with stairs leading up and down from the main hallway. The uniformed police went up, and the detective and I went downstairs to the main living area.

There were about five Sussex University students sitting around the dinner table smoking joints, drinking wine and staring rather open-mouthed at us as we entered the room. 'Detective Inspector Roberts from the Brighton CID,' he said. 'Please don't get up.'

Marianne Faithfull might not have been lying naked on a bearskin rug eating a Mars Bar when the police entered, but the scene of relaxed debauchery was nonetheless reminiscent of the recent Redlands bust, in which the Rolling Stones had been arrested at Keith Richard's nearby country house.

Inspector Roberts picked up one of the unlit joints and sniffed it gingerly.

'Marijuana?' he asked.

I nodded glumly.

Having now digested and accepted the fact that I had been raided by the police, my bourgeois upbringing immediately asserted itself. I started to feel socially embarrassed in front of my guests and guilty that, as a host, I was responsible for exposing them to this unpleasant intrusion.

Roberts dropped the joint delicately into a little plastic bag and raised his eyebrows as he looked at me. 'Yours?' he asked.

'Yes, officer. It's all mine. All the drugs here are mine. These other people are just guests, old friends who were visiting.'

Roberts smiled approvingly. 'Very well, then,' he said. 'I see no reason to detain any of your friends any longer.' He turned to address the table. 'You are all free to go,' he said.

There was an unseemly rush as my friends grabbed their coats and bags and climbed the stairs to the front door. A couple of them gave me shamefaced and sympathetic glances but most of them avoided looking at me.

'Nice friends,' Roberts said ambivalently.

The other cops had joined us after exploring the upper reaches of the house and they showed Roberts my collection of syringes and vials of Methedrine, cocaine and heroin.

'Yours as well?' Roberts asked.

I nodded.

'You have a doctor's prescription?'

I showed him where my name was printed on the label on each box of vials.

'But not for the marijuana?'

I shook my head. 'No.'

'Mr Lane, are you aware that it is against the law to possess marijuana? Did you know that this is an illicit drug?' Roberts asked, adding a few other stubbed-out joints to his little plastic bag. 'We are going to take this away for analysis but if it proves to be what you say it is, I will have to charge you with possession of an illegal substance.' He gave the bag to one of the uniformed officers. 'Not planning to leave town any time soon are you, sir?'

'No,' I mumbled.

'Good. I must ask you not to leave this house and to make yourself available for further questioning.'

The house seemed strangely large and quiet after they had gone. I fixed myself an extra-large shot of heroin in the hope it would allow me to sleep and stop me from thinking. It didn't; but then it never does.

The place was owned by a fellow student who had lent it to me for the summer while she took a lengthy tour of Italy with her parents. Babs was the only daughter of a wealthy London solicitor who had bought her the house for her to live in while she completed her studies in Brighton. Babs was one of the few wealthy people I have met who was comfortable with her wealth. She enjoyed her money and enjoyed the things it allowed her to do. She did not hide her wealth but neither did she flaunt it; she just used it sensibly and shared generously.

Babs was not a student at the university. She was studying design at the local college of art and liked to practise her design ideas on her house. Located in a working-class street of rather run-down late-Victorian terraced houses, her place was already somewhat conspicuous because of the long-haired hippies who visited at all times of the day and night. Unlike our rather dour neighbours, my friends and I had no set schedules and most of the time we were stoned. Living inconspicuously was a skill that none of us ever acquired.

Babs had a unique system for renovating and decorating her house. She would plan her projects meticulously and make sure all the paint and other materials were purchased and easily accessible. She would then organise a party for ten or twelve friends and feed us black bombers or whatever other amphetamines were on the market. After a couple of hours sitting around popping pills and smoking joints, everyone was restless. That was when Babs would describe her ideas and hand out the ladders and paintbrushes. The next 12 or 14 hours would see an explosion of activity as a dozen speed-crazed hippies obsessively polished, cleaned and painted everything they could lay their hands on and Babs' house was magically transformed into a glowing feast of colours.

I sourced some ideas for the house myself in 1967, when my girlfriend Sue and I were voted 'Coolest Couple in London' by *London Life*. The prize included first-class tickets with the British Overseas Airways Corporation to Hawaii. (The magazine sadly declared bankruptcy a month after our return but by then, luckily, we had collected all our prizes.) We were put up for two weeks in the Kahala Hilton on Waikiki Beach. Richard Milhous Nixon was staying there, too, but these were Nixon's 'wilderness years' and it was London's coolest couple, not the future president, who stayed in the Presidential Suite. I'll never forget Nixon sitting in a lounge chair beside the hotel swimming pool every afternoon in his dark suit and tie. However hot the sun, however skimpy the girls' bikinis, he never once removed his jacket or loosened his tie. Years later, I was reminded of Nixon when Alec Singh stubbornly retained his bowler hat in our Bedford hotel.

After leaving Hawaii, we spent a couple of weeks in San Francisco on the way home. We stayed in Haight Ashbury, which, in 1967, was Hippy Central for the Age of Aquarius. I returned home with books and posters of the new psychedelic art, which was all the rage in San Francisco. Babs was enchanted and wanted to copy everything. She already had a large collection of art nouveau artefacts, which she purchased in flea markets, and my samples of psychedelic artwork fired her imagination even more. I can safely say that Babs' house in our grey Victorian terrace could proudly compare with anything to be seen in Haight Ashbury at the height of the Summer of Love.

The front door was purple with the number 27 painted in a vibrant floral design, 7 ft tall. She used *trompe l'oeil* to make the windows look like large, luminous teardrops. Strangely sinuous plants and creepers interwoven with dazzling rainbows climbed all over the exterior walls. As Inspector Roberts said, 'It was a difficult house to overlook.'

He arrived at the front door the day after the bust accompanied by his wife. 'Do you mind if we look around?' he asked. His wife was an interior designer and they had met at art school many years earlier. 'I always wanted to be an artist,' he told me as I made them a cup of tea in our kitchen. 'But I needed to earn a living and my dad sent me to the police academy at Henley.' He looked wistfully around the psychedelic living room as he told me this and I sensed an inner sorrow for what could have been. I too wished he could have fulfilled his dreams instead of becoming a cop and busting people.

His wife loved the house and I had to take her through every room and explain the different designs and how we had achieved them. I was pleased to see that Inspector Roberts remained within my sight at all times and didn't open any drawers or examine anything uninvited. It was a social visit, not a bust. When Babs returned from Italy several weeks later, Mrs Roberts introduced herself and they became the best of friends.

The lab analysis on the collection of joints proved positive and I was charged with possession of a controlled substance. Inspector Roberts appeared in court, spoke highly of my character and asked for the legal minimum. I was discharged with a £50 fine and told not to do it again.

'No, Your Honour,' I said. 'I've learned my lesson. Thank you.'

My second drug bust was not until five years later, in 1973. From our offices in Warwick Place, Graham, Howard and I had been organising the movement of large quantities of Pakistani hashish in containers to Los Angeles. Their international shipping carnets identified them as sound equipment belonging to various major rock groups on international tours around the world. Ernie's people in LA would unload the containers and distribute the hash all over the US.

I was usually the person who dealt with Ernie over in California but for this particular shipment Howard had flown to LA to deal with Ernie in person. Ernie sent a message that there had been a slight problem and that Howard was to wait in his Los Angeles hotel until Ernie contacted him. It was Howard's first visit to America and he was enchanted with everything he saw – not least the seemingly infinite choice of TV stations 24 hours a day. He was fascinated. He watched everything from the extraordinary selection of evangelical religious programmes to the non-stop game shows and, of course, the endless violence displayed on the hourly news broadcasts. He was still watching when an attractive blonde Californian newscaster announced the biggest hashish bust in history, with a photograph of Ernie on the screen behind her.

Apparently, one of our seven containers had been mistakenly rerouted to Las Vegas and local officials had discovered the hashish. They quickly connected the misrouted container with the others in Los Angeles and seized those before they could be unloaded. We had lost everything!

Ernie had flown to Las Vegas to try to intercept the missing container before the police did. He sent one of his surfer dudes to collect it from the airport and drive it by road to Los Angeles. The DEA, predictably, were following Ernie's driver to see where the container was going to be delivered. Ernie was also following his driver to see if he was being tailed. Eventually, the undercover cops and Ernie all realised they were following the same truck and while one carload of cops kept following the hash, another started to follow Ernie. Driving his Cadillac Eldorado at full speed, Ernie managed to throw off his pursuers by suddenly turning off the Las Vegas Expressway into a maze of small side streets not far from the airport. Unfortunately, the place he chose to execute his dramatic U-turn and vanish in a cloud of dust was a small and obscure street called Patrick Lane. Years later, in a Florida courtroom, when the details of this story were recounted, many of the half-sleeping jurors sat up at the mention of Patrick Lane and glared reprovingly at me.

Ernie drove his Cadillac to the front door of the newly opened MGM Grand and threw the keys to a doorman. 'Got to run!' he shouted. 'Feeling lucky!' He walked rapidly through the casino till he reached a side entrance and saw a queue of people waiting for taxis. A large limo sat under the main canopy and Ernie climbed into the back seat. Two startled Japanese tourists stared incredulously at him as he pulled out a wad of $100 bills and gave them to the driver. 'Take these good people to wherever they want to go and then take me to the airport,' he said. 'Do it fast and there's an extra $100 for you.'

Ernie turned to the Japanese couple and gave them his biggest Californian surfer-dude smile. 'My wife's having a baby,' he explained. 'They just called me. It's a week early.'

They were enthralled. 'Go to the airport first,' they told the driver. 'Hurry, hurry!'

The woman clasped Ernie's hand when they reached the airport, her eyes shining with excitement, and her husband gave Ernie his business card and made him promise to send a photo of the baby. Unfamiliar with Japanese business-card etiquette, Ernie stuffed the card in the back pocket of his jeans and with a brief 'Stay cool, man!' sprinted towards the departure gates and vanished from the known world.

Although his photo was all over the TV news, Ernie successfully remained a fugitive for the next 25 years. Meanwhile, Howard, wearing dark glasses and a baseball cap, checked out of his hotel and quietly returned to London on the first available flight.

The next few weeks were a confused time. Police forces in several countries exchanged notes and painfully reconstructed the paper trail of fraudulent bills of lading. We knew it was only a matter of time before they connected us with the Vegas consignment and, because his name was all over the paperwork, Graham immediately left the country. He moved to Dublin, where Jim McCann had a safe house, and for the next several weeks I travelled between London and Dublin to deliver supplies and news. Graham insisted that I follow 'Moscow Rules', so instead of the two-hour direct flight from Heathrow, I had to travel by train and ferry via Belfast, an uncomfortable journey lasting almost two days.

Howard didn't leave the country immediately but he left his house in Oxford and changed hotels every night, moving around London. Eventually, he travelled to Amsterdam to meet Ernie and was arrested by the Dutch police. Ernie was staying in the hotel next door and once again avoided arrest by minutes. He returned to California and never visited Europe again. 'Too uptight, man.'

During this period, I continued to live at Warwick Place. My name was on none of the shipping papers and I felt relatively secure. Nevertheless, I kept my passport and a suitcase of clothes stored in the boot of my car.

Val Johnson called into the shop one day on his way back from Lebanon. 'What's happening, dude?' he said. 'How're the boys in the Pink Poodle?'

I gravely explained what had happened while he'd been away.

'They're probably watching your house in Laguna Beach,' I said. 'They've probably arrested your girlfriend,' I added cruelly. Val looked devastated. 'They're watching this place now,' I exaggerated. 'Make sure they don't follow you from here. Take the Tube to throw them off.'

Val looked around nervously and then scurried away. For Val Johnson, the idea of travelling on public transport was almost as bad as the thought of being arrested.

Unfortunately, it turned out that I hadn't been exaggerating after all. The next time I returned from a trip to Dublin I went straight to the Warwick Castle for a drink. Eddie, a neighbourhood handyman whom we used for various odd jobs, was standing at the bar.

'Old Bill's been watching,' he said.

'What do you mean?'

'Out in the street. Sitting in cars, pretending to read the papers. They've been watching the shop for the past three days. Every now and then they ring the doorbell.'

He looked at me knowingly as he drained his Guinness. 'Don't look like carpet collectors to me,' he said. 'Got Old Bill written all over them.'

When it came to recognising policemen and sensing trouble, Eddie was one of the best and I never doubted him. 'Another Guinness?' I suggested. I waited in the pub till closing time and then I left with everyone else and did not return to Warwick Place for some ten years.

The following morning, when I arrived at Newhaven to take the car ferry to France, I was stopped by a young customs officer. He had examined my passport and asked the usual sorts of questions and then he stood back and looked at me quizzically. 'You know, sir, all my senses tell me to take this car apart and examine every piece of luggage.'

He stared at me and I stared back. I could think of no other reaction except to laugh. 'Why would you want to do that, officer? It's a German car. You'd never be able to put it back together again.'

'I've just got a funny feeling,' he said.

I affected a slight lisp. 'Oh, I bet you say that to all the boys.'

His expression changed and I saw the revulsion on his face as he handed back my passport. 'Go on,' he said, 'get out of here.'

The boat arrived at Dieppe four hours later and I did not return to England for many long years. As I stood at the stern and watched the seagulls swooping over the ship's wake and the white cliffs of England receding in the distance, I thought about my white BMW. If that young officer had only trusted his instincts he would have found several thousand pounds in cash as well as a significant amount of hashish and paperwork tying us all to the big dope bust in California.

But once again, while many of my friends were arrested, I had got away with it. The luck of the Irish!

* * *

I will never forget one beautiful Saturday morning, seven years later, when I sat on the patio of my home in Molières drinking freshly brewed coffee and eating croissants. The morning air was fresh with the promise of an early spring and the meadow was filled with buttercups and poppies, just as it had been on the day when we discovered it ten years earlier. I could see old Monsieur Carrière with his small white dog as they crossed the stream looking for truffles further up the valley towards Molières. An incredible peace flowed through me as I leaned back in my smart new chaise longue.

Buying our new patio furniture had added the finishing touch to the renovation of the old mill and when Jude joined me with a second pot of fresh coffee I could not help saying, 'You know, it really does not get much better than this.'

Just then the phone rang.

We had mounted our 'Norwegian Shit' operation in Scotland earlier that year. The project had been remarkably successful: the streets of England were awash in Colombian pot and I was funnelling hundreds of thousands of pounds per week out of the country. I had rented a large house in Orme Square, overlooking Kensington Gardens and close to the Soviet Embassy, which was always under surveillance. This meant that I had 24-hour police protection, which is what you want when you have regular deliveries of cash to your house.

As I have observed already, money laundering is a demanding and strenuous profession. It involves endless counting of cash, and the packing and carrying of heavy suitcases. I had therefore employed my old school friend Charles, who would arrive at the house at 9 a.m. and spend the day sitting at a large table by a window looking into the park, counting banknotes. Since graduating from university, Charles had devoted himself to the collection of rare books and was largely innocent of the world of commerce. He happily accepted my story that the cash came from the sale of T-shirts and other paraphernalia at Rolling Stones rock concerts. 'Whether Mick and Keith actually declare this income to the tax authorities is not really our problem, is it?' I would say. 'Our job is simply to count it.'

At midday, we would go to the Victoria pub around the corner, a place frequented, according to Howard, by low-level officials from the Soviet Embassy and British intelligence types. There were many tea breaks throughout the day, too, but the rest of the time was spent counting the cash into orderly piles and packing it neatly into Hartmann suitcases. Charles would finish work at five on the dot and, after a final pint at the Victoria, take the Northern Line home to Barnet.

The tale I told Charles about rock-band T-shirts was actually the cover story I used with Juan, Alec and all the other bankers to account for the cash that I handled. The sale of T-shirts and other memorabilia at concerts was still fairly new and unregulated during the '70s. Like the groups and the huge arena concerts themselves, this was a youth-driven phenomenon that middle-aged bankers, whether in Switzerland, London or New York, simply did not understand. All they knew was that the long-haired rock idols were generating vast sums of money, so when I explained that the cash was collected at concerts, people were more than willing to believe me.

Counting the money was exhausting work but by April I had managed to move several million pounds out of the country and dispersed it through our Swiss accounts. I'd also spent a couple of weeks restoring democracy in Nepal and smuggling elephants into India. I decided I needed to get away and spend a weekend with my family in France. I did not tell anyone of my plans and in fact emphasised over the phone that I planned to be in Orme Square during the weekend. I didn't want anyone to know the house would be unattended.

Unknown to us, for the previous two weeks, the FBI and DEA had been working with London's CID and Her Majesty's Customs and Excise to follow our every move and listen to all our phone conversations. They were satisfied they knew the full extent of the conspiracy and were simply waiting till they knew where everybody was located to swoop. They planned a series of internationally simultaneous raids.

They struck at dawn. At some 30 different locations in England, Ireland, America and around the world, they executed arrest warrants on everyone known to be connected to the plot, including poor innocent Charles (who was, thankfully, acquitted of any wrongdoing at the Old Bailey). They burst into my house in Orme Square and found thousands of pounds of cash. They raided Howard's luxury apartment opposite Harrods and found money and hash. They raided a small hotel in Suffolk where Howard was spending the weekend with Judy and the children. But they never thought to raid my house in France, because nobody knew I was there. One of the reasons I had gone away for the weekend was to update all the accounts, so I had taken all the paperwork with me. I had neatly annotated records of how much cash had been received, and from whom, and where it had gone, and how it had been dispersed, and to whom. It was all written in code but it would not have taken the Enigma team to crack my system. Normally, the records would have been in Orme Square but at the time of the bust all the records were with me in Molières.

So, on that glorious spring morning, leaning back in the new furniture, I drank my coffee and lazily planned my weekend of well-deserved rest. The valley was so peaceful and the meadow filled with buttercups had such a calming effect on me that I knew I had been wise to get out of London. Sometimes a chap just needs a break.

And then came the phone call. 'Howard's been arrested. They've raided your house. They know everything. You need to move. Get out now!'

Since that morning, I have never again dared say, 'It does not get much better than this.' Indeed, I still get very nervous whenever we buy patio furniture.

After throwing all the paperwork and accounts from Orme Square into the kitchen furnace, I bundled Jude and the girls into the car. 'We have to go,' I said. 'I'll explain later.'

We drove to a café in Lalinde, where I told Jude everything. We have a very honest relationship and I have never cheated on her or lied to her about other women; however, I was less than candid with her about my business activities. She suspected a lot, of course, but she chose to ignore the signs or at least not to question me about them. In reality, she had little option. She loved me and knew that I loved her and the children. I was a good provider and I always had a plausible explanation. I was a professional dissembler.

'We have to go back to England and face the music,' she told me. 'What about my mother? I can't abandon her. What about the girls? Do you want them to grow up as fugitives?'

The café was owned by two friends of ours, and every now and then Jacques or Denise would come and chat with us and we would make small talk before reverting to the most important and decisive conversation I've ever had in my life.

'I can't go with you, Patrick,' she told me, her eyes filled with tears. 'It wouldn't be right. I can't do it to Peggy and Bridie. I can't do it to my mum. My family back in England – they would never understand. They would never forgive me.'

Still undecided, we drove back to Molières to collect some clothes for the children. From the village, you can look down into our valley, where Le Moulin nestles in the meadow about a mile further north. On a hill overlooking our house, I saw a police van and some policemen behind the hedges. As we drove past the cemetery, I saw another van and caught a glimpse of blue uniforms among the headstones. Instead of turning left towards the mill, I turned right and drove to Bergerac. Our valley had been lost to the enemy. We could never go home again.

I don't know what arguments I used, what lies I told or what promises I made, but somehow I talked Jude and the children onto the train at Bergerac, headed for Madrid. Only at that moment did I realise what a colossal fool I had been. I had risked the only things that were ever important to me, all for nothing. All that I had cared about was fun and adventure; I had taken the love of my wife and the adoration of my daughters for granted. I knew then that life without them would be meaningless. If Jude had persisted, I would have returned to England and taken my chances at the Old Bailey. But the Irish charm worked, I got her onto the train and the next morning we were in Spain. Two days later, we were in America, ready to start a new life in a new land. Again, I had got away with it – that old Irish luck was still with me!

* * *

When my wife gets out of the shower and stands naked in front of the mirror, I am always struck by her beauty and reflect on what a lucky man I am. When my wife stands naked in front of the mirror, however, all she sees are flaws and imagined evidence of age and gravity. I understand this is fairly typical of all women. On the other hand, when I stand naked in front of the mirror, I suck in my stomach, pull back my shoulders, marvel at what a good-looking stud I remain and reflect on what a lucky woman my wife is.

I was engaged in thoughts of this nature on the morning of 25 July 1988 when two men dressed in full body armour burst into my bathroom and pushed me to the floor. One pushed his knee into the small of my back while his companion held a gun to my head and asked if I was armed. It was hard to shake my head because it was wedged against the base of the toilet bowl and probably unwise to point out what a silly question that was to ask a naked man, so I just muttered, 'No.'

For the first eight years after we fled Europe, we had lived the American Dream. We arrived with little money and few friends but we worked hard and within six years had saved enough money for the down payment on our own house. We attended PTA meetings and Little League softball games. We quickly blended into the life of the community, first in Santa Cruz, California, and later in Miami, Florida.

We learned to become Americans by religiously studying *Brady Bunch* reruns each evening on television. What we didn't realise until much later was that these repeats were about ten years old and consequently everything we learned was outdated. Not only did we all have funny accents but we behaved like time travellers from the '70s, caught in a time warp.

Keeping my promise to Jude, I tried to support my family with honest work and cut dramatically back on my racketeering activities. Nevertheless, as an international fugitive and illegal alien with no documentation, getting regular work was not easy. In Santa Cruz, I worked on *The Offshore Banking Report*. In Miami, I operated the smoked-salmon factory and then launched Mr Write.

When we lived in California, I did the occasional 'black job' for Ernie Combs, who had been extremely helpful in finding me a home and supporting the family as we adjusted to life in the USA. It wasn't just that, when we first arrived, I needed the money; I also wanted to maintain the friendship and feel I was still part of the action. But gradually my contact with my old racketeering friends faded. I saw them less and less. By the time we moved across the country to Miami, I had lost contact with almost everyone from my criminal past except Howard.

In 1980, while I was safely hidden in Santa Cruz, Howard had gone on trial in London for our Scottish/Norwegian adventure. Even for a major trial in the Central Criminal Court of the Old Bailey, Howard's defence was sensational. In a previous trial, he had established that he was employed by British intelligence and now he argued that he was also employed by the Mexican secret service to monitor the activities of a group of Colombian smugglers who imported pot into Scotland for a criminal gang run by Patrick Lane and his sister Natasha. Howard was an innocent bystander who had been wrongly arrested while the real masterminds had escaped scot-free. *The Times* ran an article about me with an old photograph from my long-haired student days under the headline 'Mr Big Flees His Swiss Hideout'.

At the time, I was attending bingo games for the local PTA in Santa Cruz and poor Natasha was languishing in a Mexican prison.

To support his bizarre defence, Howard had witnesses appear before the judge and jury in a closed-door session to confirm the whole preposterous story. One witness claimed to work for the Mexican secret service and, as such, he refused to give his name or show any documentation. As he gravely explained: 'Then it would no longer be secret, señor.'

To the horror and disbelief of the prosecution, who thought they had a rock-solid case – including the ten remaining tons of evidence – the jury apparently swallowed Howard's story and he was found not guilty.

Howard, Judy and the children immediately moved to the island of Majorca. Secure in the knowledge that he could not be extradited from Spain and convinced that he was invincible, Howard collaborated with journalist David Leigh, who wrote a bestseller called *High Time*. The book told the whole story and gloatingly revealed how Howard had successfully made a fool of the British and American authorities. An epilogue to the book included the following: 'Patrick Lane, Howard's brother-in-law and "financial advisor", is living abroad under a false name. He is quite rich.' This last was an unnecessary and untrue observation that was to cause me serious problems in later years.

While the police and intelligence forces in several countries plotted their revenge for the double humiliation of the trial and the book, Howard went back to the old business but now on a much larger scale. From his base on Majorca, he travelled all over the world, especially to Pakistan, Thailand and the Philippines. He started working with Ernie again, sending large ships and containers filled with Thai sticks to California. His connection with me, however, was now mainly as a brother-in-law. Though I would occasionally move some money for him through my old Wall Street contacts, he knew that I had largely given up my bad old ways and had started a new and law-abiding life. I enjoyed listening to the stories of derring-do but no longer wanted to play an active role. After moving to Miami, the only time I did anything remotely illegal was to help one of Howard's friends, Lord Moynihan, during his visit to South Florida.

Anthony Patrick Andrew Cairnes Berkeley Moynihan, 3rd Baron

Moynihan, was the great-grandson of a Crimean War hero who'd
been awarded the Victoria Cross for killing five Russians at the siege
of Sebastopol. As a member of the Coldstream Guards during the
1950s, Moynihan was a member of Princess Margaret's fast set and a
favourite of the gossip columnists. After divorcing his first wife, a nude
model, he married a snake charmer and fire-eater's assistant, whom he
employed as a belly dancer in one of his many failed nightclubs.

In 1965, his father died while awaiting trial for importuning men
in public lavatories and Tony inherited the title, becoming the 3rd
Baron Moynihan. As a member of the House of Lords, he argued
strongly in favour of returning Gibraltar to Spain. This was the
equivalent, at the time, to a US senator proposing that Alaska be
handed over to the Soviet Union. It was argued, but never proved,
that his motives were entirely pecuniary and that Moynihan was on
the payroll of Generalissimo Franco, the Spanish dictator. Facing at
least 57 charges, mostly involving fraud but also including the theft
of a Rolls-Royce, he finally fled England and joined Franco in Spain
in 1970. Franco awarded him the Order of the Gentleman of Don
Quixote. Possibly he was being ironic, since there was never anybody
less quixotic than Lord Anthony Moynihan.

After a lifetime of shady deals with various dictators, he had
ended up living in Manila as a friend of President Marcos, whom
he had met through the dictator's sister Elizabeth. With Marcos's
protection, he ran various nightclubs and massage parlours in
Manila's top hotels and enjoyed close business relations with various
Australian gangsters. Moynihan was even implicated in the murder of
a rival nightclub owner, Robert Waldron, who had foolishly married
Moynihan's third wife after she left him. Having met in the bar of a
Manila hotel during one of Howard's many visits to the Philippines,
he and Howard had become buddies.

In 1987, Moynihan was doing a world tour while on honeymoon
with his fourth wife, Editha, whom he'd met when she was modelling
at a teenage lingerie show. He'd asked Howard if he knew anyone
in Miami, so Howard phoned and asked me to entertain the good
lord during his visit to South Florida. 'You'd be doing me a favour,'
he said, 'and you'll find him very entertaining.'

Moynihan was truly larger than life. Already 6 ft tall, he wore insteps in his shoes and was hard to miss when I met him at the bar of the Biltmore Hotel.

'How do you like to be addressed?' I asked him.

'"My Lord" will do just fine,' he said, and then roared with laughter. 'Call me Tony,' he added.

Tony had a problem and wondered if I could help him. He was carrying $50,000 in cash, which 'a friend' in New York had given him, and he did not want to get arrested trying to take it out of the country when he flew home. He offered to pay me $5,000 if I would launder it to a company he owned in Manila.

This was easily accomplished and I was happy to oblige. Leaving Tony and his wife at the Biltmore, I flew to New York and spent the night at Juan Dejesus's apartment. I should have had a premonition that something bad was going to happen to me when Juan and I watched the news that night; the Dow Jones was falling rapidly and Wall Street was in a panic. The following morning, we went to Juan's offices on Wall Street and Broadway, where we watched the meltdown of the world's financial centre. In the previous few days, the Dow Jones industrial average had plunged 508 points or 22.9 per cent. This was nearly twice as bad as the Wall Street Crash of 1929, which ushered in the Great Depression. I craned my neck to see if any bankers were jumping from their windows. As the stock market collapsed and everyone on the Street tried to go liquid, Juan's sources of cash were in great demand. He didn't even bother to charge me a commission for the $50,000 in $100 bills but simply wrote me a cashier's cheque in favour of Lord Moynihan's Philippine corporation. Wall Street was going crazy and cash was king. Though Juan charged me nothing, I would have to pay for my involvement in the 1987 financial crash at a later date.

For the next few days, after my return from New York, Tony and his wife Editha were our guests in Coral Gables. We introduced them to all our friends, who were delighted to meet real English aristocracy. I very proudly gave him a tour of my desktop publishing company and he immediately wanted to know if I could produce false passports and birth certificates.

One night, we took him to a Nicaraguan restaurant, Los Ranchos, which was owned by the nephew of Anastasio Somoza, the Nicaraguan dictator. 'I always prefer eating with dictators,' Tony confided. 'The food is usually good and you know it's been checked for poison.' Moynihan was nothing if not entertaining and played the part of the eccentric English lord to perfection. The ladies in particular all loved him.

The only people who did not like him were my daughters. Tony was very keen to visit Wolfie Cohen's Rascal House, a Jewish deli on Miami Beach. It had been one of Meyer Lansky's favourite hangouts.

'Why do you want to go there?' I asked him. 'The food is horribly greasy.'

'We want to see the curlies,' Moynihan said.

'The what?'

'The Jew boys with their long curly hair,' he explained. 'Always good for a laugh,' he added.

My daughter Peggy looked sharply at me, obviously expecting me to object to this racist comment. I'm ashamed to say I did not say anything and laughed along with Tony, studiously avoiding her disappointed eyes.

After leaving Wolfie's, we drove down Miami Beach's Collins Avenue while Tony sat in the front seat eating a large lox bagel and noisily pointing out the 'curlies' we passed on the street. Editha decided she did not like her sandwich and gave it to Tony. Rolling down the window he tossed the greasy bag into the middle of the street. Peggy and Bridie were horrified.

'You can't do that!' Peggy objected.

'That's littering,' Bridie added. 'It makes the planet all dirty.'

'But that's what we always do in Manila,' Tony said. 'It provides food for the poor people. If we were in Manila, they would all rush into the street to get that delicious sandwich.'

'Well, you're not in Manila. This is America and we don't do that.' Peggy was by now visibly appalled.

'So what am I supposed to do with this?' Tony asked, holding out his own greasy bag of lox and bagel. 'Look, it's dripping nasty grease all over my jacket.'

'Put it in the garbage can,' Bridie said.

'There's one over there,' Peggy said, pointing. 'Dad, stop the car.'

I parked the car and Tony got out with his dripping bag and walked towards a rubbish bin. He then paused and turned towards the car with a wicked grin and winked at us all. Walking a few steps further, he deposited his greasy bag of half-eaten food in a US mailbox.

'That wasn't the trash can, it was a mailbox,' Bridie said.

'I know. I was having a joke.'

'But now there'll be grease all over the people's letters,' Bridie said, her eyes filling with tears at the thought.

'It doesn't matter,' Tony said. 'They're only curlies.'

Peggy folded her arms tightly, saying not another word for the rest of the journey and when we got home she locked herself in her room. Neither of the girls ever spoke to Tony again and after he had gone they told me he was a bad man and I shouldn't have friends like that. Despite all the racketeers and smugglers they had met in their young lives, Lord Tony Moynihan was the only one of my friends they did not like. Their feelings were intense and strongly felt and I remain deeply ashamed that I could not see or acknowledge the evil that they recognised immediately. Unfortunately, I was blinded by Tony's aristocracy – and the $5,000 commission.

In fact, Tony was working undercover for the DEA and had taped all our private conversations. After the overthrow of the Marcos regime and the death of Elizabeth Marcos, Tony had been left without a protector and so Scotland Yard and the DEA recruited him to take down Howard Marks. They obviously took great interest in the certified cheque that Juan Dejesus gave me on Wall Street in return for Tony's cash. That was one of the reasons why Juan moved out of the US and currently resides in the jungles of Suriname. I had not said much to Tony that could be used against me in a court of law but I had obviously said enough for two federal agents to wrestle me to the bathroom floor and slip handcuffs on my wrists.

Simultaneous arrests were being made all over the world that morning and Howard Marks and Ernie Combs were only two of dozens of other people having their mornings unpleasantly interrupted. Howard, as usual, was the one who got the most press. The following morning, George Volsky in the *New York Times* quoted a senior official at the DEA saying: 'Mr. Marks was the Marco Polo of the drug traffic. He perfected smuggling methods and intricate laundering operations involving many countries around the globe, and this is why it took efforts in so many countries to complete this case.' The *Times* also quoted Dexter W. Lehtinen, the US Attorney for the Southern District of Florida, who said that law-enforcement agencies from 13 countries had worked together on an 'extremely complex international investigation of a large multinational narcotics enterprise'. Government officials were shown on all the TV news broadcasts pointing importantly at complex maps and charts showing the corporate structure of our 'organisation' and the worldwide nature of our illicit activities.

Apparently we had been the subjects of a massive international operation led by Special Agent Craig Lovato of the DEA, who had been monitoring our phone calls and photographing our meetings for several years. Lovato had even filmed my meetings with Lord Moynihan at the Biltmore Hotel. Eventually, I was to meet Lovato in person but that first morning he was otherwise engaged, arresting Howard at his home on Majorca. I was led out of the bathroom naked to find the house filled with armed men all wearing SWAT jackets and body armour.

'Mr Lane, I am Special Agent Brad Whites. I am a federal agent from the IRS criminal investigation unit. I am placing you under arrest. You are charged with running a continuous criminal enterprise, racketeering and conspiracy.'

Jude was standing at the back of the room, white-faced. She and Peggy had just got into the car to go to school when they were swarmed by armed men dressed in black. They had been led back into the house and told to wait while the bathroom door was kicked open.

Agent Whites allowed me to get dressed. 'Doesn't matter what you put on,' he said. 'They'll only take it away.' He stopped me as I started to slip on my wristwatch. 'You won't need that where you're going. Time is not an issue.'

The police had seen that Bridie was in her bedroom, asleep and blissfully unaware of what was happening. Whites suggested I stick my head round the door and take a last look. 'She'll be a 50-year-old woman with kids of her own by the time you see her again.' I asked if I could kiss her. 'No physical contact,' he said.

They hustled me out of the house past a distraught Jude and Peggy and pushed me into the back seat of a police car in the street. The look on Peggy's face as I passed her in the garden is something that is burned into my soul. No father should ever have to see such an unforgettable look of horror, fear and shame on his daughter's face. No child should ever have to see her father in such a position.

Then they left me alone in the car. The handcuffs dug painfully into my wrists as I sat in the back seat looking dazedly out at my once familiar street. Curious neighbours stood silently on their neatly manicured front lawns watching all the armed men as they went in and out of my house; they studiously ignored the frightened and embarrassed man in the back seat. White stencilled letters on the backs of the agents' flak jackets showed them to be from the FBI, DEA, IRS, INS and the Miami Special Crimes Unit.

Eventually, after what seemed like an eternity, Whites and another agent got in the car and drove me to DEA headquarters near Miami airport. They led me to a windowless room filled with boxes of files and folders, where they removed the handcuffs and gave me a cup of coffee. My hands tingled as the blood finally rushed back. The coffee was warm and helped my brain recover from the bleak numbness I felt.

'You've still got a chance to save yourself, Pat,' Whites said in a kindly tone. 'Give us Howard and Ernie and we'll see what we can do to help you. You've got a lovely wife, a lovely home, lovely kids. Silly to throw it all away.'

The room was very cold and I wrapped my hands around the warm coffee. I shivered slightly but said nothing.

'You realise we've got you cold, Pat?' he said, swinging his arm lazily around the room to encompass all the boxes and files. 'Seventeen years of evidence,' he said. 'Photographs, recorded conversations, witness statements, hotel receipts. The works.'

He pulled out a file at random. 'What have we got here?' He put on his reading glasses. 'Hotel receipt dated 1972 from the Shannon

Shamrock Hotel outside Limerick. You, Howard Marks and James McCann.' That was the hotel we used when we were running hash through Shannon airport. He looked at me over his glasses. 'What were you doing there? Canoeing holiday on the Shannon estuary?'

Of course, it was all carefully rehearsed. They had practised exactly which files to pull out. At the time, though, it seemed as though the whole room was filled with evidence relating solely to me.

One of the other agents was reading from another 'randomly' pulled file. 'Transcript of a phone call from Howard Marks in Majorca: "Are you still in business?" Howard asks. What sort of business was that, Pat? Accounting?'

'More hotel receipts,' read another agent. 'Mandarin Hotel, Hong Kong, October 1979. Same time as Ernie Combs was staying there. Friend of Ernie's, are you, Pat?'

'Here's a photograph of you in the street outside Howard's home in Majorca in July 1985.'

They were all pulling files from the boxes and enjoying themselves enormously. 'Statement from Tom Sunde explaining how he helped you bribe a Mexican judge to get your sister out of prison in Tijuana.'

'Here's a statement from a Scottish police officer, formally attesting that he personally met you at a country house on New Year's Eve where 20 tons of marijuana was later discovered to have been stored.'

'You'll like this one, Pat. It's a photo of you in the Biltmore Hotel, just round the corner from your house, and Lord Moynihan is handing you $50,000 in cash.'

It was endless. They seemed to have recorded and documented everything I had ever done in my whole life. They even had details of my Brighton bust for a couple of joints in the '60s. I would like to claim that my stoic silence in the face of this barrage of evidence was due to courage or loyalty to my friends. In reality, my brain and my spirit were simply overwhelmed and had shut down on me. I was a dead soul.

Finally they grew bored with their game and tired of my silence. 'All right, Pat. Have it your own way. See you in court.'

I was handcuffed again and bundled once more into the back seat for the long drive out to Miami's Metropolitan Correctional Center, or MCC, as I soon learned to call it. It was late at night when we arrived and, after a humiliating strip search, I was given some grubby prison overalls and led to my cell. It was a proper cell, just like you see in the movies, with two bunks and bars on the doors and windows. The bars were thick steel and cold.

Wrapped in a thin blanket, something sinister grunted and shifted on the bottom bunk and two eyes glinted resentfully at me in the half-light. The top bunk was mine. The guard's footsteps receded along the corridor and cries of 'Shut the fuck up, you cocksucking motherfucker' came from neighbouring cells.

The door clanged shut behind me and I found myself locked in an American prison cell in the dark. After a lifetime thinking I was invulnerable, breaking the law with impunity and a total lack of remorse, justice had caught up with me. My luck had finally run out and my innocent wife and children were left to pay the price.

AFTERWORD

After so many years, some of the events of my life have become rather hazy. Not only have I forgotten the names of some of the minor characters (or the names they were using) but even their individual identities have become indistinct and, as a consequence, some of them have blended together in my memory. Likewise, some of the many organisations and banks with which I was associated have blurred together in my mind, or their names have faded from my recollection. I was president of so many financial holding companies in so many countries, from Liberia to Liechtenstein, from the Isle of Man to the Cayman Islands, and all with such vague and silly names that, at this stage in my dotage, I could never begin to remember which was which.

I was convinced for many years that my brother George had remained in Kabul long after the Russian invasion. I had no reason to question my memory until publishing this book. In fact, he had been expelled from Afghanistan by the Daoud regime, long before the arrival of Soviet tanks. Similarly, I firmly believed that my sister Natasha's yacht was carried into Key West by a naval helicopter. My memory was at fault; she was towed into Key West by a Coast Guard cutter. Other sources suggest that if I took the ferry between Cork and South Wales in the early '70s, I must have embarked at Swansea. Despite all the evidence, my memory insists that my port was Pembroke or Fishguard.

Some names and details have been deliberately changed, but for any accidental lapses of memory, I apologise profusely.

For those interested in other perspectives on some of the activities described in this book, the following works, some written much closer to the time, might fill in some of the blanks.

- *High Time* by David Leigh, William Heinemann, 1984. Written by a *Daily Mirror* journalist and with Howard Marks's active cooperation, this tell-all book enhanced the Marks legend. Following his acquittal at the Old Bailey, it emphasised his victories over Scotland Yard and the DEA – with predictably unfortunate consequences.

- *Hunting Marco Polo* by Paul Eddy and Sara Walden, Little, Brown, 1991. Written by two *Sunday Times* journalists, this excellent and well-balanced book not only chronicles my life and Howard's but also follows the police team who eventually brought us down.

- *Mr Nice* by Howard Marks, Secker & Warburg, 1996. This is Howard's own version of the story, in response to *Hunting Marco Polo*, which he found *too* well balanced. It deservedly continues to be a bestseller all over the world and has been translated into many languages. It is being made into a feature film starring Rhys Ifans, Chloë Sevigny and Jamie Harris.

- *Grass* by Phil Sparrowhawk, Mainstream Publishing, 2003. Philip Sparrowhawk was one of our partners in crime, an East End barrow boy with a heart of gold. His book is a delight to read and reflects Phil's sardonic humour, natural intelligence and stoical good nature.

- *Mr Nice and Mrs Marks* by Judy Marks, Ebury Press, 2006. My sister Judy married Howard and gave him two daughters and a son. Her book provides a female perspective on our *Boy's Own* adventures.

- Finally, keep an eye out not only for Marcus Scriven's forthcoming book *Splendour and Squalor* (Atlantic Books, 2009) but also for his follow-up, devoted entirely to Lord Anthony Moynihan and associates.

AFTERWORD

This book ends with the clanging shut of a prison door and the conclusion of a whole way of life. But life has a way of continuing and humans have a wonderful way of surviving. That prison door opened to a whole new life and a fresh beginning, which I hope to describe in *Redemption of a Racketeer*.

ACKNOWLEDGEMENTS

This book began as an email response to a journalist who asked me for my recollections of Lord Anthony Moynihan. Marcus Scriven was writing a book about aristocrats who had disgraced themselves and their families; Moynihan appeared to be an obvious candidate for inclusion. As it was, research subsequently suggested that he was in a category of his own, hence his omission from Marcus's forthcoming book *Splendour and Squalor*. It is thanks to Marcus's generous encouragement and support, however, that my original email eventually became a book.

For making it read like a book, I must thank Claire Rose, my editor at Mainstream, for her limitless patience, her professional guidance and her excellent suggestions. For bravely taking on and representing an unknown writer, I thank my agent, Andrew Lownie. I would also like to thank Peggy Morel, my eldest daughter, for suggesting a new title for Chapter Five, which was originally called 'Norwegian Wood'.

I would like to thank Roy Harper and Science Friction Records for generous permission to quote from his song 'Watford Gap'. The album *Bullinamingvase* can be found, along with much else, at his very interesting and useful website.

Lyrics to 'Truckin'' by Robert Hunter, copyright Ice Nine Publishing Company, used with the generous permission of Ice Nine.

The quotation from *Greenmantle* by John Buchan is reproduced with the permission of A.P. Watt Ltd on behalf of Jean, Lady Tweedsmuir, and the Executors of the Estate of Lord Tweedsmuir.